P9-DMA-963

Acclaim for
HOW TO FATHER A
SUCCESSFUL DAUGHTER

"[This] book can teach both moms and dads how to help their daughters use and appreciate their talents."

The Charlotte Observer

"There's energy and enthusiasm here, Marone's advice is useful and inspiring."

The Kirkus Reviews

"[Nicky Marone's] personal narratives interject prescription with sentiment. Recommended for *both* parents."

Library Journal

"A thoroughly positive and empowering approach for fathers and daughters.... *How to Father a Successful Daughter* demonstrates how one man can make a crucial difference in his daughter's life."

Harry Brod
Editor
The Making of Masculinities

HOW TO FATHER A SUCCESSFUL DAUGHTER

Nicky Marone

Foreword by Gilbert Simon, M.D.

FAWCETT CREST • NEW YORK

Library of Congress Catalog Card Number: 87-3840

ISBN 0-449-21687-X

This edition published by arrangement with McGraw-Hill Book Company, A Division of McGraw-Hill, Inc.

The graphs on page 31 of G.P.A.s for achievers versus underachievers originally appeared in an article entitled "The Onset of Academic Underachievement in Bright Children," in *Journal of Education Psychology,* 51, p. 105 (1960), copyright by the American Psychological Association. Adapted by permission of the author, Merville C. Shaw.

Manufactured in the United States of America

First Ballantine Books Edition: June 1989
Fourth Printing: December 1990

*To the memory of my father, Al, and for
my mother, Maxine*

CONTENTS

FOREWORD

❦

You could see it coming. The vacuum, created by mothers leaving the home to enter the labor field, pulled the traditional breadwinning father into the domestic childcaring scene. This push-me pull-you trend was furthered by the feminist movement.

Women demanded that their husbands become more active in the family so that they'd be free to pursue their aspirations outside the home. Men, whose consciousnesses were also being raised, chose to abandon the peripheral Dagwood Bumstead-like role, preferring to become an integral factor in their children's development and socialization.

However, the exact nature of the father's role needed to be clarified. Research was needed. In the late 1960s, not much was known about the paternal role in child development since all of the major theories about child rearing focused on mother–child, and not father–child, relationships. By the mid-1970s, enough evidence had accumulated to justify the statement that fathers were "the forgotten contributors to child development."

The first important fact we learned was the importance of the father's *salience*—his physical presence, accessibility and closeness. What a father actually *did* while present didn't seem to matter as much as his being on the scene. His salience was consistently shown to matter most when it came to motivating his child to high academic achievement.

The next area where a father's influence was found to be pre-eminent was in the development of his son's masculinity and his daughter's femininity. We learned that men, much more than women, hold rigid sex-role stereotypes, and are more likely than mothers to treat their children differently according to gender. Fathers, it was found, are the principal transmitters of culturally based attitudes on masculinity and femininity. This occurs through an insidious process of encouraging one type of behavior from sons, and another from daughters. Ironically, this process has its greatest impact not on sons, but on *daughters*.

If it's the father's role to motivate his child to academic achievement, and at the same time help her assume an appropriate sex-role, then depending on his style, he can either be a help or a hindrance. When it comes to a father's effect on *gifted* girls, Marone discovered that, all too often, he's a hindrance.

Marone points out that it is customary to define femininity in terms that stress passivity, helplessness and dependency—not the sort of traits often associated with success. Many well-meaning fathers unwittingly deliver traditional feminizing messages that damage their daughters' self-esteem, restrict their goals and undermine their confidence. Hoping for exactly the opposite, they inadvertently squelch their daughters' intellectual and academic development.

What a waste! And the more gifted the girl, the greater the potential waste. But it doesn't have to happen that way. If the predictable outcome of certain types of fathering behavior is negative, then the behavior has to be changed. Marone gives us more than a few suggestions for change.

Nicky Marone, whose background includes teaching junior high school students and educating gifted girls with corresponding workshops for their fathers, explains *how to father a successful daughter*, how to *encourage*, and how not to retard a daughter's intellectual development. She does this by blending her own insights, derived from her experience, with a review of the latest research in childhood development and education, and then lets us hear the exact words of successful daughters as they describe their relationships with their fathers. We also hear the words of those who would have liked things to have been different. Through the liberal use of very readable vignettes, Marone awakens male readers to what their daughters know and feel. The lessons are clear, and the effect is powerful.

A theme running throughout the book is that a father's actions count more than his words. The words we use become meaningless if we infantilize our wives, denigrate their achievements, tell or *allow to be told* sexist jokes—in effect, we are saying to our daughters that we don't value or respect women. When our sons are required to master the complexities of mathematics, finance and computers, and our daughters receive lessons in sewing, tap dancing and politeness, we are saying to our daughters that we don't think much about their abilities. When knightly fathers swoop in to rescue their daughters from predicaments that they would have left their sons to sink or swim in, they are telling their daughters that they're expected to sink. Fathers may be offering love and warmth, but the vote is "No Confidence." Making matters worse, Marone points out, fathers have *two* votes to cast—one as a parent, and the other as the paradigm for all men.

Readers will especially appreciate the pointers on recognizing subtle expressions of giftedness. It's no problem if a child is a straight A student, virtuoso and poet. But how many of us see the untapped potential in the wise-cracker, the daydreamer, the very young child with an adult sense of humor, the child who assumes adult responsibilities in the home, or the child who is able to empathize with and minister to the emotional needs of her distressed friends? The message here is: "there's gold in them thar hills," and if nobody knows it's there, nobody's going to get rich.

I was reminded of how exquisitely sensitive teenage girls can be to the comments of their fathers on certain topics, particularly when it comes to their popularity, weight or developing womanly shape. I can still hear the familiar sound of plaster falling off the walls of my oldest daughter's bedroom from her slamming her door in a fit of embarrassed rage. I didn't think *then* that my teasing was anything to get her that upset. I promise to behave better for my fourth daughter.

Marone shows us the bad ways and suggests the good ways for fathers to show love for their pubescent daughters, to tease without torturing, to discuss difficult and often shunned topics, to offer encouragement without pressure, and to discipline without punishing. She's even found ways for television watching to be instructive. She suggests that we make a game out of searching for sexist messages in commercials and on a positive note, we can watch movies from the forties and fifties and appreciate how attitudes are changing.

Throughout the book there are charts and checklists that simplify the points and deliver the messages unmistakably. For those who are rippers and tearers, these pages would not be wasted on your bulletin board. At the end of the book, there are two appendixes: one offering thumbnail biographies of successful women, and the other, consisting of the right questions for parents to ask in evaluating their school district's gifted student program.

In this age of bottom lines, we might ask ourselves: what do we want for our daughters? We certainly don't want them masculinized. We do want them to be loving, warm, tender and sensitive when the circumstances call for nurturing. Come to think of it, I'd like no less for my son. We should also want them, if the situation calls for action, assertiveness and strength—just like our sons—to go out there and "kick ass."

Fundamentally, your daughter should be free to and capable of making whatever response she needs to bring her closer to *whatever* goal, personal or professional, she chooses. What she opts for is entirely her business. As a father, it's your business to remove the limits that others have placed before her. After reading this book, you should have a better idea of how this can be done.

Gilbert Simon, M.D.
Associate Clinical Professor of Pediatrics
University of California, Davis

Father of Tanya Linn, 28, lawyer and wife; Lesley Ellen, 26, financial analyst and wife; Alicia Ann, 23, mother and wife, and Helen Elizabeth, 6, plans to be a vagina doctor, dancer and builder of tree houses for her children.

ACKNOWLEDGMENTS

I would like to send my love and deep appreciation to the following people: to my dear friend D.B., who put her money where her mouth is—without her support this book may never have happened; to my professors, Dr. Linda Silverman and Dr. Connie Platt, for their scholarship and skillful mentoring; to my editor, Leslie Meredith, for her careful reading, her enthusiasm, and her commitment through some difficult times of her own; to my birthday twin, K.R., who lovingly tended my mental state through the creative process; to Tim Pestotnik for his steadfastness and sense of fun; to Kathy Green, who kept reminding me of the cosmic jokes; to Pam Goodman, for her help in compiling the biographies; to Mr. Calm, whose kindness, patience, and intelligence are a constant source of that valuable commodity—male support; and finally, to my mother, who encouraged me to show a little guts and write this book.

PART 1

Getting a Grip on the Problem

AN OPEN LETTER TO FATHERS

Dear Dad,

I wonder if you have noticed the changes in your little girl, and I wonder if they bother you? I know they bother me. I see your daughter six hours out of every day, one spent in my class and the other five in the hallways of our junior high school. When she entered my class two years ago, she was bright, sparkling, and competitive. Today, as a ninth-grader, the vital and lively girl I knew has disappeared to be replaced by a shy, submissive, subdued teenager who wears tight jeans and too much makeup. She seems to have lost interest in her grade-point average and deliberately pretends not to know the answers to questions raised in class. She is hiding her light behind two shades of eye shadow and values her body more than her mind.

Before you become too alarmed, let me tell you that she is not alone. As is typical with teenagers, she is one of a pack. Many of her equally bright and once-active girlfriends suffer from the same disorder. I wish I could reassure you that this is only a passing phase that stops when puberty ends. Unfortunately, my years of experience and the current research on your daughter and others like her indicate the opposite. This is the time at which she is likely to go permanently underground with her abilities and never resurface to realize her potential.

I know you love her very much. I know you want what is best for her. You care. Otherwise, you would not be reading this book. Rest assured you *can* make a difference, for you hold the keys in your hands. More than you realize, you can have an impact on her life. You can equip her with the self-esteem and psychological health necessary to achieve her potential, and you can do it in spite of the obstacles of peer pressure and societal expectations to which she has been exposed.

Your importance as the man in her life cannot be underesti-

3

mated. Consider this: research studies on female achievers consistently show that a father's role is critical to his daughter's development—particularly in the area of achievement. Fathers who act as mentors to their daughters have a profound influence. By being the first supportive male in your daughter's life, you will be giving her the edge: the self-love and confidence mandatory for the rigors of personal and professional achievement and a lasting foundation on which to build her life.

I am also dedicated to her success, and in this way you and I share a common bond. That is the reason I wrote this book.

CHAPTER 1

❧

Out of the Mouths of Babes

Pregnant Doctors

On a bleak January morning my friend Sue and I sat at her kitchen table drinking coffee and talking. In the middle of our conversation her six-year-old daughter, Sharon, and her four-year-old playmate, Christine, strolled into the kitchen carrying the "doctors' kits" they had received for Christmas. (My friend would ask me to emphasize that these were doctors' kits not nurses' kits, as she was making an effort to give nonsexist gifts.) What caught our attention was that these two little girls had stuffed something under their clothes, next to their abdomens, giving them the appearance of having great big bellies. My friend asked her daughter, "Who are you? Starving children from Biafra?"

"No," was the reply, "we're pregnant doctors!"

Driving home later that day, I couldn't get Sharon's reply out of my mind. There was something disquieting about it. "Why not just doctors?" I kept thinking to myself. "Why *pregnant* doctors?" Gradually, I began to realize that the unnamed anxiety I was feeling was the same feeling that had been haunting me each day as I taught school. . . .

The scene is a typical, middle-class junior high school in Anytown, U.S.A. It is the first day of school, and I am watching my ninth-grade students file in, reflecting on the changes I have seen occur in them since I knew them as seventh-graders. This age, in particular, is a fascinating one to teach precisely because it is so fraught with change and growth. Unfortunately, my pleasure in my students is intruded upon by a vague disquiet I have not yet identified. Take Christy Barnes, for example. When she first entered my class as a seventh-grader, she was bright, exuberant, fresh, unaffected, and high-achieving. Now, as a ninth-grader, she appears a wholly transformed person. Her jeans are too tight, her neckline too low, and she is wearing two shades of eye shadow (one for depth, the other for highlighting), plus enough blush on her cheeks to qualify as stage makeup. Her repertoire of facial expressions seems somewhat limited—either disdainful petulance or wide-eyed vacancy. While noticing this, I'm not really alarmed, chalking it up to the experimentations of puberty and adolescent sexuality.

As the days become weeks, however, I notice other, deeper changes in Christy. She volunteers less information in class, seeming to hold back purposely. Her performance on tests and papers has noticeably declined. I check her report card and discover that her grade-point average has plummeted. She has adopted what seems to be a whole new personality. The bright, assertive, natural child is gone and has been replaced by a shy, submissive, cutesy young woman who giggles too loudly at jokes made by boys and pretends not to know the answers to questions that she does, in fact, know perfectly well. Finally, at parent-teacher conferences, Christy's mother is distraught. Christy has "gotten stupid" at home, too, refusing to take responsibility for homework and verbally expressing less and less confidence in herself. Her mother informs me she has dropped out of sports, where she was once an active athlete, and cares little about her grades.

What is happening to Christy is happening all over the country to countless bright, high-achieving females as they reach the precarious age of puberty. The subliminal lessons that society, family, and the media have taught them are finally surfacing—that "femininity" is *still* the most potent attribute a girl can have. Boys still eat it up, and girls still play it to the hilt. The game is still *on*, as hot and as intense as ever.

These mating rituals are to be expected as boys and girls search for sexual identity, but they undermine a girl's progress toward achievement because "feminine" behavior (which attracts the boys) is not necessarily congruent with achievement behavior. At this age, girls who suspect they come on too strong realize that this strength threatens the boys, who symbolically hold the keys to their acceptance and recognition as desirable females. This realization causes many girls to force underground and out of sight the assertive behavior required to achieve.

Let me take a moment here to clarify a point about achievement. I do not wish to represent success and achievement as exemplified only by corporate executives handing down proclamations from boardrooms on Madison Avenue, or the cutthroat tactics of multinational mergers, or even the daily drama of, say, a courtroom trial lawyer. Throughout this book, the terms "successful person" and "achiever" will also refer to the individual who wishes to paint watercolors in her attic or start a small business on little capital, become an apprentice electrician or write string quartets as more than just a spare-time activity. You see, for a female, almost *any* nontraditional aspirations can be thought of as achievements, since refusing to accept society's limited expectations of her requires both risk-taking ability and mastery-oriented behavior. If your daughter believes femininity alone is the requisite to her acceptance as a human being, she may never develop assertiveness, never cultivate and refine her talents, never realize her dreams.

Although the tension created by the conflicting demands of achievement and femininity does not surface until puberty, girls perceive it on a subconscious level at an extremely tender age. This is why a six-year-old girl acts out what she senses is the future conflict of her adult life. She attempts, through play, to fuse the divergent requirements of femininity and achievement by becoming a pregnant doctor! In this way she covers all her bases and resolves the conflict. She meets both the demand to achieve and to prove her femininity. Later, at puberty, this game takes on more serious dimensions.

Femininity and Achievement: A Father's Role

I have observed adolescent behavior for the past eleven years, and what I see is unsettling.

First, little has changed. If the feminist consciousness that developed in the sixties were going to have any effect on our daughters' behavior, it would be visible by now. It isn't. The roles adopted by adolescent boys and girls reflect the same old, worn-out, self-defeating poses of twenty years ago. Sure, the girls now *say* they want to be doctors instead of nurses and a few *say* they want careers before they marry and have children, but their *be-*

havior remains eerily resistant to change. If we continue to delude ourselves and pretend that major changes have occurred when they haven't, we will continue to lose the talents of half our population and its collective potential contribution.

Second, the girl who receives the least amount of male attention and approval at home is the one to seek it most aggressively *outside the home*—namely, at school. There, it is frightfully easy to get the kind of attention (which translates as approval) that she does not receive at home from her own father. Any girl who has doubts about her worth can find encouragement by capitalizing on her helplessness, flaunting her youthful sex appeal, and abandoning (in many cases permanently) achievement-oriented behavior.

Third, while mothers and female teachers try valiantly to change the behavior patterns of girls, the fact is they can't do it alone. The models they offer are crucial and must not be taken lightly, *but* if a father, the first and most important male in any girl's life, continues to reinforce only stereotypically feminine behavior, his daughter will get the powerful message that one can elicit male approval simply by conforming to a prescribed standard of femininity. At puberty, when the need for male approval becomes more intense, conforming to this standard will become the focus of her energies.

For a girl, then, puberty is a time of great decision. If she perceives that femininity and achievement are mutually exclusive, she will be sorely tempted to sacrifice one for the other. She cannot avoid the conflict. She is living in the latter half of the twentieth century in America. The conflict exists, and she will have to confront it.

Your job, as a concerned and loving father, is to help ensure that she doesn't get stuck at this stage of her growth. You can help make puberty a rite of passage to a higher plane of maturity and development. Whether your daughter is so young that the conflict lies ahead of her, or old enough that she is in the midst of the struggle, you can make a difference.

Research on female achievers consistently shows that fathers who act as mentors to their daughters exert a powerful influence on the daughters' life accomplishments.[1] Therefore, your understanding and advocacy can become a vehicle through which your daughter will learn to reject the labels that undermine her confidence, restrict her development, and confine her choices. Your unique contributions as the first and most important male in her young life will have significant and far-reaching consequences.

The message is clear and simple. If your daughter is to succeed in the demanding world of her *future*, it is imperative that she feel the respect and involvement of her father *today*.

A Shining Example

"The whole time I was growing up my father expected everything from me," says a thirty-five-year-old Denver businesswoman, "so when I had a terrible experience my first year away from home, he found a way to help me turn it around into a positive, growth experience.

"The reason I was so devastated by this event is that it was my first direct experience with sexism. It was my first realization that the blinders worn by other people could actually affect *my life*!" She laughs. "Ah, the naïveté of youth.

"Anyway, what happened was I lost out on a job that I wanted terribly to a man who was obviously not as qualified as I. I was destroyed. I just didn't think this kind of thing happened. It was inconceivable to me that anyone would pick an unqualified person over a qualified one just because of his sex! Obviously, I had a lot to learn. It was the kind of knock I just didn't think I could live through.

"I jumped the first bus home. When I got to the bus station, I called my father to come and get me. As far as I was concerned, my college career was over.

"My father left work—which was a major deal—to pick me up. The minute I got in the car, I broke down. He listened attentively, let me cry, hugged me, reassured me that he knew I was the best man for the job (ha, ha) and all that sort of thing.

"Anyway, I remember he made the perfect remark. He said, 'It's not the sex, it's the person. He is not entitled to that job just because he's male. Why don't you appeal your case and make the people who hired him account for their actions?'

"This may not seem like a big deal now, but this was 1967. I think he was very enlightened to encourage me not to sit still for that kind of treatment.

"I got up the next morning under the assumption that I was going to get to stay home permanently. I just figured I had been through something so horrendous that I couldn't possibly be expected to go back." She laughs again. "Anyway, my dad came in and said to me, 'Hurry up and get dressed. I'm dropping you off at the bus station on my way to work.'

"Well, I was stupefied. We didn't even discuss it. I dimly realized that I could always come home and tell my dad my problems and he would always listen, *but* he would not let me hide. I was expected to go back out into the arena regardless of how difficult it might be. I did appeal my case, by the way, and got nowhere. After all, it was 1967.

"Anyway, it was the best thing he could have done because later, as a college counselor, I saw the fathers who allowed their daughters to come home after the first day. If they just would have been supportive and loving but held firm, their daughters would have made it, just as I did.

"From that day on, there were many times when he was there. He would support me over the rough spots or help me see the lesson to be learned, but then it was back out into the arena once again.

"Now that he's gone," she says wistfully, "I do that for myself. I pamper myself immediately after a hard knock. I occasionally even allow myself to wallow in self-pity for a day. But then it's over. I know no one is going to rescue me. I must be my own savior. So, I pull myself together like the little soldier he taught me to be and march right back out to the battlefield."

Every girl should be so lucky. This father demonstrated his love and respect in a variety of ways. He was *there*. He left work to be there. He listened, hugged, and reassured. He gave sanctuary when it was needed, but not a permanent hiding place. He encouraged her to fight the inequity blocking her path rather than to be helpless in the face of it. And he did not take the reins of power out of her hands.

You can be this kind of father. Your decision to read this book is an indication of your desire to help. You will be required to summon your courage and your foresight, for the issues that you will be dealing with are complex and powerful. If you love a challenge, this is for you. Remember, awareness is the first step. I guarantee it will be a rewarding journey.

CHAPTER 2

❧

What Kind of Daddy Are You?

A Variety of Daddies

There are all kinds of daddies. Soft daddies. Stern daddies. Fun daddies. Demanding daddies. Each kind of daddy produces a different kind of daughter. There is no one best prescribed mode of behavior. Every situation that a daddy faces with his little girl will require a different kind of behavior on his part. There are times to be soft and times to be stern. Unfortunately, many parents (not just daddies!) get locked into one particular kind of behavior and play out every scene using the same tape. Regrettably, men seem to have this problem more than women.

I might as well lay it on the line before you read any further: many of the ideas you will confront in this book will challenge you to make some changes. If you are unprepared or unwilling to do so, you may face some psychic discomfort. This will be particularly true if you are in agreement with an idea but reluctant to make changes. Once you have realized the effects of your behavior on your daughter and have accepted as reality the kind of impact you can have, then fathering her becomes more than just a passive kind of experience. It may become the challenge of your life.

While all this has a decidedly melodramatic ring to it, you should know that these sentiments have been expressed by fathers who attend seminars that I teach. They have asked me to warn my readers that they will make some leaps they hadn't anticipated.

One father in particular was able to verbalize both the anxiety and the sense of purpose that accompany this new awareness.

"I guess I'm going to have to make some changes. Up until now I hadn't realized the kind of messages my daughter was receiving. I didn't understand the significance of some of the pressures that were on her. Now, I have a better perspective on where she is coming from.

"I used to feel that I had to be satisfied with being on the border of her life. Now I know what an important part I play in her development. I feel as though I have a purpose."

Later, this same father came to me privately to say, "You know, my wife has said some of the very same things that you have been saying. To tell the truth, I'm glad she's not here or I'd have to eat humble pie." I smiled. He added, "From now on, maybe I'll pay closer attention."

What this father was trying to say was that he was beginning the painful process of having his consciousness raised. He had begun to understand the complexity of the forces that act on females and affect their lives significantly. And he was beginning to understand that he could apply this new knowledge in a positive and productive way to help his daughter.

That is the purpose of the quiz offered in this chapter. It will help to heighten your awareness of the kind of daddy you are. Are you overly protective? Do you secretly believe (maybe unconsciously) that females are inferior to males? Does your behavior toward women in general, your wife in particular, send a message to your daughter that she would be better off not receiving?

"I thought I knew it all," one father confessed, "but my eyes have been opened. This is very valuable information, not only in raising my daughter but in understanding myself. I only wish I had had this information when my other daughter was younger."

Sometimes instituting changes can be painful. On the other hand, it can be the start of a whole new approach to your role as a father—an approach that ultimately will be more rewarding, refreshing, and humanly gratifying than you had imagined.

A Quiz for the Courageous

UNDERSTANDING THE QUIZ: SOME INTRODUCTORY REMARKS

Although there is some overlap, the questions are loosely configured around five main categories. They are:

1. Femininity
2. Risk taking
3. Male advocacy
4. Male superiority and devaluation of the feminine
5. Activities and quality of time spent together

As you can see, these categories are very broad and encompass a wide variety of issues. Each one will be addressed often throughout this book. It is not important that you agree with the implications of each and every question. What is important is that you begin thinking about these issues. Then you can make enlightened decisions regarding your daughter's upbringing and help make her the strong and independent woman she will need to be in order to achieve her potential.

The point of this quiz is to emphasize and raise awareness of rule number 1 in all effective parenting: *What you do is vastly more influential on your children than what you say.* Commit this to memory. In other words, verbal encouragement is important, but the true barometer of what you are teaching is your behavior. You may tell your daughter from now until forever that she is capable, talented, competent, and beautiful, but if your behavior undermines your words, their power will be lost in the revealing light of pretense.

Bear in mind that children learn early to block out what they perceive as the constant barrage of parental chatter, advice, warnings, admonitions, and words of wisdom. What they are unable to block out is the impact of parental behavior and the unspoken messages it carries. If you want your daughter to believe in herself, to value her talents and trust her insights, *you* must believe, value, and trust first, for it is from you she will learn her worth. Your behavior, not your words, will be her guide.

Each set of questions will help you characterize your behavior and the messages it carries. This will promote a higher level of understanding concerning the types of behavioral changes necessary on your part to make a measurable impact.

Remember that there is no laying of blame intended here. If, on occasion, you feel a little defensive, remember that my purpose is not to be like the Sunday preacher who rails at the congregation in attendance about the people not in attendance. *You are reading this book.* I admire you for it. As you read along, you may feel everything from guilt to anger to amusement. That's good. Consider it an indication of your involvement with and commitment to your daughter. Again, it is not important that you agree with everything presented, but rather that your degree of awareness be raised.

Most fathers do not have a gut-level grip on the obstacles, both subtle and blatant, facing their daughters. They don't realize that the more talent and inclination to achieve a female possesses, the greater the dispiriting impact of these obstacles. Awareness of the realities facing her and of the impact of your own behavior constitutes the most potent force you have to help you guide her through the precarious times and choices she will face. The more you understand the forces at work on your daughter, the better armed you will be to help her get where she wants to go.

If you have been wondering how you have been doing as a father so far, now is your chance to do some evaluating. There is no score on this test. It is not meant to be a measure of your love as a father. Its purpose is to stimulate thinking about the controversial issues dealt with in this book and to help you formulate some of your own notions, so that you can actively use the information and techniques presented later in the text. Good luck, and remember, it is not your "score" that counts, but rather, the degree to which you think about these ideas.

ON FEMININITY

1. Do you have a hard time disciplining your daughter if she turns on the tears?

2. Do you ever tell your daughter to "act like a little lady"?

3. Do you say things like, "She's really going to be good-looking some day," or do you take an inordinate amount of pride if someone else says it? (If you have a son, do you discuss how good-looking he is going to be?)

4. Does it bother you if she is totally unconcerned or in-

different about her appearance? Do you think she should try and stay neat and clean when she is playing?

5. Does it bother you if she rejects dolls and dress-up and chooses instead to play with robots, tinker-toys, soldiers, and cars?

6. Do you excuse inappropriate emotional displays by saying or thinking, "That's just how girls are. They're more emotional." (Would you excuse inappropriate emotional displays in a son?)

7. If your daughter has done poorly on a math assignment, have you ever said (or even thought!), "That's OK, honey. Girls aren't supposed to be good in math."

8. Does competent behavior in an adult woman bother you? For example, if a woman puts on overalls and fixes her kitchen sink, does she seem unfeminine and unattractive?

If you answered yes to any of the questions above, then to some extent you have accepted the traditional stereotype of the female as an appropriate role model for your daughter to follow. This would be fine except, in cultivating traditionally female behaviors—being sweet, polite, attractive, emotional, and dependent—you discourage the development of the traits required for personal and professional achievement—being competent, taking risks, and mastering skills.

Later, this discrepancy will be further emphasized when your daughter perceives that society, too, has a different set of expectations for a female and for an achiever. At the precarious point of puberty, when her primary concern will be male approval, she may choose the behavior of the stereotypical female in order to attract boys, affirm her femininity, and please her father. The traits that need to be developed for achievement may be forced underground.

Remember, to a certain degree this is to be expected. Experimentation with different kinds of gender behavior and the need to know if one meets prescribed standards of attractiveness are the natural process of adolescence. However, the degree to which *you* indicate through your behavior that she should adhere to a stereotypical role may bear on the degree to which she embraces the behavior. It may also influence whether she gets stuck at this stage of development or moves on to more mature behavior mandatory in meeting the rigorous challenges of life and career.

ON RISK TAKING

1. Do you encourage your daughter to explore her environment, seek new experiences, and challenge her physical limits? In other words, do you encourage her to take risks?

2. Are you inclined to rescue your daughter whenever she becomes frustrated or upset? Do you hover, ever-watchful to ensure her comfort and security?

3. If another child hit your daughter on the playground, would you tell her to hit the other child back? (Would you tell this to a son?)

4. Have you ever shown your daughter how to defend herself or enrolled her in a self-defense course?

5. Do you accept "I'm scared" or "I don't want to" as a legitimate justification for avoiding a challenge? (Would you accept this justification from a son?)

Your answers to the above set of questions will help determine two things: your tendency to rescue your daughter prematurely and to shield her from natural consequences. This behavior on your part can cripple her ability to *act* by perpetuating one of the most debilitating of feminine traits—the perception of herself as weak and in need of protection.

Because of realistic fears concerning our daughters' safety, we train them to be careful and cautious. We do this out of love, but love can make mistakes. When we rescue prematurely or protect too aggressively, we send a powerful message: "You can't do this alone. You need help." The result of this training is that girls become fearful and dependent and seek shelter under the protective wings of the risk takers of our society—males. Unfortunately, any glory that comes from the risk taker with whom they are associated is vicarious at best, a pale substitute to the personal fulfillment of individual risk taking and success. Finally, they rarely get the opportunity to experience the sheer exhilaration of a risk successfully negotiated. Consequently, girls are often cheated out of the growth and self-knowledge that come from pushing beyond one's comfort zone.

We do not do this to boys. We recognize, correctly, that over-protection of boys results in fear and that which we used to call "sissyish" behavior. We are unwilling to accept this in our male children, and so we put aside our parental fears to let them test themselves. With our female children, however, we seem willing to accept "sissyish" behavior and consequently produce fearful and dependent individuals. Once again, these are not the qualities we want to develop if our daughters are to succeed.

As we will see in a later chapter, risk taking is a critical component of achievement. The individual who values safety and security over challenge and excitement is not the individual who rises to a position of prominence. Safety and security are goals in themselves, whereas risk taking is part of a process toward a larger goal.

We must develop in females the same courageous attitude, derring-do, and self-confidence that we admire in males. Certainly there may be times when little girls find themselves in perilous situations and need adult help. Boys, too. But the insidious messages sent by overprotection and premature rescuing must be avoided—they foster only dependency and fear.

ON MALE ADVOCACY

1. Do you voice your approval for nontraditional female role models? Have you even thought about who these role models might be?

2. Have you ever acted as a mentor to a girl or woman?

3. If you are in a position to do so, do you demonstrate your support of female talent by hiring and promoting competent women on the job?

4. Do you belong to any professional groups that recognize and actively support women's issues?

5. Have you ever voted for a woman wishing to hold public office?

The purpose of these questions is to help you ascertain to what degree you actually put your money where your mouth is. Encouraging your daughter to realize her potential, make a contribution to society, and achieve worldly goals does not begin or end at home. It is a philosophy that must be carried out into the workplace if you are to help create a world where feminine contributions, including those of your daughter, are taken seriously.

Social change is a painfully slow process, so slow in fact that the chance of seeing a sex-equitable world in our lifetime is a slim one. But the process must begin somewhere. It can begin with you. Every small step taken on an individual basis will be your contribution to a world more willing and able to respond to the achievements of women, in general, and your daughter, in particular.

ON MALE SUPERIORITY AND DEVALUATION OF THE FEMININE *

1. Do you make the final decisions in your household? Is your word considered law?

2. Does your wife complain that you interrupt her a lot during conversation?

3. Do you resent the extra time your wife may spend on a job, a project, or a class, if it takes her away from you?

4. Do you shrug off the sexual sell in advertising, which uses females as objects to sell a product, as just another gimmick?

5. Do you refer to women as "girls"?†

6. Do you ever joke with your friends (or sons) about females when your daughter is around?

7. Do you think of a "wimp" as a feminine man?

If you answered yes to any of the questions in this section, it might be wise to examine the extent to which you assume that males are superior to females. It indicates the degree to which you may be subtly devaluing females by belittling their minds, their goals, and their work. And it indicates the degree to which you are undercutting your daughter's self-confidence and self-image.

While many contemporary men are far too enlightened to admit

---

*"The feminine" refers to any set of traits, attitudes, opinions, or behaviors which people *believe* are characteristic of females.
†"Gal" is not much better. Although I am not in the habit of quoting Joan Rivers, she makes a good point when she says a "gal" is just an old girl.

to putting down females in obvious ways, their behavior often betrays a deeper (but unexamined) belief in the superiority of male authority. Insistence on the final say in controversial family decisions, frequent interruption of daughters, wives, or women relatives, resentment of time a wife gives to projects other than domestic ones, all are symptomatic of a man who, at that most profound level of his belief system, presumes his sovereignty of the household.

What effect does this have on a daughter and her potential to succeed? It teaches her that despite her father's vociferous verbal support of her abilities, he doesn't really believe she is as capable as the males around her. Why not? Because she is female and male authority always supersedes female authority. The only logical conclusion she can reach is that male authority is superior.

This section will help you determine if you are sending this type of message. If so, you are undermining your own teaching with your behavior. You are sending a double message. You have forgotten rule number one—the impact of actions over words as the most powerful determinant of a child's behavior. Lip service paid to female potential, without the solid backup of behavioral evidence, will be seen by your daughter as hypocrisy when she is old enough to understand the concept. Therefore, be aware that pep talks alone are an empty and false kind of support. They are not sufficient to create the independent and autonomous female with the inclination and will to achieve.

ON ACTIVITIES AND QUALITY OF TIME SPENT TOGETHER

1. Do you spend uninterrupted and focused time *alone* with your daughter, just the two of you?

2. Do you take your daughter fishing? Hunting? Golfing? Camping?

3. Have you taught her how to climb a rope, swing a bat, dribble a basketball, read a compass, shoot a gun, throw a football, or bait a hook?

4. Have you ever taken your daughter to your workplace to show her what you do?

5. Do you ever discuss the nature of the business or professional world with your daughter? Do you explain what is expected of the participants in this world?

6. Do you ever discuss finances and investments with your daughter?

7. Do you ever take your daughter with you on Saturday to do traditionally masculine errands like going to the dump, the auto parts store, and the hardware store?

8. Have you ever lifted the hood of the car and explained to your daughter how the engine works?

9. Do you teach your daughter how to fix things?

10. Do you teach your daughter the names of tools and show her what they are used for?

11. Do you take your daughter to ball games or other athletic events?

12. Do you attend your *daughter's* athletic events?

These questions are designed to stimulate your thinking about worthwhile activities to share and discussions to have with your daughter. One of the most interesting things I have learned from fathers is that many of them want to spend time alone with their daughters but don't know what to *do* with them. One poor father actually said, "I thought all I could do was take her out to lunch or out shopping." While she may have enjoyed this outing, it is the time with her dad she would have truly enjoyed.

The problem for many fathers is that they believe the myth that there is a prescribed set of activities for males and a different set for females. They also believe an even more dangerous myth. They believe that a mother is needed as a go-between, an emotional mediator. Nothing could be further from the truth. A father and his little girl can enjoy as much camaraderie as a father and his son. One basic rule of thumb applies: Whatever you can do with a son, you can do with a daughter.

You say you have no son? Great! Take your daughter on those fishing trips, to that football game, out in the garage to work on the car. Whatever! In most cases, she will be so pleased to have you all to herself that she won't care what you are doing together. This may change drastically during the adolescent years, of course, when *any* activity engaged in with parents is just too dumb to be believed—although you can usually find something—but it shouldn't be much of a problem while she is still small. An elementary school child will be thrilled to spend time alone with her Daddy.

Little girls will be highly individualistic in this area. Some may love working on the car or going fishing, others may hate it, but it is wrong to assume that your daughter will not enjoy participating just because she is a girl. Even in adolescence, a daughter may be so delighted to have time alone with her dad that she becomes unexpectedly compliant and nonargumentative. Moreover, these activities will provide valuable time to talk and get to know each other. Since the time that most men spend with their children is limited, every opportunity to spend time together should be seized.

As you read through the rest of this book, keep in mind your answers to this quiz. Check back periodically to see if you would answer a question differently. Remember that the purpose of the quiz is to stimulate your thinking about the crucial issues outlined in the five categories of the quiz. Since the best kinds of tests are those which teach as they test, I hope you will capitalize on this opportunity to use the quiz in that capacity—as a learning tool for further exploration into your relationship with your daughter.

Types of Dads

The first paragraph of this chapter referred to the wide variety of daddies in the world. I realize that many people resent labels, feeling they are too confining and oversimplified to be accurate. By the same token, naming things gives us a tool with which to think about them, and sorting fathers into categories does offer a convenient tool by which to examine behavior. Faced with this dilemma, I decided to compromise and present a brief discussion of each type. If you find the descriptions too narrow, disregard them. If, on the other hand, they help you understand your behavior and the unspoken messages it carries, use them.

THE AUTHORITARIAN

This type of father is likely to send the message that the only avenue of behavior open to his daughter is submission to men. What this does is reinforce the imperative that females always submit to male authority. It is incongruent, not to mention counterproductive, to expect a daughter to acquiesce to a father's wishes all her life and then, suddenly, one day, out of the blue, acquire the chutzpah to take on her boss or some other male authority figure with whom she must be assertive, or even (God forbid) an attacker.

The issue to bear in mind is this: Does it really serve your goal of building a strong, independent woman to insist on your authority? Stop and ask yourself, "Would it really hurt anything to let her make her own decisions?" If that is too threatening, try this: "Would it really hurt anything, just this *one* time?" In other words, learn to separate those encounters which truly require your experience and superior world knowledge from those that are just a test of who's in charge. Relaxing the authority image just a little will make you easier to get close to.

THE SOFTIE

This daddy, although he will be greatly loved by his daughter, will be easy to manipulate. He will send the message that she can control male behavior by turning on the feminine charms and wiles. Although this may seem OK, it is important to remember that many men in the business and professional worlds resent being treated in this fashion. If they suspect they are being manipulated, they will pass up a woman for a promotion or raise, even if she is competent and deserving.

In many ways, being a softie with your daughter is an excellent quality. It will show her your nurturing, feminine side. It will make you easy to trust and confide in. Do not give up the tender qualities of your soft side. Softies are greatly loved.

On the other hand, if you become putty in her hands every time she turns on the tears or uses cute behavior to get her way, you reinforce her idea that this behavior is an effective and appropriate tool. In fact, the exact opposite is true.

Instead, teach her how to present an argument. Show her that she can make a point (perhaps even get her way) by planning ahead, using logic, and relying on the strength of her convictions. Reinforce this behavior rather than that of a charmer.

THE PROTECTOR

It is hard to fault this kind of daddy. He truly loves his little girl and wants with all his heart to keep her safe from harm. But by overzealously protecting and rescuing, he sends an insidious and debilitating message.

First, he creates in *her* the belief that she is vulnerable and in need of male protection. This fosters inappropriate dependency and the belief that a knight in shining armor will always arrive in the nick of time to save her. After all, Daddy always did. Second, protecting her from the natural consequences of her actions establishes the notion that she will not be held responsible for her behavior. If she never has to face the music, she never matures to the level of a fully responsible adult. Finally, this childlike dependency will result in the rudest of rude awakenings when your daughter realizes the world requires her to be strong, responsible, and brave.

THE PAL

This father is the closest to being on the right track. Authoritarians, protectors, and softies just reinforce old models of male/female relationships. But pals, friends, buddies—that's a different story. The implications that a friendship carries—two individuals who care about each other and enjoy each other's company—can be an extremely useful model for fathers to use in relating to their daughters. A genuine but relaxed concern for her well-being, combined with an honest desire for her company and a belief in her abilities, will send the strongest message that she is an equal and valuable individual.

Some fathers react to this concept negatively because they *want* to be authority figures. They want to be able to lay down the law and not be challenged. Unfortunately, the daughter of this type of individual will not learn to think for herself. If she does learn to think for herself, she may be too timid to assert herself.

The concept of father as person-mentor-pal strikes some men as wimpy. In fact, it is a powerful model. It does not preclude advice giving or even, on occasion, laying down the law. What it does do is reinforce the message to your daughter that she is a competent and trusted individual.

If you find yourself reacting negatively to the idea of a friendship with your daughter, go back and read the section on the authoritarian. Look inside to determine what you are proving by remaining an authority figure. Is it really worth creating a barrier between you and your daughter?

SHADES OF GRAY

In reality, of course, most fathers fall somewhere in between. That is why the labeling technique can be so limiting. Nevertheless, these descriptions can be a handy tool to examine your own behavior and determine to what extent you may be sending messages that are not conducive to your daughter's achievement.

Use your own judgment. The basic message is simple. Be an authoritarian, and you teach submission. Be putty in her hands, and you teach manipulation. Be her knight in shining armor, and you teach dependency. Be a person, a mentor, a pal, a father who has acquired the awareness and sensitivity to vary his behavior to meet the demands of the moment, and you create a female who believes in herself and surmounts obstacles with dignity and grace.

07-02-91

3 TX *4.95 1
       *4.95 ST
      *0.15 TX 1

              1 Q
       *5.10 CK

* 4-19
001-0008A

CHAPTER 3

Academic Success and Femininity

One of my workshop participants, a mother, made me realize that I was conveying a false idea when I said that striking a balance between achievement and femininity is a problem limited to *teenage* females. She didn't mince any words when she said, "What do you mean it's a teenager's problem? I'm thirty-five years old, and I haven't figured it out yet." Imagine, then, how difficult it must be for a girl who has little worldly knowledge to help her.

The conflict your daughter will face at puberty is the one you must begin preparing for now, whether she is twelve months or twelve years old. The crisis will not just be the result of raging hormones or teenage rebelliousness. It will be an observable manifestation of the conflict your daughter feels because of the messages that society sends females every day. Basically, these are the messages: achievement requires mastery-oriented behavior, and mastery-oriented behavior is seen by our society as essentially masculine. Consequently, many teenage girls come to perceive that achievement must be at the expense of femininity. In many ways, they are right.

The Rock and the Hard Place

This next section is critical. It outlines the two principal issues you must handle as you struggle to prepare your daughter for the world of achievement. These issues are part of the fabric of our contemporary culture. Although you may be tempted to pretend these issues won't affect your daughter, particularly if you have raised her in a nonsexist environment, to do so is unrealistic and ignores the power of the culture.

The first issue:
The discrepancy between the traits that define an achiever and those that define femininity

Its challenge:
To raise a daughter who sees a range of behavioral choices available to her, who doesn't see femininity and success as mutually exclusive, who doesn't believe she must sacrifice one for the other

The second issue:
The perception of females as victims that prevents parents from training them to take risks

Its challenge:
To raise a daughter who is aware of her vulnerability without feeling like a victim so that she is *able* to take the risks required to achieve

Let us begin with the first issue—the gap separating achievement from femininity. This gap creates great conflict in a teenage girl as she attempts to determine which potential to fulfill. Unfortunately, from her perspective, the seeming exclusivity of the two makes it a painful and confusing choice.

The best way to illustrate this impasse is to relate to you what happens in the seminars I teach on fathering successful daughters. (Most of the participants are fathers of daughters, but not all of them are.¹) I ask participants to make three lists: On one list they "define" success by naming its rewards and the traits required to achieve it. On the second list they give the traits that characterize masculinity; and on the third, the traits that characterize femininity. (You might want to do this yourself right now, if you are feeling in an introspective mood.)

Below is a compilation of how fathers define success. The first three items under each category are ordered by priority. (My personal experience has shown me many more people would put money at the top of the list but are embarrassed to do so in a group setting.) Here is that list:

SUCCESS

External (observable rewards)	Internal (required traits)
Power and authority	Belief in self
Money	Willingness to take risks
Responsibility	Independence and autonomy
Status or rank	Willingness to change
Nice clothes, car, house	Willingness to risk failure
Expense accounts	Willingness to accept success
Freedom to travel	Energy
Freedom to set own schedule	Humor
Stability	Curiosity
Good mental health	Creativity
Happiness	

As is readily apparent, some of the attributes listed here are subsumed under others. For example, a willingness to change must be preceded by a willingness to take risks, and a willingness to take risks is preceded by a belief in oneself. This is no great revelation, since it has been part of our folk wisdom for years. Phrases like "No guts, no glory" and "Nothing ventured, nothing gained" convey the same message and world view.

Now, here is a compilation of the typical lists men devise when asked to characterize masculinity and femininity.[2]

MASCULINE		FEMININE	
Positive	*Negative*	*Positive*	*Negative*
Adventurous	Violent	Nurturing	Weak
Assertive	Aggressive	Caring	Helpless
Aggressive	Inflexible	Emotional	Emotional
Independent	Stiff	Sensitive	Sensitive
Confident	Hard	Sweet	Talkative
Intelligent	Coarse	Curious	Powerless
Logical	Rigid	Domestic	Defenseless
Objective		"Connected"	Impotent
Reasonable		Understanding	Conniving
Athletic		Flexible	Vacillating

MASCULINE		FEMININE	
Positive	*Negative*	*Positive*	*Negative*
Active		Intuitive	Fickle
Vigorous		Compassionate	Inconsistent
Strong		Intelligent	
Forceful		Playful	
Powerful		Gentle	
Firm		Sensual	
Virile		Sexy	
Sexual		Attractive	
Decisive		Self-sacrificing	
Rugged		Passive	
Sturdy		Soft	
Brave		Pretty	
Daring		Refined	
Stoic		Slight	
Courageous		Dainty	
Tough		Fragile	
Muscular		Frail	
Robust		Submissive	
Straightforward		In need of protection	
Protective		Childlike	

Here is the point: when you compare the success list and the masculinity and femininity lists, you discover that *the traits listed as those exemplified by successful people are the very traits described as masculine by groups of men.* There it is. It is that simple. Even in a time when the society at large has been educated to understand that these stereotypes are limited and limiting, our responses and expectations continue to be influenced by old standards. Our daughters' perception that being attractive, sexy, and desirable as women is radically discordant with mastery-oriented behavior is right on target.

The internal qualities deemed necessary for success are actually fueled by the so-called masculine traits but *undermined* by the so-called feminine ones. For example:

Belief in oneself:
Requires confidence, decisiveness, firmness, and vigor

Is undermined by emotionality, sensitivity, frailty, and submissiveness

Willingness to take risks:
Requires daring, courage, adventurousness, robustness, decisiveness, and confidence

Is undermined by passivity, fragility, frailty, helplessness, vacillation, softness, and excessive refinement

Autonomy:
Requires assertiveness, vigor, courage, straightforward behavior, and power

Is undermined by passivity, impotence, softness, sweetness, childlikeness, excessive connectedness to others, and a need to be protected

Although there are a few feminine traits mentioned in the men's list of requirements for success, for the most part the feminine traits are the ones that must be *overcome* in order to succeed in the marketplace. As I say to the fathers in my workshop: suppose you were allowed to converse with God (or whomever or whatever is in charge of your personal universe) at your daughter's conception and were given permission to choose the traits your daughter would possess. Assuming you want her to be a successful individual, would you choose that she be emotional, childlike, self-sacrificing, passive, and frail? Or would you prefer her to be assertive, confident, independent, powerful, and decisive?

At first glance, it seems like an easy choice. But the more a father examines the traits required for success, the more he may feel queasy about raising a masculine daughter. This alternative is not attractive either. This is the same queasy feeling your daughter gets, only usually, she hasn't the understanding, experience, or vocabulary to express it.

Before anyone accuses me of presenting an oversimplified view of men's attitudes, let me be the first to point this out. However, in my defense please allow me to say that the social forces which are redefining the status and role of females have produced a population which finds itself at all points along the "awareness continuum"—with females as vassals at one end and females as Amazon warriors at the other. Naturally, fathers taking my class and reading this book will also be at all points along this continuum. It is not my wish to insult those with a heightened degree of awareness or to oversimplify the problem.

However, it is safe to say that in general our gut-level responses to an issue change much more slowly than our intellectual responses do; particularly if the issue is charged with an emotional investment, as is the issue of sex roles. (This slow-moving change is what is revealed in the lists of feminine and masculine traits that fathers in my class devise.)

The adolescent boys your daughter will know are operating on a very simple level, as you well know from having been there yourself. They are struggling just trying to figure out what it means to be masculine. Their grasp of the concept is fairly tenuous, even if their grasp of *their* masculinity is firm (pun intended). They have an easier time exhibiting the masculine behavior required of them if they clearly polarize it against feminine behavior. As our lists indicate, even grown men rely on stereotypes; so adolescent boys can be expected to rely on them even more. These are the boys your daughter will be wanting to attract when she reaches puberty.

Precarious Puberty and the Academic Struggle

Puberty and the junior high years are critical. Whether your daughter is still small and these years lie ahead or she is in the midst of the struggle, there are certain facts you need to be aware of in order to prevent or correct a negative situation.

During adolescence your daughter will sense, perhaps only unconsciously, that her competence threatens the boys, whose responses she uses to gauge her desirability as a female. Let's face it: being competent, assertive, independent, intelligent, and decisive are not the traits usually considered attractive by adolescent boys. In fact these traits are probably just the opposite of what boys consider sexy. If a girl acts cute, coy, compliant, sexy, and in need of protection, she is much more likely to get the kind of attention that affirms she is attractive to the opposite sex. Given the choice, the age factor, and society's expectations, male attention and approval are a lot more seductive than achievement at this time.

A perfect example of this all-important male approval was provided by one of my ninth-grade students, a handsome all-American boy, a football player and honor student of whom any father would approve and for whom any girl would gladly hand over her grade point average on a silver platter. He casually picked up the rough draft of the first chapter of this book and began reading it. When he came to the part describing how adolescent girls wear heavy makeup, skintight jeans, and low-cut blouses in order to win male approval, his comment was, "They sure get mine!"

You may be thinking, "Yes, but boys also need approval from

the opposite sex at this time in their lives.'' True. However, there is a fundamental difference. The role expectations for a boy to go out there and compete are not in conflict with the masculine traits he has been brought up to emulate. For a boy, the requirements for being masculine and receiving female approval are congruent with the traits he has been taught are necessary for achievement—power, strength, courage, assertiveness, and confidence.

Not so for our contemporary young female. Suddenly, at puberty, femininity requires that she exhibit a whole set of traits which have absolutely nothing to do with, and may even be in direct opposition to, the qualities necessary for achievement. It is no wonder she becomes ambivalent.

Many fathers waste hours of precious time in the vain attempt to convince their daughters they shouldn't care what the boys think. They say things like, ''You've got plenty of time for boys later.'' Come on. Get real, Dad. This kind of counseling is extraordinarily ineffective. All it does is reinforce your daughter's belief that you don't understand, that you can't relate to her problems.

THE BAD NEWS

In 1960, two researchers conducted a study to determine the onset of academic underachievement in bright children. The following graphs compare the achievement patterns of both boys and girls in grades one through eleven. The dotted lines represent underachievers and the solid lines represent achievers.[3]

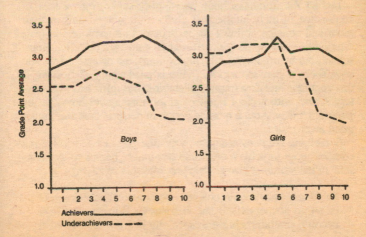

Achievers ———
Underachievers — — —

These graphs illustrate a disparity between male and female students. The female underachievers *begin* with a higher grade-point average than either the male or the female achievers. The grades of female underachievers begin to plummet at approximately seventh grade, the age of puberty for many girls, and continue a relentless decline through the eleventh grade.

Another very recent study supports the 1960 findings and confirms that, indeed, we have made little progress in our concept of femininity despite twenty years of "progress" in this area.

A group of researchers traced the performance of girls from sixth grade through their senior year of high school. In an interview which appeared in an Associated Press article in the *Philadelphia Inquirer* of March 6, 1986, Anne Petersen, head of Pennsylvania State University's program of individual and family studies, said, "Especially high-achieving girls seem to find status (good grades) inconsistent with having a positive self-view in seventh grade and they reduce their achievement. Girls may be making compromises that are detrimental to their long-term futures."

Furthermore, another researcher in the group states, "When boys drop out of the high-achievement group, their self-image drops . . . but for girls there's a tendency for self-image to *increase* when achievement declines."[4] (Italics mine.)

During the middle school years, girls suffer from a lack of confidence in their intellectual abilities in general and in their math and science abilities in particular. Furthermore, on tests rating self-esteem, girls score higher than boys in elementary school, but by middle school (junior high), the reverse is true and boys score higher than girls. What is particularly distressing is that cognitive and developmental studies show girls leave elementary school with a clear intellectual advantage over boys, yet by junior high they show a marked deficit in performance and grade-point averages.[5]

Something happens along the way: the pressure to resolve the conflict between achievement and femininity begins to assert itself. In the words of two researchers into this problem:

> She must either acquiesce to the stereotypical feminine role
> or try to be herself. If she chooses the former, she may
> become an underachiever, especially in areas such as math

and science. If she chooses the latter, she risks incurring censure and peer rejection.[6]

As a junior high school teacher I saw the ease with which boys and girls assume their roles. Boys automatically assume privilege and girls *automatically surrender it*! One of my teaching strategies was to put students into groups to solve problems, share ideas, etc. Without direction from me, a curious thing occurred with nauseating regularity. The groups would automatically divide up into two task categories, the decision makers and the secretaries. That's right, the girls would immediately take out pencil and paper to take notes and the boys would sit there like little chairmen of the board and dictate!

I immediately made a new rule. In my class there would be no, repeat no, female secretaries. The boys yelled and screamed that this was unfair. I admitted it. They said I couldn't do that. I asked them why not. When they informed me that it was because it was unfair, I pointed out that in "real life" it wasn't fair either, but nobody stopped men from exercising this prerogative in their hiring practices. This remark was greeted with silence and sullen expressions. I told them that in my class they would receive the rare opportunity to experience life on the other side of the fence. I asked them to pay careful attention to their feelings of resentment and anger. I asked them to remember these feelings and store them away for when they were older and in a position to hire women for other duties.

The girls, on the other hand, were smiling and nodding. I didn't hear one word of opposition from them. I pointed this out to the boys. "Isn't it interesting that the girls are not saying anything? Why do you suppose that is?"

"Because they're lazy," one boy shouted out.

"Does that mean that all you boys have been lazy in the past?"

"No!" he screamed at me, red-faced and furious, "it just means that we're supposed to be the boss!"

At this point all hell broke loose with boys and girls shouting at each other. I let the bedlam continue for a while before interrupting. But I did not change the rule. It remained in effect for the ten years that I taught school, and over the years I received scores of thank-yous from girls and their parents.

The real problem that girls face, if they knuckle under to the pressure to be feminine, is that by the time they realize they want to go to college or pursue a career, they have not taken the hardcore classes like calculus and physics that they will need for acceptance into the better schools. Then they must either play catch-up, which can be a stressful and frustrating process, or redefine their goals. This is why we must encourage them to keep their options open throughout their schooling.

Furthermore, we must teach them they can be studious and ambitious as well as feminine and attractive—that one does not preclude the other. The way to do this is to illustrate how any individual, male or female, can choose which way to act based on the moment (which will be elaborated on at great length in Chapter 5).

Another study whose findings substantiate a female's tendency to avoid success can be found in attribution theory:[7] when successful men and women were asked what they attributed their own successes and failures to, their answers were most revealing. Men, on the whole, tended to attribute success to internal qualities, such as ability and motivation. They attributed their failures to external problems, such as bad timing or difficulty of task. Women, on the other hand, were exactly the opposite. They were more likely to attribute their success to the outside influences of luck or ease of task, while failure was attributed to a lack of ability. In other words, females have a difficult time "owning" their achievements. They are more likely to take the blame for their failures but refuse credit for their achievements.

Puberty is a most critical period for intellectual development in girls. It can make the difference between a life of growth and achievement that proceeds in a more or less direct fashion and one that gets sidetracked with other considerations.

THE GOOD NEWS

Wouldn't it be nice if your daughter could bypass this precarious stage of development? She cannot. Puberty and its crises will happen no matter what. However, the good news is that you as a father can be instrumental in seeing to it that she doesn't get stuck at this level of development but instead passes through it as part of a greater process toward maturity. But you must begin your work now.

You will be walking a fine line. If you encourage only the development of her so-called feminine traits, you contribute to the creation of a dependent, passive personality; one that will be reluctant to assert itself against the dominant model of femininity. If you encourage only the development of her so-called masculine traits, you exacerbate her confusion by forcing on your daughter what seems to her a choice between love and achievement. If she is like most others her age, she will show indifference to achievement behavior if it means being passed over for an important dance or party. As we said before, attracting boys and winning popularity is the name of the game.

You must teach your daughter that it is not necessary to sacrifice boys, love, and popularity, for if she believes this is so, you may lose the battle, perhaps only temporarily, but perhaps permanently. Instead, help her understand that attracting the attention of a boy she has a crush on is one thing and getting an A on a math test is quite another. She must understand that it is possible to do both. Teach her that she has a range of behavioral choices open to her; that traits are just traits and it is unnecessary to laden them with connotations of feminine and masculine. (This will be elaborated on Chapter 5.) When she believes this, she will be more willing to expose all sides of her personality and capabilities.

Even more important, puberty is the time when you must give her all the approval and reassurance about her appearance and femininity that you possibly can. It will be her main concern. Although you may be concerned with more important issues in her life, like her grade-point average, remember that you must talk to her from where *she* is if you wish to be effective. Therefore, the greatest gift you can give at this time in her life is *male approval.* You have it in your power to give the very thing she needs and craves the most.

This is the time to tell her she is pretty, that you like her new outfit, that the boys will be lining up at the front door to take her out. Please don't misunderstand me. I'm not advocating that you abandon the development of her skills, talents, and competence; in fact, the rest of this chapter is devoted to just that. However, being a good father at this point in her life means realizing the extent to which her self-image is dependent on feeling confident *as a female*, which means believing she is attractive and feminine. Since this is the issue of puberty that drives girls underground, this is the one you must be ready to accommodate.

As her father, you are still the most important male in her life, and your opinion counts, believe me. Even if she puts on a great act of bored nonchalance, or worse, open hostility, it is your job to see past it, to see the neediness that is just below the surface. She will be flattered, honored, and encouraged to hear that dear ol' dad notices that she is becoming a young woman and that he approves of the woman she is about to become. It will be that extra touch that contributes to her overall self-esteem, and she will love you for it.

Remember, for girls, puberty is a time of great indecision. Their conflict is usually subconscious, and most of them are unable to verbalize it, but the more they are divided by the conflict between femininity and success, the less they have to give to the achievement of their goals. To be forced into such a limited and premature decision is tragic. Make that extra difference in her life by being the kind of father who, while teaching her skills and developing her competence, takes the time to recognize her femininity as well.

More on the Academic Struggle: Girls and Computers

Perhaps there is no greater symbol of our technological, electronic age, no more useful metaphor for our human intellectual processes, no more appropriate indicator of our future than the computer. Similarly, there may be no more accurate gauge of the reluctance of females to succeed in what they perceive as a male world.

Recent data on the use of computers both at home and in school indicates that society continues to propagate the myth that computers are primarily male machines. This notion will have dire consequences for females if they refuse to become familiar with computers. Not only will they lack the skills necessary to acquire the best-paying jobs, indeed, perhaps any job at all, but they will be left behind in a technological society and lack the cognitive and intellectual skills required by that society for survival.

The data on males and females and how they relate to the computer lies in four basic areas which I call the four A's: appreciation for, attitude toward, access to, and application of the computer.

Let's begin with the good news.

The young female population does show an appreciation for the computer as a tool of the future and recognizes its importance to career opportunities. A 1983 Gallup youth survey showed that 65 percent of girls between the ages of thirteen and nineteen planned to take college computer courses.[8] In another study, nearly three-fourths of all twelfth-grade girls, and two-thirds of sixth-grade girls in California agreed with the statement, "A knowledge of computers will help me get a better job." In a required high school computer science class fully 80 percent of the girls enrolled agreed that knowing about computers was important to their futures. These studies reveal that schools, parents, and the media have done a good job of making young people aware of the value and importance of computers.[9]

Now the bad news.

Despite their appreciation for the computer, many girls have acquired negative attitudes toward them. This incongruence has been reported many times in the research. Several studies have confirmed repeatedly that males are more positively disposed toward computers than females. Also, males report a much higher use of the computer than do females. More boys than girls take computer classes, learn to use micros, play computer games, and learn programming. In a study of at-home computer use, 70 percent of users were male![10] In the words of Marlaine E. Lockheed, a researcher in the field, "Males and females express similar appreciation for computers, but males report using and liking computers more than females do."[11]

What are the reasons for this discrepancy? The view of technology as a male domain is only one of many explanations. A variety of attitudes accounts for female reluctance to become involved with computers. Some attitudes are subtle and some are quite overt, but either way, their impact is severe and debilitating.

One is the connection between mathematical aptitude and programming ability. Several studies have confirmed that both males and females are socialized to perceive mathematical ability as a male trait.[12] This perception has two consequences. First, when a young female does display mathematical aptitude, she may be reluctant to develop it. Fearful of seeming unfeminine, she may hide her ability altogether. Second, if she doesn't show mathematical aptitude, she is often predisposed to give up more quickly than her male counterparts, believing that since she is female, and therefore mathematically inept, she shouldn't bother trying.

In another study, math skills were rated as both feminine and masculine by elementary school children, yet by adolescence, students ranked mathematical ability as a masculine trait.[13] The decision whether or not to take algebra I in the eighth grade was shown to be a critical factor in another study.[14] As recently as 1982, in an era in which we are supposed to have conquered these narrow stereotypes, boys and girls both continued to reflect stereotypical conforming patterns in their class selections. For example, in one study (which we will examine in depth in Chapter 5) students gave the following responses to the question, "If you were to wake up tomorrow as a (girl) (boy), how would your life be different?"[15]

> "I would drop my math class and take more classes like cooking, English, and ones that would make me look good as a girl." (Twelfth-grade boy)

> "I would not want to take all of the math and science classes I am taking now. I would take mostly art, food, and clothing classes." (Tenth-grade boy)

> "I'd drop my sewing class." (Eleventh-grade girl)

> "I would take classes like drafting and woodshop." (Eleventh-grade girl)

Generally speaking, math, science, and computer classes are seen as male classes, while cooking, sewing, and typing are seen as female classes. (Girls may enjoy a bit of revenge later on when they are able to type with speed and utilize the time-saving capabilities of the computer much better than the boys, who have been observed wasting hours of precious time hunting and pecking at the keyboard—but that's another story.)

Another negative influence on girls and computers involves video games and arcades, which are targeted as male-oriented activities and appeal to male-oriented value systems. Any quick peek into a video arcade will reveal that it has become the modern technological equivalent of the pool hall, complete with a males-only atmosphere. Groups of young men cluster around game booths or just hang out with their friends. Any girls observed there seem to be hanging on the protective arms of their boyfriends.

This atmosphere can be quite intimidating to a girl alone. If she wants to go in and play a game, she feels she needs a male escort. If she goes in with a girlfriend (assuming she can find one who will brave the scene), she is likely to experience being "hit on"[16] rather than being able to play. Furthermore, many parents discourage their daughters from going in because of the den-of-iniquity atmosphere that surrounds these arcades. Since a primary motivational factor in computer use is game playing, this fear of arcades can have negative consequences for girls.[17]

In another study, a random sample of seventy-five different software titles was taken from entertainment, education, and general interest software developed for three major microcomputer manufacturers. These titles were rated by 150 junior high school students. Only 5 percent were judged to be primarily of interest to females. A group of thirty adults also rated the titles. There was no difference. In other words, boys, girls, men, and women all agreed that software games and titles are male-oriented.[18]

Another fascinating study shows the more subtle ways that our stereotypes concerning females and computers are shaped. A study by Mary Ware and Mary Stuck, of the State University of New York, explored the pictorial representations of males and females in three mass-market computer magazines.[19] They analyzed the pictorial content of a total of 2,637 pages to determine three things:

1. The number of men, women, boys, and girls illustrated
2. The roles in which they were portrayed
3. Whether they were shown using the computer, rejecting the computer, or just standing by

In an era when girls need as many media and visual role models of female computer users as they can get, the results of this study are disconcerting.

A total of 426 illustrations containing 727 individuals was analyzed. Of these individuals, nearly 70 percent were male.

Even more important than sheer numbers were the activities and roles of the individuals in the pictures. The role classifications for the individuals portrayed in the magazines were as follows: expert, manager, clerk, teacher, learner, repair technician, game player, seller, buyer, sex object (yes, even in computer magazines!), and "other," which was defined as "no classifiable role."

First, women were overrepresented as clerks, sellers, and sex objects. They were underrepresented as managers, experts, and repair technicians. Sex differences were also apparent for boys and girls. Boys were shown in the roles of learners, game players, repair technicians, buyers, and "other"; girls were portrayed *only* as learners and "other." Males were much more likely to be actively engaged in using the computer (82 percent male, 55 percent female).

Finally, it is very revealing to note that there were two areas (one activity and one role) in which *only* females were portrayed. No males were observed in these roles or activities. You guessed it. Only females were shown rejecting the computer, and only females were portrayed as sex objects. Males never were.

The second area of negative impact on females involves access to the computer. Several studies have suggested that parents and teachers discriminate between boys and girls, giving boys greater opportunity to use the computer.

One study, conducted in 1982, questioned twenty-three directors of computer training programs or summer computer camps serving 5,533 students. Data was provided by these directors concerning cost and enrollment, type of program, sponsorship of program, and level of difficulty of course offerings.[20]

Three times as many boys as girls were enrolled! The ratio of males to females increased with age, difficulty of the course, and cost of the program. We will look at each item separately and attempt to explain these findings.

First was the correlation between age and enrollment. The percentage of females was as follows: 30 percent in elementary grades, 26 percent in middle school or junior high, and 24 percent in high school. This data is congruent with the earlier studies we discussed concerning the declining performance of females during puberty as well as data indicating that math is seen as a male activity among adolescents.

Next was the striking difference that was exposed when the data was tallied by the difficulty of the course offering. The percentage of females in beginning and intermediate classes was 28 percent; this dropped to 14 percent in advanced programming and plummeted to only 5 percent in assembly language courses.

Finally, the highest disproportion was related to the cost of the program or camp. The high-cost residential camps had the highest proportion of males, while the camps offered by public schools contained the most females.

This last statistic deserves some special attention. It is the most interesting one to ponder. Could it be that parents are more willing to invest in this expensive type of training for their sons? Do they foresee a better return on their money? Is it yet another example of the obsolete notion that males need to earn more money than females? Considering the fact that female participation is much greater when provided by public schools at low cost to parents, it certainly seems like a plausible explanation.

A Department of Education study showed that boys were given more computer time by educators both in the lab and at the terminal. In my own junior high school boys just naturally assumed that if they were vying for computer time with a girl, they would take precedence. Many were angry and voiced their indignation when I informed them they would have to sign up and wait their turn.

One bright boy actually said, "You mean *she* gets the computer before *I* do?" He was incredulous. *I* was incredulous over the ease with which he assumed his male privilege and dismayed by his disgust that a mere girl came before he did. I then took it upon myself to make certain that the girls were able to use the computer at least as often as the boys. I didn't realize the battle I was setting myself up for. Even when the boys knew this was the rule, they continued to badger me. They accused me of being sexist and unfair because they weren't being given free access to the only computer in my classroom.

Finally, when females do score on a par with their male peers regarding the computer, it is in the use of the computer as a tool. No sex differences are reported there. Are you breathing a sigh of relief? Well, don't. Even this seemingly positive statistic has a downside for females. Unfortunately, girls are signing up for more courses in word processing and database retrieval than are boys.[21] Although this helps them to use the computer and acquire skills, the skills they acquire qualify them for clerical and secretarial jobs only, not the high-paying careers of those who know how to control the "thinking" processes of the computer and the information it houses.

Recommendations

As her father there are many things you can do, both subtle and overt, to encourage your daughter's intellectual gifts.

First, be aware that you must work on your daughter's belief system. If her belief system is allowed to develop freely without some corrective information from you, she will most likely come to believe that mathematics, computers, programming, engineering, and science are strictly male activities. It is your job to convince her that this viewpoint is false and limiting.

Begin by never presuming to know what subjects will interest your daughter. As a matter of fact, do just the opposite. Assume she is interested in *everything* until she proves otherwise. Even if she rejects scores of subjects, never jump to the conclusion that you know what will capture her interest. Your daughter may be utterly fascinated by electronics or mechanical engineering.

You may find this hard to believe. Many fathers in my class sort of snicker when I say this. But what if someone in Terrie Ann McLaughlin's family had assumed that she would not be interested in electronics or mechanics because she was a female? Who is Terrie Ann McLaughlin? She is the young woman chosen as Outstanding Cadet in the U. S. Air Force Academy's graduating class of 1986 and the first woman to receive such an honor. Not only was Terrie chosen as outstanding cadet overall, she was also named the outstanding cadet in the engineering school at the academy. She is pursuing an advanced degree in electrical engineering at Stanford University. Terrie is important not only for her achievements but because she gives lie to the concept that females show less aptitude than males in the fields of math, mechanics, electronics, and engineering.

When I asked her why she chose such a nontraditional field, she said, "During high school I always found math and science to be the most fascinating courses, so that's how I got involved in computers and engineering.

"My father, with whom I have always had a really strong relationship, never specifically encouraged me to go into electrical engineering or anything like that. He was just supportive of anything I wanted to do and, above all else, he wanted me to be happy.

"There are still some people that have some doubts about women in certain career fields, but from what I've seen, women have so much to contribute that men are beginning to notice."

One woman who has a lot to contribute is Barbara Grogan, about whom you will learn more later. She is the founder and president of Western Industrial Contractors, Inc., a business which grew in four short years to a $5 million firm whose clients include Anheuser-Busch, AT&T, IBM, Nabisco, Ralston-Purina, and United Airlines, just to mention a few. When she was a little girl, a man who apparently did not know that girls were not good in math changed her life forever.

"When they put glasses on me, this man in a big, white coat said to my mother, 'She'll never be able to spell or read worth a damn, but she's gonna be a whiz in math.' Well, when I heard that, I just programmed myself to do it," she said.

"I never got any less than an A in any math class I had in my entire life through graduate-level calculus. I've always loved math. I have a very logical mind."

A female computer programmer and math major in college said to me, "When I was a math major, I really never had a good grasp on what I was doing until I got to the next-level math course. Then it all became miraculously clear. I think females need to learn to be patient with themselves and not jump to the conclusion that they can't understand it just because they are temporarily confused. *Anyone* who does higher-level math gets confused."

When your daughter shows frustration with math, indicate that it is a challenging subject for all those who confront it, not just for females, because even if she doesn't hear it at home, she is likely to hear somewhere that "girls are just not good in math." Make her aware that males become just as frustrated with math problems. The difference is they aren't taught that they are genetically incapable of solving them, so they persist. Relate to her Einstein's famous quote, "No matter how great your difficulties in mathematics, mine are still greater, I can assure you."

Let her know about females and their early involvements with the computer. The world's first programmer was a woman. Augusta Ada Lovelace wrote the instructions for a computing machine in the 1800s. The first programs for the ENIAC, which was built in the 1940s, were written by Adele Goldstine. One of the chief developers of COBOL, a language used for programming digital computers for business applications, was Grace Hopper, who was also the first person to coin the term "bug," referring to an error in a computer program. Of the 2,000 computer operators in 1960, when the computer industry was still in its infant stages, 65 percent were women.[22]

Acclimate your daughter to computers early in life. When she is a baby, sit her on your lap and let her pound away at the keyboard. It will only be a game at this point, but the screen will be fun to look at, and she will learn to feel relaxed around the computer. Search out video games that appeal to females; that is, ones with less shooting and fewer militaristic themes. Take her into video arcades, where, with you for moral support, she can learn to play the games and not be intimidated by the males. "Joust" and even the old standby "PacMan" are good arcade choices, as they tend to appeal more to females.

Expose her to popular high-tech and computing magazines at the same time that you discuss the sex-stereotyped portrayal of females in these magazines. In other words, teach her to be aware and critical of the sexism she will be confronted with so that she does not absorb it passively. Again, emphasize that ignorance in high-tech fields will keep females out of many of the highest-paying jobs of the future.

If she has a brother, see to it they each get equal time at the computer. Do not the send the subtle message, through providing greater access to a boy, that his time at the computer is more valuable than hers.

If she shows interest (and if you can afford it), send her to computer camps and encourage her to enroll in programming classes. If you see her beginning to fall into the trap of "boys program; girls word process," nip it in the bud by igniting her enthusiasm for the wonderful tool that a computer is and all the marvelous things you can make it do for you, if you have acquired the knowledge and learned the thinking processes.

Buy her one of those beginner's electronics kits that teaches the basics of electricity and electronics. The two of you can work on it together, providing not only a great teaching tool for her to become familiar with how computers and other electronic gadgets work, but also the time for you to talk to one another.

An early interest in math, electronics, and mechanics was revealed in the life of Judith Resnick, the only female NASA astronaut aboard the ill-fated shuttle. In an interview with her father, he revealed that Judy had always shown an interest in math and things mechanical.

"We would go to the library on Saturdays, and I would read science fiction, but Judy would pick more factual things. She wasn't much of a fiction reader but was very thorough in her interest in mathematics, science, and how to do repair work.

"She liked to watch me fix things around the house, too. She would say, 'Daddy, show me how,' and I said, 'Sure,' and I would show her. She was interested in electrical things, so I taught her how to fix base plugs, put in electrical wiring, and put in chain pulls when she was still just a little girl.

"When she got older, she was very interested in cars and automobile repair and stuff like that, so I helped her there as well."

Obviously, anyone who snickers at the idea of females being interested in math and mechanics has never been around females like these. Perhaps it is simply because no one ever told them they should not be interested in math and science because they were boys' subjects. Dr. Resnick was very matter-of-fact about teaching Judy how to do electrical wiring. He did not even realize it was an unusual thing to do. He said, "I always taught her that she could do as well as any man. I taught her that if she worked hard, she would achieve. It just so happened that she had high ability in many areas (particularly math and music), and so she was able to achieve quite a bit."

Above all, these efforts on your part will teach her that the technological, electronic age is *hers*, too. It is your job to show her that it is more rewarding, fun, lucrative, and exciting to be an active participant than a passive observer. Teach her that if she has the aptitude and the interest, programming is an ability, a skill, and a thinking process, not a trait of femininity or masculinity. Being feminine or masculine is something quite apart from the processes of thinking and problem solving. When she understands this, she will feel free to develop her abilities without the fear of negative consequences.

Another way to encourage her interest in these subjects is to buy her subscriptions for magazines not usually considered girls' magazines. Buy her a subscription to *National Geographic* or *Omni* or *Popular Science* instead of *Seventeen*. Please notice I used the phrase, "buy *her* a subscription." Purchasing a subscription for the family and hoping she picks it up has a great deal less impact than actually putting the subscription in her name and being able to say, "Mary, your copy of *National Geographic* arrived today." After she has had a chance to read her magazine, she may choose to share it with the rest of the family, but making it *her* magazine gives her a sense of ownership of the ideas therein. This sort of thing goes a long way toward building her perception of herself as someone who is interested in ideas and issues.

As you will see in Chapter 5, one way an individual's self-concept is formed is through finding out what *other* people think. Buying your daughter a subscription to a nontraditional magazine is a reflected appraisal. It says that you think she is the type of person who would enjoy and understand this subject matter. The same goes for computer games that teach programming skills. Give her these as gifts also, and send a powerful message concerning your beliefs about her capabilities.

If you have a professional library, encourage her to browse through your books. If she is very young, sit her on your lap, open up a technical book or magazine which contains illustrations or diagrams and show her the pictures, explaining what she is looking at and what its function is. (If you don't tell her, she will never know that most little girls don't look at these pictures with their daddies!) It makes absolutely no difference that she will not understand what she is looking at; what matters is that she will be exposed to this type of material and learn to see herself as a person capable of understanding it because *you* see her as a person capable of understanding it.

Teach your daughter how to play intellectual games, particularly those requiring strategic thinking like chess, backgammon, and "Go." When we had game day in my junior high classes, these games were played almost exclusively by the boys. While they were busy training their minds in strategic thinking, the girls were writing notes or drawing on the board. This is pathetic. When I inquired as to why the girls never requested to play, they informed me they didn't know how. Some of the boys then volunteered to teach them. I asked myself what kind of a society teaches its males to play chess but somehow overlooks its females? This is not as minor as it seems on the surface. It concerns the skills that can be learned from these activities which may be applied later in life.

Another strategic game that teaches important skills is poker. It, too, is considered a primarily male activity. I have often thought that corporate wheeling and dealing is just another sophisticated variation of poker. Learning to psych-out your opponent, to master the art of bluffing, and to call your opponent's bluff are skills that have been put to good use in many a smoke-filled boardroom. Once learned, these skills contribute to situational aplomb, the ability to think on one's feet, and self-esteem.

Yet another male activity which I have observed teaches thinking skills is the making of paper airplanes. In all the years that I taught junior high school, I never saw one girl make a paper airplane. I never thought much of it until I had the good fortune to observe a gifted boy who was utterly fascinated by paper airplanes. He would create his own original designs or elaborate on old ones. He would improve them aerodynamically by weighting them with paper clips or staples, making cuts on the fins, etc. By watching him, I realized that he was *learning* in the process of this activity. Sure enough, he went on to become an engineer.

Making paper airplanes and playing poker or chess or "Go" are great rainy-day activities to indulge in with your daughter. Not only will you be teaching her new skills, you will have time to talk, get to know each other, and have some plain old fun.

If she indicates an interest in attending an all-girl school, by all means, send her! Research findings have emerged concerning young women who graduate from these schools. According to Dr. Elizabeth Tidball, of George Washington University Medical Center, more than twice as many graduates of women's colleges, as compared to female graduates of coed schools, go on to earn doctorates or attend medical school. Furthermore, women who attend women's colleges are more likely to graduate than are females who attend coed schools, and graduates of women's colleges are twice as likely to be cited for career accomplishments in *Who's Who of American Women*![23]

The reasons for this are varied. First, there are more leadership opportunities for women in girls' schools. Second, there are more females on the faculty and therefore more opportunities to see women as serious scholars. Third, the study atmosphere is more pronounced than at coed colleges, where social events may intrude on class and study time. (That is not to say there is no social life at girls' schools. Girls' schools traditionally mingle with boys' schools, but social events are more detached from everyday campus life than at coed colleges.) Fourth, achievements by females may be taken more seriously by the student body at large. Finally, there may be fewer females attending who are seeking what used to be called an "MRS. degree."

Many young women who have attended girls' schools, even at the high school level, say that without the boys around to show how sweetly feminine and noncombative girls can be, the girls retain their spirit of inquiry and debate. Furthermore, they have a greater chance to practice it.

For instance, Barbara Grogan, the president of Western Industrial Contractors, whom you met earlier, attended girls' schools from first grade through twelfth. Here is what she has to say about the experience:

"You know, at the time I didn't think it was so hot, but in looking back I think it was real important, because girls were the leaders, girls were the jocks, girls were the scholars. It was a very normal course of events to see females assume these roles, because we were all there was!

"We had an hour of sports, and it wasn't optional, it was mandatory. We ran our fannies off for an hour a day. We played hockey, we played soccer, we swam, played tennis and basketball." She chuckles at the memory. "I can't play basketball. I mean, there I was, 5 feet tall, playing basketball. But it didn't matter. You just were expected to get out there, by damn, and play ball."

As she reminisces, I am aware of how feminine she is. Just as most other people, I suppose, I had assumed before I met her that to survive and thrive in the world of industrial contracting, she might be forced to behave like a pseudo-male. How thoroughly refreshing and encouraging to know that is unnecessary. This petite, blonde mother of two is highly intelligent, competent, and energetic. These are the qualities which enable her to succeed in her field.

"There were these two components in my life. There was my father expecting me to excel in school, and then there was the school providing the environment where I could excel without worrying about competition with the guys.

"What I mean is, you didn't have to think, 'Oh, maybe he won't ask me out if I beat him in this election for class president.' That didn't exist. I dated guys during high school and had lots of male friends, but they were all outside my school, so it is still possible to have a social life, too."

Although Judy Resnick attended a coed public high school, she dealt with boys in much the same manner—she dated ones who did not go to her school.

"At Firestone High, Judy was known as Judy the Brain," says her father, "but she dated boys further from home who attended a Catholic high school. They knew she was a smart girl, but they didn't see the brainy side as much."

Let your daughter know that even if she attends an all-girl school, she does not have to be alienated from the male population. Make her aware that she can meet boys just about anywhere and that attendance at a girls' school does not preclude dating or socializing with the opposite sex.

Another skill you can teach her is how to handle money. You can begin this at a very early age. Don't just give her money; when she is old enough, insist that she earn it. Do not relegate her labor to only traditional female activities like baby-sitting. Hire her as your assistant (apprentice?) in building or repairing something. By late elementary school you could help her establish her own little business. (Put your heads together to come up with ideas.) If she needs "capital" to get started, stake her a loan with interest and require monthly payments.

Teach her how to save by making a deal that she must save a certain percentage of her earnings (50 percent is a good number). When her savings have reached a certain level, allow her to spend the money on anything she chooses. Resist the temptation to tell her what to buy. Let her make her own spending decisions. Give her the right to folly and the license to make mistakes with her money. (After all, you do!) Experience will teach her more than any amount of advice.

When she is a little older, you can upgrade her financial education. Let her witness the kind of decision making that you and your wife engage in while making family financial decisions. Show her your own family budget and how it was planned. Let her participate in paying the bills every month by putting her in charge of recording the checks in the checkbook.

When she is still older, talk to her about investments, real estate, stocks, bonds, and financial planning. According to Marty McNellis, financial planner of Hanifen-Imhoff and the father of two daughters, "Women sometimes seem thrown by financial jargon. I would suggest that fathers begin to teach their daughters some basic financial planning, as well as the fundamental concepts around economics and investing.

"It is important for their daughters to know how bonds are valued, how and why interest rates move, the causes of inflation and its effect upon investments, that sort of thing. These are subjects on which most of the population is ill-informed, but women often seem more reluctant to learn about these concepts than men do."

Finally, discuss women you would like your daughter to respect and emulate. Make pointed remarks that these women are good role models and then give your reasons why. Do not always focus on just the brilliant women, or the famous women, or the women in nontraditional occupations. Although these are certainly good choices, they are usually already in the spotlight. Don't forget the "ordinary" women; in particular those who have not always sought to please, those who have chosen unpopular causes, those whose behavior some would label aggressive but to others is merely principled, and those who have displayed strength of character in a quiet, day-to-day sort of way.

A Story of Three Sisters

The story of Deana Bennett and her two sisters illustrates the results when daughters are encouraged by their fathers through word *and* deed to be independent, self-reliant, and courageous.

The Bennetts' father produced three extraordinarily successful daughters. We are talking about a 100 percent success story! All are the principal breadwinners in their families. All have held highly unconventional jobs for women.

One daughter was graduated summa cum laude from her college and was immediately wined and dined by the Big Eight accounting firms. She became the youngest (as well as the only female) financial director of the United Way at the tender age of twenty-six.

Another daughter became the first nonmedical head of a medical department at a large university medical school after convincing them that her credentials were superior to those they had been requiring from their other applicants.

The oldest daughter, Deana, took over the family business with her brother, where she deals with farm and drilling equipment as well as all aspects of managing the business—hardly a traditional female occupation.

"My father never differentiated between his son and his three daughters in terms of what he expected us to achieve," says Deana. "The things that society labels as successful, like financial ability and job success, came because my father never saw any difference in his son and his three daughters. He wasn't a boy, and we weren't girls. We were all just Bennetts.

"My father told all his daughters from the very beginning that we had to be able to take care of ourselves. He never once told us that a man would take care of us. That's because he didn't believe it himself. He watched his two sisters marry complete nerds and have to support both themselves and their children, and he wanted to make sure that all of us were capable of doing that in case we found ourselves in a similar situation.

"In fact, it was a real surprise when I became an adult and heard that other women had been told as children they would grow up and a man would take care of them. That was never a message from my father. Even subconsciously. In fact, the opposite was true.

"And, of course, I'm still single, so obviously I'm responsible for myself. And even though both of my sisters are married, they earn the most money in their families."

Deana is quiet for a moment, remembering something important, if the look on her face is any indication. Then she says, "You know, my father actually made my brother come back from Dartmouth, where he was doing very well, because he said he had three daughters to educate and he couldn't afford it if my brother stayed at Dartmouth. At the time I didn't think much of it, but now I realize how incredible that was.

"When I was in high school, there was an Italian girl whose father wouldn't let her go to college because he didn't believe in girls going to college. She was a National Merit Scholar! When I told my Dad, he absolutely flipped. He was just appalled. He thought it was such a ridiculous waste, and he was very vocal about it. He just couldn't understand treating boys and girls differently, *as if life demands less of females than males.*

"The funny thing is," Deana says with an ironic smile, "he doesn't think he did anything unusual. His attitude was there just wasn't any question of ability, you know, you were born to it. You're a Bennett, so you do what has to be done. It doesn't have anything at all to do with your sex.''

At this point in our conversation, I asked her to give me some specifics she could remember that went beyond verbal encouragement. She laughed.

''Actually, we didn't get that much verbal encouragement! It was more in the form of expectations. Like I remember when I was sixteen, I totaled the only family car we had. Completely smashed the hell out of it. Undriveable. My father bought a brand new car, drove it home on Saturday, walked upstairs, knocked on my bedroom door and said, 'Get up. You're driving.'

''God, I didn't want to drive that car. I never wanted to drive another day in my life. I was scared, you know. Hadn't had enough time to recover from the shock of the accident. But with him, you weren't allowed to hide. It was just, get back on the horse and all that.

''And at each step of the road as we were growing up, there were things that when they came up, you just did them. You did them because they had to be done. It was immaterial whether you were male or female. What mattered was that there was something that needed doing, and responsible people took care of business. Responsible people, not just responsible men. It made me very self-reliant.

''I can remember my French teacher, whom I hated. She put me in the hospital with an ulcer. What a bitch. Anyway, my father told me I didn't have to be good in French. It was OK to be good in the things I was good at. *But*, and here's the catch, I still had to take the course. I had to take French and possibly not do well. Or perhaps even fail. You see, you were allowed to fail. But you weren't allowed to give up. The worst thing, in his eyes, would be not to try at all.

''Looking back, it must have been difficult for him to make me stick it out, especially because it was making me sick. I guess he realized that there would be other life situations that had the potential to make me sick and I might as well learn how to handle myself.''

Because Deana's father did not rush in to rescue his daughters from anxiety-provoking and even perilous situations, he produced three women capable of taking risks and taking care of themselves. These three women do not consider for a moment that their well-being is someone else's responsibility. They have demonstrated they are capable of taking risks—the first step toward achievement. And achieve they have. Perhaps by some standards their self-reliance and knack for risk taking would be considered masculine, but to the extent that the quality of their lives demonstrates the rewards of feminine autonomy, it is worth the criticism.

The Difference between Encouragement and Pressure

I must bring up a common but disturbing fact about the nature of successful individuals. It won't be the first time you have heard it, but it is an issue which must be discussed because it is crucial to your job of fathering a successful daughter.

In interviewing successful people (in this case, women), one comes to notice that there seem to be two basic types of successful individuals: those who enjoy their success and those who don't; those who acquire a sense of gratification from their accomplishments and those who feel perpetually inadequate. Unfortunately, there are some successful people who never really feel good about themselves regardless of their achievements. They are plagued throughout their adult lives with a sense of inadequacy that even the most grandiose accomplishments do not seem to assuage, or if they do, they do so only temporarily.

The successful individual who feels secretly inadequate often projects a persona that is not congruent with his or her inner feelings of self-worth, a kind of false bravado, if you will. This is the type of person who, when success comes, feels like an impostor, even though he or she may be quite competent and intelligent, even brilliant. The other type of individual succeeds with an inner feeling of self-worth that is independent of accomplishments, a self-confidence that springs from an internal belief rather than one requiring external validation. In other words, one individual succeeds trying to *get* self-esteem, the other succeeds because the self-esteem is already there.

Individuals trying to get self-esteem are usually functioning on a belief system which disallows any good feelings concerning themselves. At the very core of their beings, they believe that they are not OK people. They believe they are stupid, or bad, or inadequate, or as one woman put it, "improperly tested."

People with this kind of belief system often had parents who withheld approval, believing that it "spoiled" a child and that criticism made the child try harder and perform better. This tends to be more of a male style of parenting than a female style, more of a fathering issue than a mothering issue. Fathers in my workshop have told me they think it comes from the old sports model of bearing down, toughening up, and never giving an inch, a kind of army boot-camp approach to child rearing. In reality, it is not encouragement but pressure.

Most fathers do this unconsciously and with the best intentions. For example, suppose a child is having trouble in math evidenced by a string of D's on daily assignments and quizzes. One day, the child brings home a B. Instead of showing great joy at this accomplishment, many fathers say something like, "Well great. Now next time get the A!" Or suppose a daughter runs a mile in ten minutes and Dad says, "That's terrific, honey, but let's get it down to nine!" By constantly setting a higher goal for a child, so that he or she must always run faster, throw further, climb higher in order to get parental approval, a subtle but compelling message is sent: the current performance, no matter how good, is never good enough. This can leave a child with a profound sense of inadequacy as well as the message that love is conditional and based on performance.

As the father of a daughter whom you want to be successful, you will find it very easy to fall into this trap unless you are aware of it. Remember that it is easy for pressure to masquerade as encouragement.

Don't get me wrong. I'm not saying this technique doesn't work: scores of parents have produced successful children who constantly drive themselves trying to prove that they *are* adequate, intelligent, energetic, or whatever they feel the requirements are. I know. I have interviewed many of them.

The problem is they never really get to enjoy the fruits of their labor—that is, the joy of an accomplishment, the feeling of self-worth at a job well done. Perhaps for a few fleeting moments they allow themselves a respite, but the old belief that whatever they do is never "enough" resurfaces quickly to drive them to the next accomplishment. This addiction to perfection can have devastating psychological consequences as we will see later. (Some of these repercussions are discussed in the chapter on eating disorders.)

Contrast this successful but insecure personality with the type of successful individual who functions from an inner feeling of self-worth. This type is as energetic, productive, and achievement-oriented as the one who lacks self-esteem, but is less driven, less desperate. These individuals allow themselves to feel good about their achievements. They get a lasting sense of satisfaction from their accomplishments. They do not become complacent or smug, but both their attitude toward success and the pleasure they get out of success are quite different from the reactions of their less-confident peers.

These individuals' parents gave them a sense of self-worth regardless of their achievements. They let their children know they were loved unconditionally whether they brought home an A, a B, or even a D. They didn't push and shove their children; they simply let the desire for achievement evolve as the child acquired more of an identity and more self-love.

The point I want to emphasize is that either style of fathering may work and produce a successful daughter, but those fathers who relentlessly criticize and pressure are risking failure more than the others. There is the chance that they may not produce a successful daughter at all, but instead one who feels perpetually inadequate and unlovable, one who is timid, unable to enjoy success and sometimes even life itself.

How, then, does a father walk that fine line between encouragement and pressure? First, by examining his motivations. A father who constantly pressures for more and better achievements may be selfishly motivated, may feel that his daughter's accomplishments reflect on him. He may be more concerned with his own self-image than the success and welfare of his child. Second, by allowing the child herself to initiate the goals. If your daughter brings home a B on her math assignment (up from a D), simply show your pleasure, give hugs, etc., and wait for *her* to say she wants to try for the A. Then, and only then, should you encourage her to seek the higher goal. This accomplishes three things.

First, it gives your daughter an opportunity to enjoy her achievement. (Remember the research that showed that females have a tendency to disown their achievements and give the credit to external forces?) Allowing her a little time to bask in glory builds her belief that *she* was the one to accomplish this goal. Furthermore, it reinforces the desire to do more. Second, it helps her learn to do things because *she* wants to, for her own reasons and her own esteem, rather than to please Daddy. Third, it establishes a sense of autonomy by allowing a daughter to chart her own course and determine her own direction.[24]

In summary then, if you are the type of father who tends to drive yourself or those around you, the best way to encourage your daughter without pressuring her is, simply, to lighten up.

Remember, once she has had time to experience the good feelings that come with accomplishments, she will want to seek out those good feelings again. She will most likely do this by setting higher goals for herself. Then, when this happens, you can seize the moment and be the supportive, encouraging father. Remember, her timetable may be different than yours.

AMBITION OR ANXIETY?

Suppose she doesn't continue to set higher goals. Suppose she seems perfectly satisfied to stay put, right where she is. Suppose her "ambition" is not really ambition, but just a desire to please her parents. Now we come to a more complex and philosophical issue.

The stress on achievement for children of the eighties is excessive indeed. More and more child psychologists are expressing alarm at the pressure being placed on even very young children to get good grades so they can get into the "right colleges," etc. It's part of the yuppie syndrome.

I am in no way a supporter of excessive pressure and expectations on children to begin climbing the ladder of success complete with ulcers, insomnia, and anxiety attacks. I firmly believe that children must be allowed to be children, must be allowed to make mistakes to experiment, to fail. When we are overly critical, we teach our children to constantly strive toward a level of performance that doesn't exist. It doesn't exist because we always raise it. The end result is frustration. The end result is a daughter who may be successful in her career but unhappy, prosperous but discontent, 'triumphant" but dissatisfied.

In seeking to mold your daughter into a successful female, be vigilant about your own behavior and loving in your responses. The loving responses are those that demonstrate your belief in your daughter by allowing her to create the next goal for herself and strive toward it under her own steam and on her own terms. In other words, to encourage, support, inspire, reassure, and embolden is commendable. To pressure, wheedle, threaten, intimidate and discourage is not.

The authoritarian type of father may want to take the reins of control out of his daughter's hands by setting her goals and charting her course. (The protector and the softie may have trouble as well. They may be too eager to rescue. The result is the same: Daddy takes control.) Instead he must learn to say, "I trust you to make your move when you are ready and only you can know when that is.''

Armed with your awareness that encouragement and pressure are two different things, you will be the kind of daddy who contributes to the self-esteem your daughter needs to meet the challenges that will face her. You will not undermine your encouragement with a needling pressure that says she isn't good enough, but will encourage confidence in your daughter and foster her belief in herself. When she ascends the podium to accept her Nobel prize, you can smile confidently that you have played a major role in her achievement. If you're lucky, she may even mention you in her acceptance speech!

A Final Word

This chapter reveals the complexities and ironies of fathering a successful daughter during the latter part of the twentieth century. You have many paradoxical influences to contend with: feminine behavior versus achievement-oriented behavior, and feminine vulnerability versus risk taking. Do not become discouraged. Chapter 5 will reveal how your daughter's self-concept is formed, how this will affect her capacity and inclination to achieve, and how different fathering styles can affect this important process. Then, you can begin to pick and choose those behaviors you would like to emulate and those you wish to change or avoid altogether.

CHAPTER 4

❦

A New Look at Underachieving Girls

I might as well just say it: the great unspoken responsibility placed on the public schools is to maintain the status quo, to produce the next generation of workers who will meekly take their place in society's machine. Questioning authority and thinking for oneself are not priorities, and they are not encouraged by the system. Teachers who attempt to change this system are discouraged most of the time.

Even in school districts where the official philosophy and policies of the school board state a desire to help students initiate and/or deal with change, upon examination, one finds very little of this actually taking place in the curriculum or the classroom. This interest in maintaining the status quo has two important consequences for your daughter.

First, the search for potential leaders and high achievers continues to take place in fields which are traditionally male. Since the culture does not value traditionally female activities, the school system (which is extraordinarily paternalistic) will simply reflect these same values.

Second, in a system designed to maintain the status quo, good grades are not necessarily an indication of superior intelligence. They reveal instead how well a student has learned to play the game, that is, please the teacher and regurgitate information. Very few grades are actually based on a student's capacity for original thinking or ability to solve problems. In my experience some of the most talented, creative students had rather mediocre grades. Some were even failing. Therefore, grades alone are not sufficient to determine your daughter's achievement potential.

The upshot of this is that it may be a mistake to automatically assume that a girl with traditionally feminine interests, or one who is earning B's, C's, or even D's, is not a candidate for achievement. If you have a daughter who by all outward appearances is fairly average, yet something in her development over the years has given you the gut feeling that she is more than average, my advice is: follow that hunch. It is better to err on the side of high expectations than low ones.

Furthermore, as we will see later in this chapter, fathers are more hesitant than mothers to identify giftedness in their offspring, particularly daughters. This may have severe repercussions on a daughter's development. If a father is suffering from the same bias as the school system, that good grades or an interest in male-dominated fields are the only indications of ability worth rewarding, then he may overlook talent being displayed by a girl who has "gone underground."

Before we examine the different masks the underground girl may wear in order to be acceptable to her peers, however, several issues need to be clarified.

First, throughout this chapter I will be using the terms "high-achieving" and "gifted." They are not interchangeable. While it is true that one can be high-achieving *and* gifted, one can also be high-achieving and *not* gifted. Similarly, one can be gifted and low-achieving. To those unfamiliar with "educationese" this may sound quite confusing, but really it is quite simple.

The difference between the gifted population and the rest of us is that they are capable of producing *new* knowledge, designing new techniques, inventing new widgets. While the rest of us may be high-level consumers, able to appreciate a symphony by Beethoven or an orchid by Georgia O'Keeffe, for example, we remain, nevertheless, consumers. We do not produce these works ourselves. We must rely on the gifted to do it for us.

By the same token, giftedness does not automatically ensure achievement. I have seen many gifted students, too many of them girls, become low achievers, while other, so-called average students, have applied themselves and become high achievers. So, the labels "high-achieving," "low-achieving," and "gifted" are separate and distinct.

Second, my awareness of the disguises that high-potential girls use to hide their abilities comes from my years of teaching experience with gifted girls. However, these disguises are not limited to gifted girls but used by any girl who may be trying to put her talents to use in a more socially sanctioned way. Therefore, although you will find that I refer to the gifted quite often in my description of these disguises, bear in mind that what I am discussing is a matter of degree rather than substance. Therefore, it may apply to your daughter, gifted or not.

Finally, while all the information presented here is applicable both to the gifted girl and the high achiever, I have included a special section dealing with the gifted girl and her problems in particular. I advise you to read it even if you don't think your daughter is gifted. You may be surprised at what you will learn.

The Feminine High Achiever: A Master of Disguise

The girl who has already made the decision to go underground may exhibit her potential in traditional ways, donning different disguises in order to be accepted. Therefore, we must look for her where she is most likely to be found—in that realm where she can apply her special talents and gifts surreptitiously and without fear of discovery. Although she may have become quite skilled at hiding her abilities, she can still be outfoxed if you know what to look for.

DISGUISE 1: THE MIDDLE-AGED TEENAGER

The girl who receives only B's in school but also manages the family household (including budget, shopping, cleaning, and cooking), works on the campaign of a local politician, is president of the pep club, volunteers at a nursing home on the weekends, organizes the school fund-raising drives, participates in student government, has the lead in the school play, and still finds the time to date boys and socialize with her friends is exhibiting some mighty sophisticated developmental achievements.

I had just such a girl in my class. When her mother died, she took over the role of managing the household for her father and brother as well as participating in all the other activities I listed. She was in the eighth grade when I nominated her for the gifted program. Some members of the identification committee protested because she had "only" a B average. When I listed her other activities, they took more careful notice, for even though her activities were traditionally female, they indicated a degree of social conscience, motivation, responsibility, and organization mastered by very few adults.

Another girl was quite similar. In her case, she ran her father's office on Saturdays, answering the phone, keeping the books, scheduling appointments, handling customers with questions and complaints, talking to her father's business associates, and ordering supplies. Talking with this adolescent was like talking to a thirty-five-year-old adult. Once again, her grades were rather average, but her out-of-school activities were anything but average.

The girl who consistently prefers older companions, even adults, may be a potential achiever. I hesitate to make this recommendation because there is a type of female adolescent who prefers adult companionship because she feels safer with adults than with her own age group. This is not necessarily an achiever. The girl with potential is the one who prefers adult companionship and adult conversation because it is more interesting and challenges her intellect in a way that the simplistic conversations of her peer group are unable to do.

DISGUISE 2: THE COMIC, CUTUP, OR SMART ALECK

Another characteristic which may give away the bright girl who is hiding is a sophisticated and well-developed sense of humor.

When I taught Mark Twain to seventh-graders, most of them thoroughly enjoyed Tom and Huck's trip down the river and were completely enraptured by their adventures on the raft. They did not, however, laugh at Twain's wit. They lacked the maturity to understand his deep and insightful humor. The gifted kids, on the other hand, would howl at a well-turned phrase or ironic pun. If your daughter consistently understands humor which is beyond her years; if she is a punster, a wisecracker, and a joke maker; if she is able to perceive irony, sarcasm, and satire at an early age, she may be gifted.

Another possible candidate to keep your eye on is the leader of a clique, even if she is a rebellious or smart-mouth type. The important thing to realize is that the traits and characteristics which produce a leader—ability to organize, willingness to make decisions and solve problems, courage to blaze new trails and question authority—all are traits and characteristics of the high-level thinking skills that pinpoint a leader. Furthermore, the tough type of girl may be exhibiting a willingness to take risks by rejecting the traditionally female role of submissive compliance expected of her. (On the other hand, she may just be a smart aleck. There has to be more evidence than just a rebellious attitude, or all teenagers would be in the gifted program!)

DISGUISE 3: THE TOMBOY

Although this is not a traditionally feminine role, it needs to be included. Somewhat like the rebellious clique leader, the tomboy may be a risk taker who is dissatisfied with her role as a female (and the unspoken message, to be a "good girl"). She may seek adventure, excitement, and thrills. She may see boys as more interesting companions than girls because of their propensity for adventure, risk taking, and physical exertion. Do not discourage this behavior or her camaraderie with boys. She is likely to learn some valuable lessons from hanging around with them which will serve her interests in the future.

DISGUISE 4: SLACKER OR SCHOLAR

Yet another candidate may be the girl who gives a very erratic academic performance, the one who teeters on the edge of failure, yet is able to achieve a passing grade at the last minute by acing her final exams. Her report card may only reflect a series of D's or C's and not the last minute A+ which was required in order to pass and of which she proved capable. This type of behavior can be evidence of an academic conflict or boredom with traditional classroom fare.

DISGUISE 5: THE DAYDREAMER

Another possibility is the girl who withdraws into a world of fantasy and books to an unusual degree. Seeking to stimulate her mind and wishing to avoid the realities of her boring role as a female, she may find that books provide the perfect escape. If she has an unusually large vocabulary and reads books beyond her age-level ability (a seventh-grader reading twelfth-grade books, for instance), it is worth paying attention to. If you are unsure of the level of her reading material, check with her English teacher at school. Also, try to direct her reading so that she becomes exposed to nonstereotypical heroines. Biographies of famous women are very good for this. (See Appendix A.) Ask her teacher for other suggestions.

DISGUISE 6: THE ADOLESCENT SOCIAL WORKER

Another traditionally female activity at which the underground girl may excel is in the role of rescuer or nurturer: the girl everyone turns to when they have a problem. She may possess unusual insight or emotional wisdom beyond her years which is sensed and appreciated by her classmates. This is a role which may be severely misunderstood and devalued by a traditional academic system, yet it may reveal an emotional depth, wisdom, or maturity which few but the gifted exhibit.

The message to be gleaned from these disguises is that there are girls of high potential who try to become more "acceptable" to their peer group by exhibiting their talents and abilities in traditionally feminine ways. If one looks closely, however, one can see the abilities that are being utilized just below the surface. Your job as her father is to look beyond the traditional role your daughter may be playing, or the mediocre grades she may be receiving, to see what may be a more accurate picture of high-level abilities at work.

The School Side of the Problem

The different treatment of bright boys and bright girls has been well documented in the professional literature (see the bibliography for further reading), and there are still too many sexist teachers who make subtly denigrating and destructive comments to females. Talk to your daughter to find out what she hears from her teachers at school.*

One day a gifted girl stormed into my class and threw her books on her desk with a thud. "What's the matter with you?" I asked. "I hate Mr. Norlund," she replied. "He's such a sexist."

---

*"Talk to your daughter" does not mean grill her mercilessly to plant ideas in her head. Unfortunately, this often happens when a parent is suspicious of the school system. It simply means that *if* you have open communication with your daughter and take the time to *listen* when she talks to you, you will hear what goes on in school.

"Oh really?" I said, arching my eyebrow and burning with feminist curiosity. "What happened?"

"He was showing a filmstrip on dinosaurs. You know the carnivorous one that stood on two legs and had great big teeth? I think it's called Tyrannosaurus Rex. Well, anyway, in the filmstrip, the dinosaur had its mouth open, getting ready to devour some poor creature, obviously, but Mr. Norlund said, 'As you can see, this is a female dinosaur. Its mouth is always open.' Then he just laughed and laughed with the rest of the class as if it was the funniest thing he ever heard."

Unfortunately, this kind of humor occurs more often than it should, and it is not always just men who are guilty. Sometimes, it takes the form of "advice." A school counselor came into my classroom to do career counseling with my ninth-graders. She said, "Shop and auto mechanics are open to girls, but most girls don't really like them. They just take them to be with the boys."

Imagine the effect this has on girls who want to enroll in these courses. Not only does it discourage exploration and repress risk taking, it plants the seed in the minds of all the students that any girl enrolled in those classes is only there to flirt. Suddenly, what started out as the promise of a new challenge or the opportunity to learn practical skills has been downgraded to the level of an adolescent manhunt. Her intentions have been denigrated in front of the whole class. At this point it would take a brave female to sign up for the class and suffer the teasing and derision. To put it bluntly, a school representative (particularly a counselor!) has no right to prejudice the whole class against girls in these courses because some have been less than serious.

If I were a parent and heard from my daughter that teachers or counselors had made sexist remarks in the classroom, I would make it a point to say something at the next parent-teacher conference. After all, if a teacher made a racist comment in the classroom, I would not tolerate it, so why should I tolerate a sexist one?

It is not necessary to be obnoxious or threatening to the teacher. Simply state your case. Tell the teacher that sexist comments are discouraged in your home because you want your children to grow up free of the negative programming inherent in sexual biases. Inform the teacher that your daughter is very aware of sexism. If the teacher presses for details as to why you have initiated a discussion on this particular subject, you might say something like, "The comment you made about the carnivorous dinosaur (or the auto mechanics course) runs counter to everything we are endeavoring to instill in our daughter regarding her self-esteem and capacity to achieve.''

The last thing teachers want to deal with is irritated parents, so you can be pretty sure most of them will refrain from making sexist comments in the future. You would be doing a service by speaking out, not only for your own daughter but for all the other children being exposed to sexism in the classroom as well.

Recognizing Giftedness

One of the most disturbing realities I had to face as a teacher of gifted children was that, as a general rule, fathers were more reluctant to recognize giftedness in their children than were mothers. Furthermore, they became even more disinclined to believe the evidence if the child was female. When I brought this up to a colleague, Dr. Linda Silverman, president of the Gifted Child Development Center and a professor who has worked with gifted children for over twenty-five years, she said, ''I think fathers are more reluctant than mothers to identify any child as gifted due to a male perception of giftedness. They are operating from a masculine perspective,'' she continued, ''which seems to view the true test of genius in terms of the quantity and quality of one's influence *as an adult*. This is, of course, of little practical use to parents and teachers.

''Mothers, on the other hand, more closely involved with child care, observe the daily developmental achievements of a gifted child. This grows into an awareness and concern about meeting the child's intellectual needs *in present time*.

''In short, the masculine view emphasizes prediction of *future* achievements and productivity; the feminine view emphasizes the impact of developmental differences on a child's *immediate* needs.

''I think fathers need to learn a new view of giftedness if they wish to capitalize on the potential already there,'' she concluded.

I pointed out, ''I have found that when a father realizes his daughter may be gifted and is forced to reconcile this knowledge into his understanding of a system that does not support female genius, his protective reaction is to block his daughter's development in that area.'' Dr. Silverman agreed.

''Consequently,'' she said, ''the male perception of giftedness combined with his instincts to protect his little girl thwart the full recognition of gifted girls.''[1]

Early Signs

Identification of a gifted child can occur long before she enters school. Research has shown that, contrary to popular opinion, not all parents think their children are gifted; in fact, many are quite accurate in identifying a gifted child. So, don't be timid. If you believe you have a gifted daughter, you probably do.

To properly identify a gifted daughter, you should have an overall picture of what giftedness is. The easiest way to explain it is to use a pictograph designed by Joseph Renzulli:[2]

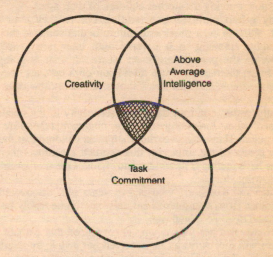

These are the three ingredients of giftedness. Where they intersect, the cross-hatched section, represents the gifted population. All three characteristics must be in evidence, for alone, each is not sufficient. I have seen creative kids who had no task commitment. I have seen highly intelligent kids who lacked creativity. I have seen committed kids who lacked either one or the other.

A word of warning about task commitment. This term does not apply to a task designed by a teacher or parent. Even if your daughter is gifted, she may have absolutely no interest in the completion of a task designed by someone else and therefore no commitment to it. However, on a task of her own design which has captured her interest, she will remain steadfastly committed, often in spite of great obstacles.

Gifted children often begin talking in complete sentences rather than the random single words spoken by most children. One mother told me her daughter's first words were, "Mother, the dog wants to eat the cat." Not only was it a complete sentence, it expressed a relatively complicated set of interactions that the daughter was able to deduce without benefit of adult instruction.

Similarly, gifted children are able to think abstractly and reason logically before their peers. They are able to deal with abstracts like time and will understand the concepts of past, present, and future more quickly than other children of their age.

Many gifted children are reading before they ever enter school. What is even more astounding is that some of them are self-taught, amazing their parents with their newly acquired skill before the parents are even aware of what is going on. Many teach themselves from television commercials, newspapers, magazines, and children's shows, all unbeknownst to their parents!

Finally, gifted children develop a sensitivity to the needs and feelings of others long before their less mature and therefore more selfish peers. They realize earlier than most children that they are not the center of the universe, that sentient creatures other than humans have feelings, thoughts, and rights. One mother told me the following story.

"When my daughter, who is five years old, discovered that meat comes from slaughtered animals, she immediately became a strict and devoted vegetarian.

"This worried her father, who is convinced that without meat a person will die. Anyway he deceived her awhile by telling her that hamburger wasn't really meat. One day she said to me, 'Mommy, is Daddy telling the truth about hamburger?'

"Of course I had to tell her the truth, since she was already suspicious," her mother said apologetically.

"When my husband came home, she confronted him. He was embarrassed and promised never to deceive her again. She then went on to give a rather well-thought-out philosophical statement concerning the immorality of eating meat.

"Now she jokingly calls her father 'the carnivore,' but she still refuses to even consider what she calls 'eating animals.' "

As you can see, the gifted population is unique. These guidelines have been offered as a blueprint for identifying your gifted daughter before she enters public school:

1. She is creative, intelligent, and task-committed.
2. She begins talking in complete (or nearly complete) sentences.
3. She is able to think abstractly at an early age.
4. She is able to read before entering school.
5. She shows an early sensitivity to the needs of others and awareness of the sanctity of life.

If you have a gifted daughter who is already enrolled in school and has gone underground or is on the verge of doing so, you need a set of strategies. And you will have to recognize the harsh realities of the public school system with which you must deal.

First, since gifted girls who have not been identified and placed in special programs by the fifth grade are at risk, comprehensive training in the early identification of gifted children, with special emphasis on what happens to gifted girls, is a must for teachers in grades one through four. If you have a daughter whom you believe to be gifted, make it your business to find out if your school district adequately trains the regular classroom teacher in the identification of gifted students. Ask your daughter's classroom teacher the hard questions found in Appendix B at the end of this book. If we can locate the gifted girl before socialization conceals her, we may be able to have an impact on her later achievement.

Second, research shows that underachievement can be somewhat alleviated by a student's identification with a strong role model. In a study of gifted women and achievement recently completed at the University of Southern California (USC), Dr. Betty Walker found that some women felt they lacked a positive female role model to show them what they could become, what the possibilities were. They believed a role model would have made a difference in their professional lives.[3]

You should try to find female mentors who can establish relationships with gifted girls, if such a program does not exist through the school district or individual school. Take it on yourself to organize such a group. Some teachers might be willing to volunteer their help. Other parents will certainly want to organize just such a group. Most schools appreciate this kind of parental involvement and will volunteer classrooms for your meetings, at least.

Since underachievement for the gifted is almost always a counseling problem rather than an academic problem, contact with sympathetic school counselors and psychologists can be invaluable. Small discussion groups to reveal the special problems faced by gifted girls are essential. These discussion groups should be girls-only so that they won't be inhibited in their discussions, which they would be if boys were invited to participate. These groups would be particularly beneficial at the junior high level, when the girl is seeking to establish her feminine identity within a culture basically hostile to her accompanying intellectual needs.

In the study of gifted women by Dr. Walker referred to earlier, nearly all the respondents were critical of the counseling they had received in high school. Furthermore, nearly 75 percent of them did not consider themselves gifted, even with IQs of 130 and above! This is a sad commentary on the inadequate counseling received by gifted girls, since a basic responsibility of the schools should be to make the gifted girl aware of her ability. In most cases, if women don't recognize their potential, they cannot fulfill it.

Remember that being gifted is hard enough in our society without the extra burden of being female as well. Along with their male counterparts, gifted females must endure the general atmosphere of anti-intellectualism that characterizes American culture and causes a large portion of the public to dislike smart folks. But a female must also cope with the attitudes of those who are skeptical that intelligence can exist in a female body at all and those who believe women can be intelligent but think their intelligence should be squelched, "for their own good."

Even giftedness that has been repressed will rise to the surface repeatedly. For that reason, you must help your daughter accept who she is and learn to value her talents rather than hide them. If she spends a lifetime, or even part of a lifetime, trying to drive her talents underground, she will suffer a great deal—intellectually, spiritually, and emotionally, as well as financially and professionally. You can help her find herself and develop into a well-adjusted, accomplished personality.

Girls to the Rescue

The feminine tendency toward early awareness and sensitivity to the needs of others is a particularly cogent point and deserves further elaboration.

The early sensitivity to the needs of others in conjunction with the development of social responsibility in girls is truly a double-edged sword. In his theory of "positive disintegration,"[4] Kasimierz Dabrowski (a Polish psychologist not well known in this country) posited that emotional sensitivity was essential to the higher-level development shown by people like Gandhi, Mother Teresa, and Jesus. In that sense, then, the emotional sensitivity of girls (which is particularly developed in gifted girls) serves them well as they strive toward higher development of the ''self-less'' nature.

On the other hand, a high degree of emotional sensitivity can prompt the kind of altruistic behavior that results in self-sacrifice in service to others. In principle, this behavior should be promoted for all members of society. But our culture does not value sacrifice or reward it. When only one segment of the society is doing the sacrificing, an unjust and unbalanced situation is created. The result is underachievement on the part of girls and women according to the criteria of the male value system.

In Dr. Walker's study at USC, it was shown that a major obstacle in the professional lives of gifted women is the same old problem faced by nongifted women: the conflict between professional responsibilities and motherhood.

''Sometimes gifted women stop themselves before they take that extra step; because they still believe they are there only to support men and children and be the comfort-giver, their own interests take a backseat,'' says Dr. Walker.

This is analyzed in great detail by Dr. Carol Gilligan, a professor of education at Harvard University, in her book entitled *In a Different Voice*, which examines the differences between male and female moral development.

In the past, many educational researchers, Jean Piaget, Lawrence Kohlberg, and Janet Lever among them, have belittled females by suggesting that they have a less finely tuned awareness of moral issues than do males. In fact, they simply have a *different* awareness of and perspective on moral issues.

According to Dr. Gilligan, the difference is this: males define a moral issue primarily in terms of rights, while females define a moral issue primarily in terms of responsibilities. Males are more concerned with whose rights are being violated or which rule is being broken, while a female wants to know who is responsible and how the people involved will be affected. While the male is more inclined to be stimulated by the elaboration of rules, the female is more likely to consider the individual circumstance and the need to make exceptions. One is not necessarily more moral than the other, they simply come from different perspectives.

Says Dr. Gilligan, ''The assumption . . . is that the male model is the better one since it fits the requirements for modern corporate success. In contrast, the sensitivity and care for the feelings of others that girls develop through their play have little market value and can even impede professional success."[5]

This has great repercussions for girls. We must teach them how to balance their inclination to serve the needs of others with their own achievement potential. We must teach them that serving others can be accomplished through channels other than the traditional care-giving occupations of teaching and nursing. They must be shown the alternatives, the great contributions in the fields of science, government, and engineering that have also benefited humankind, many times touching the lives of far greater numbers than the few who can be reached on a one-to-one basis.

Presenting Alternatives

Remember that showing off her skills in traditionally feminine ways is an easier path for your daughter to follow, especially in terms of her feminine self-image. Therefore, remember to show compassion for the girl who has gone underground or has chosen a traditional path while you continue to develop her risk-taking capacity.

Seed her mind with progressive ideas and encourage her aspirations by presenting alternatives to the limited future that awaits her as a traditional female. Find support groups for girls with high potential; acquaint her with happy, gifted women; give her biographies of famous women to read; and have heart-to-heart talks with her during which you encourage her to express her talents. When combined with the other suggestions offered throughout this book, these actions can make the difference between staying stuck and moving on.

PART 2

Sending the Right Messages

CHAPTER 5

❦

Self-Concept and the Importance of Daddy

Since, historically, mothers have been the primary caretakers, in the eyes of many they have become the ones who *should be* the primary caretakers; that is, what was descriptive became prescriptive. Consequently, parenting books have been aimed at mothers, and fathers have been forced to go by the seat of their pants.

Even when Dad took an active role as a parent, popular myth fostered the belief that fathers could not understand their female offspring. One of my interviewees, the eldest of three girls, said, "I remember my dad saying there was nothing he would rather have than girls, and I think that was true. But he also thought he couldn't understand us, so he left communication to Mom. He acted like his daughters mystified him."

Be mystified no more! The research on typical fathering styles sheds light on the father-daughter relationship and shows how even an aware father can be guilty of inadvertently perpetuating sexist programming. As you read the research findings, periodically refer back to the quiz in Chapter 2 to help you ascertain to what degree you consciously or unconsciously expect your daughter to adhere to stereotypically feminine behavior. You will see that you indeed have a choice, that your behavior can have a predictable outcome, and that by altering your style of fathering, you can alter the behavior of your daughter.

In order to do your job well, you must be aware of how a child's self-concept is formed and what you as a father do to contribute to or undermine this important process.

An individual's self-concept is in a constant state of flux; it depends on the circumstances in which one finds oneself, the work one is doing in the world, and the current level of one's performance and reward. At the same time, however, it is true that one's first impressions of oneself are acquired at an extraordinarily early age and form the initial self-portrait upon which one paints a series of modifications and changing images as one negotiates through life and acquires more information about oneself.

Females begin with a good self-concept which deteriorates as they reach puberty. Many adult females never truly recover and live their lives under a cloud of hesitancy and self-doubt. Your goal is to help your daughter paint her first self-portrait in vivid, strong, self-confident colors, with bold strokes of character that can withstand the ravages of time and change, so that her self-image remains steadfastly secure through all the trials and tribulations that are attendant upon achievement. It can be done.

Gender Identification

One aspect in the formation of self-concept that needs to be defined is a process called gender identification. This refers to the process by which young human beings learn which types of behavior are appropriate for their sex.

By age three, children have learned whether they are little boys or little girls and have begun to exhibit behavior congruent with socially sanctioned patterns of sex-role conduct. Our little pregnant doctors in Chapter 1 intuited that being a successful physician did not satisfactorily fulfill the expectations that society places on females to nurture and reproduce. In other words, they were already strongly gender-identified. By incorporating pregnancy into their play fantasy, they were able to fuse the divergent roles, fulfill society's expectations, and relieve their own psychic discomfort.

In the process of learning what behavior is appropriate for her sex (becoming gender-identified), the young girl receives many other messages concerning femininity. You may want to refer back to the list of adjectives in Chapter 2 listed by fathers as characteristic of femininity. Bear in mind that not only is femininity a well-defined code of behavior but also, to a large degree, a matter of physical appearance, both of which will be discussed in this chapter as we examine how your daughter forms her self-concept.

A DAY IN THE LIFE

The purpose of the scenario you are about to read is to re-create an average day in the life of an average little girl in order to examine the variety of ways she becomes gender-identified and to highlight the number of gender-specific messages she receives on a daily basis. I have taken pains to create a fairly average family life situation in which the parents are loving to their daughter and to each other. The little girl feels secure and content. I have made every effort not to turn males into the bad guys but at the same time to portray them accurately and according to information provided by my workshop participants, both male and female.

Our scene opens on a bright Monday morning and the sweet, serene face of a four-year-old deep in sleep. She has red hair, freckles, and a scab on her knee.

Shelley Grant's day begins when Mommy wakes her up with a kiss and some sweet talk. Mommy carries Shelley into the kitchen, where she fixes breakfast while getting ready for work. While Mommy prepares breakfast and lunch, Shelley stares at the cereal box in front of her. On it is a picture of an all-American family. Dad is seated at the breakfast table with his children. Mom is in an apron serving cereal to her family.

Shelley doesn't get to see too much of her Daddy in the mornings except to get a good-bye kiss and a ''Luv ya, sweetie'' on his way out the door. After Mommy finishes breakfast, she takes Shelley to the sitter; a sweet, motherly type of woman whom all the kids call Aunt Jenny. She obviously loves kids and is quite good with them. The Grants have complete faith in her. Shelley likes her a lot, too. The Grants are grateful after some of the horror stories their friends tell about how their kids hate the sitter.

Shelley spends her day with three other children that Aunt Jenny takes care of—two boys and another girl. They do the usual kid things, consisting of random cruelties interspersed with bonding secrets and joys. Today one of the boys challenges the girls to a race by saying, ''Everybody knows girls can't run fast.''

At lunchtime, Mr. Healey (Aunt Jenny's husband) comes home for lunch. He says hi to the kids, sits down at the table, and is served lunch by his wife. She does not sit down to eat until after he has been served. They try to have adult talk around the noise of the kids. Luckily, Mr. Healey is a good-natured fellow so the chaos created by four children doesn't bother him too much.

After work Shelley's mother picks her up. She stops at the post office to run an errand, and Shelley accompanies her. Inside, Shelley sees a poster. On it are four cartoon people, three men and a woman. Each one is wearing a different facial expression meant to convey his or her feelings toward the post office. Above a man the caption reads, "Ideas?" and he is shown with eyebrows arched and a light bulb glowing above his head. Above the second man is written, "Complaints?", and he is shown waving his fist and scowling. Above the third man is the word "Questions?" and he is shown resting his chin on his index finger and wearing a perplexed expression. Finally, above the woman, who is smiling a huge smile and beaming at the viewer, the caption reads, "Compliments?" Mommy finishes her errand, and they head for home.

Shortly after they pull up in the driveway, Daddy arrives home too. Shelley is so happy to see him. He kisses her and holds her and looks at the drawing she made at Mrs. Healey's house. Mom prepares dinner and throws a load of clothes in the washer.

They sit down to a pleasant dinner of warm conversation and strong familial feelings. Shelley feels very loved and very protected. Mommy and Daddy seem to like each other a lot. They smile at each other frequently and laugh at each other's jokes. That makes Shelley feel good. Daddy gives Mommy a hug. He clears the table and Mom rinses the dishes and loads the dishwasher.

That night watching television is pretty uneventful. Mommy gets up three times to put in another load of clothes and to retrieve the dry ones out of the dryer before they wrinkle. She folds clothes as she watches television with Shelley and Daddy. They all enjoy each other's company and talk to each other as they watch television.

Shelley sees three commercials that night.

The first one is about cavities. The little girl in the commercial has just been to the dentist and has several new cavities. Her mom tells her she is going to have to tell her father. She is sitting in her bedroom when she hears the front door open, indicating Daddy has arrived home. She says to her faithful dog, "Uh-oh, Wally, Dad's home," and waits for him to come upstairs to discuss her dental visit.

The next commercial shows how parents learn about computers—from their sons! Shelley enjoys this one. It is late at night, and a father sneaks into his son's bedroom to use his Apple 2C. The son wakes up and catches his dad at the computer. The dad seems to be embarrassed.

The last commercial is for an antacid, but Shelley doesn't know what an antacid is. There are three people in this commercial, two men and a woman. The first man is a coach and appears to be quite angry. He says, "You've been traded, Rolaids. Your performance isn't up to Tempo." The next man is a boss. He, too, is angry. He shouts, "You're fired, Maalox. Your performance isn't up to Tempo." The last character is a woman. She doesn't seem angry as the men are. She is soft-spoken and quiet. She says apologetically, "I've found someone new, Tums." She appears again at the end of the commercial getting ready to retire for the night. Before turning out the light, she coos in a low, sweet voice, "Tempo, I'm so glad I found you."

It's bedtime for Shelley. She kisses Daddy goodnight and Mommy tucks her in. Shelley ends her day by drifting off to sleep, secure in a cocoon of love and stability created by her nurturing parents.

Since becoming gender-identified means learning what behavior is appropriate to one's sex, the process takes place in all homes, be they secure and loving or unstable and hostile. Let us examine the variety of ways that little Shelley will become gender-identified through a look at the types of unspoken messages she has absorbed throughout her average day.

First, we will examine what she has learned about females:

1. *Females are the primary caretakers of children.*
   Mommy awakens her in the morning. Mommy takes her to the sitter. Mommy picks her up from the sitter. Mommy tucks her in. The sitter is also female.

2. *Females have the primary responsibility for domestic duties.*
   Mommy makes breakfast and lunch before going to work. Mommy prepares dinner. Mommy does the laundry and folds clothes while "relaxing" in the evening with her husband. Mommy rinses the dinner dishes and loads the dishwasher.

3. *Females try to please others and serve them.*
   The cereal box shows mom serving dad and the children. The poster at the post office shows only the female

in a supportive, pleasing role, giving compliments. The sitter serves her husband lunch and waits until he is served before sitting down herself. (He gets a break, she doesn't, even though she is working, too.)

4. *Females are inferior to males.*
Fathers learn about computers from sons (a double whammy, since both participants are male). "Everybody knows girls can't run fast," says her male playmate. On the post office poster, males have the ideas, females give the compliments. In the antacid commercial, only males are in a position to judge performance, while the only female is portrayed as concerned with her personal relationships.

Let us now turn our attention to the insidious messages little Shelley has received concerning the nature of men, and therefore, by extension, her Daddy.

1. *Males express anger and may be more likely to punish.*
One male on the poster (waving his fists) and two males on television (the coach and the boss) are shown expressing anger. In the toothpaste commercial a little girl is worried about her daddy finding out about her cavities. No females are shown expressing anger.
In 1984, a study was conducted which suggests that preschool-age children (ages two to six) already have pronounced sex-role stereotypes concerning the expression of emotion. To these tots, anger is a male emotion, while fear, sadness, and happiness are female characteristics.[1] If I were a father, this study would disturb me greatly. I would not want to be perceived as one who expresses only anger. I would not be pleased that this may be the only emotion my children learn to expect from me.

2. *Males are freed from domestic duties.*
Daddy has cleared away the dinner dishes. That's it.

3. *Males do not have primary responsibility for child care.*

4. *Males understand technology like computers.*

Before I am accused of presenting only one side of the issue, let me say that *all* of the examples listed above have either been submitted by fathers in my class, been observed by me, or in the case of television commercials, been taken word for word from the screen. What we are discussing is a matter of degree not verisimilitude.

I am aware that children are exposed to men doing housework, etc.; *however*, it is in fact more likely that they receive a much stronger dose of the messages shown above than they do nonsexist messages. Maybe in your household, your daughter receives fewer traditional sex-role messages than the example shown above. On the other hand, maybe she receives more.

These examples are submitted for your consideration to show the subtle ways in which children become gender-identified. If these events were isolated or infrequent, if they were less consistent in their messages, they would have little power to influence. Unfortunately, that is not the case. You and your children are bombarded with them daily. It is easy to become so accustomed to them that only the really blatant examples of sexism, such as using the female body to sell products, are noticed. Learn to recognize the more subtle examples and point them out to your daughter. (There is a family game offered in Chapter 8 that will help you do this.)

Obviously, no one individual incident, event, comment, or commercial teaches children what behavior is expected of their sex. It is rather the cumulative effect, the subtle but unrelenting pressure in a particular direction over many years, that achieves the goal of gender identification, which is: teaching children to behave in ways which are socially sanctioned and maintain the status quo. Remember this metaphor: If you wanted to straighten your child's teeth, you would not attempt to do so by hammering them into their proper places. You would use braces to apply the steady and constant pressure needed to coax the teeth to grow in a particular direction until they are set. Such is the pressure of society on all its members.

To some degree and with some frequency your daughter (and son) will experience this "gender pressure." It is impossible to avoid. *However*, to whatever degree you reinforce it in your own household, either through parental behavior or the oversight of ignoring opportunities to discuss it with your children, you will be encouraging your children to soak it up like a sponge. We cannot lay the blame totally at the feet of media; as was shown in the scenario of little Shelley's day, we must also look inside our own households as well.

Here are some other common practices of the average household for you to ponder. Remember to be alert for the unspoken message that is being communicated to the children of these households.

1. When it comes to the traditional holiday family dinner, the usual practice is for females to prepare the food and males to eat it. Furthermore, in most traditional settings, the males retire after the meal to watch football. The females clear away the dishes and clean up.

2. PTA meetings and parent-teacher conferences are attended almost solely by mothers. Although some fathers do attend, their numbers, in comparison, are quite low. During my years as a public school teacher (from 1974 to 1985), my principal had us tabulate the numbers of mothers and fathers who attended. The ratio was nine to one, females over males. Those fathers who did attend *always* attended with their wives. Someone once joked we should rename PTA (Parent-Teacher Association) to MTA (Mother-Teacher Association).

3. Several studies have shown that males interrupt females at a ratio that can go as high as four to one. It must be noted, however, that females *allow* themselves to be interrupted. (I ask you to pay special attention to what kind of an unspoken message is being delivered *here*.)

4. When the whole family goes out together in the car, it is almost always Dad who operates the vehicle. (This will be discussed later in terms of decision making and being in charge.)

5. Division of labor by sex remains firmly entrenched in the average household. Mom usually has charge of household duties, cooking and cleaning, and Dad usually takes care of the car, household repairs, and heavy yardwork. (I realize this is often the case because one or the other spouse may not be skilled at a particular task; e.g., Dad can't cook and Mom can't change the oil, but it wouldn't hurt to begin to learn these specialized skills from each other!)

How Self-Concept Is Formed

The process by which females become gender-identified and simultaneously learn to be fearful and underachieving involves a complex and interdependent set of forces. Most experts agree that there are at least four identifiable forces which shape an individual's self-concept:[2]

1. Individuals assess their worth by comparing themselves with others.
2. Individuals learn to see themselves as *others* see them.
3. Individuals prioritize their personal traits so that some traits become more important than others for overall self-esteem.
4. Individuals describe themselves by observing their behavior, its consequences and outcomes.

By understanding how these forces shape your daughter's self-concept, you will see how some rather typical fathering styles need to be altered in that they contribute to low self-esteem in females. Furthermore, where it applies to you, you will be able to alter your own specific behaviors to build the high self-esteem you want your daughter to have.

COMPARING ONESELF WITH OTHERS

An "other" may be one person or a whole group of people. For the sake of simplicity, these are called "reference groups." One of the primary reference groups girls measure themselves against is boys. As you will see in a study we are about to discuss, the underlying implication which colors the attitudes of both sexes is: *It is better to be male than female.*

In 1982, a study, fascinating in its simplicity, was conducted by Dr. Alice Baumgartner Papageorgiou. She distributed a questionnaire to students in grades three through twelve. The population surveyed included approximately 2000 boys and girls in both rural and metropolitan public schools. The questionnaire was an open-ended type which required students to give a response to the question: If you woke up tomorrow and discovered you were a (boy) (girl), how would your life be different?[3]

The results were chilling. Despite twenty years of activism, debate, and research concerning female potential as well as sincere efforts to remove gender-based constraints, the overwhelming majority of students indicated that their lives would change dramatically if they were to change sexes. This confirms that sex-role socialization is alive and well and continues its inexorable, relentless influence on our children's perceptions of their choices and abilities. As will become evident when you read their responses, these children remained locked into the belief that traditional sex roles were still the only choices available to them.

Although Dr. Papageorgiou groups the students' comments around several different themes, I have chosen one particular theme around which to discuss the results of this survey because it encompasses all the rest. That is the belief that it is better to be male than female; that males are inherently of more value than are females. The belief that it is better to be male than female has special significance for fathers trying to raise daughters with high levels of self-esteem. I guarantee that the children can say it better than I ever could. The insightful comments of contemporary children shown below will both frighten and enlighten you.

If You Woke Up Tomorrow and Discovered You Were a Boy, How Would Your Life Be Different?

"I could do stuff better than I do now." (Third-grade girl)

"If I were a boy, I would be treated better." (Fourth-grade girl)

"My grandparents would treat me extra special." (Fourth-grade girl)

"If I were a boy, my whole life might've been easier." (Sixth-grade girl)

"I think I would be more outspoken and confident, but I really don't know why." (Tenth-grade girl)

"I wouldn't have to worry how I look." (Sixth-grade girl)

"I wouldn't have to be neat." (Fourth-grade girl)

"I would put down all the girls." (Sixth-grade girl)

"Obviously, males are allowed to do more than females." (Fourth-grade girl)

"Life on the home front would be a lot easier. I know that for a fact, since I've got a brother." (Fourth-grade girl)

"I'd have different opportunities in jobs." (Eighth-grade girl)

"I want to be a nurse, but if I were male, I would probably want to be an architect." (Fourth-grade girl)

"I could run for President." (Tenth-grade girl)

"I would consider careers in math or science." (Tenth-grade girl)

"If I was a boy, I'd drop my typing class and start taking really hard classes, since my Dad would let me go to college and he won't now." (Eleventh-grade girl)

"I wouldn't have to baby-sit." (Sixth-grade girl)

"I would not have to put up with the kids." (Sixth-grade girl)

"My goal as girl is to be nothing." (Fourth-grade girl)

The following comments had no age provided:

"I could do more. I'd have more independence."

"I could play baseball or go hunting without being hassled."

"I would be able to take shop without feeling out of place."

"I could use the weight room without feeling funny."

"I could play football without being laughed at."

"I could stay out later."

"There would be fewer rules."

If you are still not convinced of your importance in the life of your little girl, perhaps the following will persuade you.

"If I were a boy, I could go hunting and fishing with my dad." (Sixth-grade girl)

"My dad would respect me better than usual because I would be a boy." (Fourth-grade girl)

"If I were a boy, my dad would do more things, like teach me how to work with wood." (Sixth-grade girl)

"If I were a boy, my father would be closer because I'd be the son he always wanted." (Sixth-grade girl)

"If I were a boy, my daddy might have loved me." (Third-grade girl)

These responses clearly indicate that in comparing themselves with boys, girls are convinced that it is better to be male.

Before I list some of the comments from the boys, I would like to quote Dr. Papageorgiou:

Perhaps the most disturbing theme which consistently appeared in the responses to the student survey was the implication that males are inherently of greater value than females.

Even though an occasional female would state that she did not want to be a boy, or that being a girl is "more fun," by far the greater number of comments which denigrated the opposite sex were written by boys. Elementary boys often selected titles for their responses using phrases such as "The Disaster," or "The Fatal Dream," or "Doomsday."[4]

If You Woke Up Tomorrow and Discovered You Were a Girl, How Would Your Life Be Different?

As you read the boys' comments, bear in mind one aspect of self-concept we have not yet discussed: individuals come to see themselves as others see them. As you read the boys' comments and their appraisals of females, it will become clear why it is so important for you to provide male approval as a counter force.

"If I were a girl, I would have to be stupid and weak as a string." (Sixth-grade boy)

"I would refuse to work as a secretary or something stupid like that." (Eleventh-grade boy)

"If I were a girl, I would kill myself." (No age provided)

"If I woke up and I was a girl, I would go back to sleep and hope it was a bad dream." (Sixth-grade boy)

"If I were a girl, I would want to be a boy." (Fourth-grade boy)

"Girls can't do anything fun. They don't know how to do anything except play dolls." (Fourth-grade boy)

"I would almost have to change career plans. I would probably consider being a housewife." (No age provided)

"I would start to look for a husband as soon as I got out of high school." (No age provided)

"I couldn't be a mechanic." (Eighth-grade boy)

"I'd have to smell pretty." (Eighth-grade boy)

"As a girl, I would use a lot of makeup and look good and beautiful to everyone, knowing that few people would care for my personality, and the majority of people would like to have me just as a sexual object." (Twelfth-grade boy)

"I would have to be around other girls for safety." (Eleventh-grade boy)

"I would always carry a gun for protection." (Fourth-grade boy)

"Instead of wrestling with my friends, I would have to sit around discussing the daily gossip." (No age provided)

"I would become less outgoing and more polite. I may become shy and be looked upon as a fragile glass doll." (No age provided)

"I couldn't go out as much." (No age provided)

"I'd have to come in earlier." (No age provided)

"I couldn't have a pocket knife." (No age provided)

"If I were a female athlete, I'd expect fewer people to come to the event." (Twelfth-grade boy)

"When you're a girl, you cheer sports instead of joining them." (Fourth-grade boy)

"Everything would be miserable." (No age provided)

"I would have to be goodie-goodie." (No age provided)

"I would have to wait for others to talk to me first." (Tenth-grade boy)

Such are the attitudes young males have about females. It is difficult to gauge just how damaging are these supremely arrogant attitudes of young males who feel superior just by virtue of the fact that they are males, but that ought to be enough to convince you that you need to provide a counterexample of male attitudes.

Without you to provide this counterexample, to show approval and admiration for females in general, your daughter may accept her inferior status without question. I want to emphasize, however, that *how* you praise female accomplishments is important as well. For example, emphasizing the atypicality of female accomplishments just serves to reinforce their uniqueness and make your daughter more aware of how different she will be. When she reaches puberty, and "different" is synonymous with "weird," your strategy may backfire. Therefore, you will have to trick her. While taking the opportunity to point out female accomplishments, act as though they are not unusual occurrences.

For example, during the 1970s some school districts introduced women's history week into the social studies curriculum. At last women were being recognized as having had a role in history. Most educators felt good about correcting a previously unbalanced situation.

Gradually, however, it became apparent that while the intentions of this addition were certainly democratic, the effect was not. One week of women's history compared to nine months of regular history began to look feeble in comparison and to feel like tokenism. For many teachers, a vague and uneasy feeling began to stir that students interpreted the new addition as, "Oh yeah, and women did something, too." It was not the content but its presentation that was flawed.

Smart social studies faculties slowly began to incorporate women's history into regular history so that women became part of the fabric, rather than an obligatory afterthought. Students exposed to this approach acquired a more honest and realistic picture of the female contribution to society.

You can accomplish the same thing by being sensitive to the words you use to phrase your admiration.

1. Omit references to gender when referring to women in nontraditional occupations, like woman pilot, female athlete, or woman executive. Simply use their names. For example, "Amelia Earhart was a courageous pioneer in the field of aviation," rather than, "Amelia Earhart was a great woman pilot."

2. Omit references to gender when referring to individuals of accomplishment. Instead of, "Eleanor Roosevelt, now there's a woman to admire," or, "Albert Schweitzer was a great man," how about, "Eleanor Roosevelt and Albert Schweitzer were exceptional human beings who are great role models for all of us."

3. When discussing fields usually restricted to males, like math and science, try to use noteworthy females in your discussion of the important milestones and evolution of that field. For example, "In 1948 the study of physics was advanced by Maria Mayer's discovery of the structure of atom's nucleus. She also won a Nobel prize for that discovery."

   Note: Unless you have a feminist in the house with an impressive library, you may spend hours researching the achievements of accomplished but often obscure women. For this reason, I have provided an appendix with brief biographies of these women, categorized by their fields. You and your daughter may want to use this as the basis for further investigation at the library.

4. If your daughter points out some way in which males are superior to females, like speed in running, be prepared to acknowledge the differences (because she is right) *and* to point out the ways in which females are superior to males, like endurance in running. Be ready to discuss how in some instances, speed is more important and in others, endurance is more important, so that she doesn't come to the conclusion males are better than females. We have our separate strengths and weaknesses. Also, be sure to teach her that physical body size bears no relationship to mental size.

Furthermore, you may wish to point out that given two trained runners, one male and one female, the male will be the faster, but Grete Waitz can certainly outrun most males in the world.

Comparing Daddy's Love: Brothers and Sisters

Remember the little third-grader who said, "If I were a boy, my daddy might have loved me"? I wish I could report that it was an unusual response, but in my interviews with women, many expressed a similar feeling. It is not that most of them felt *unloved*, they just didn't feel *as loved* or *as cherished* as their brothers.

One of the saddest things to emerge from my research is the degree to which so many little girls miss their daddies and wish they were a part of their lives in a more concrete way. They often observe their brothers receiving more fatherly time and attention. Some little girls are hurt by this. Others feel resentful. Some get angry. To one degree or another, little girls who are given only token time by their fathers begin to nurse a profound loneliness for their love, attention, and approval. Even benign neglect is still neglect.

When a little girl perceives that she does not receive as much attention from her father as her brother does, she can become suspicious of her importance in his life.

One woman said, "I can remember wishing my father would take me all the places he took my brothers. I never understood why he didn't ask me to go. I guess he thought I wasn't interested. I wasn't. But I wanted to be with him anyway, and I would've gone."

In a 1978 study, men showed a preference for sons over daughters by nearly four to one. This kind of attitude is subtly and inevitably communicated. In another revealing study two researchers observed fathers at home with their babies at ages three weeks and three months.[5] They found that fathers were more involved with boy babies than with girl babies. They stimulated boy babies more than girl babies by touching them and showing them a toy. They even looked at their sons more than their daughters. This was also true during feeding; fathers made more attempts to stimulate feeding of boys by moving the bottle around than they did with girls.

Some recent studies conducted in the United States and Sweden suggest that fathers showed more willingness and persistence in interacting with "difficult" boy babies than "difficult" girl babies.[6]

On the positive side, there is research to show that when fathers are primary caretakers, daughters benefit.[7] Being a primary caretaker was defined as having child-care responsibilities approximately 60 percent of the time, in comparison to traditional fathers, who had child-care responsibilities approximately 22 percent of the time. The study showed that both sons and daughters of these nontraditional fathers benefited in that they had a higher degree of "internality," a term which refers to children's belief in their ability to control their destiny and the external events which influence their lives. As will be noted in a later chapter, this is a crucial need in all human beings. Furthermore, in the case of highly involved fathers, girls benefited to a marked degree.

Don't emotionally abandon your little girl due to some internal but unexamined preference for boys. Look into your heart and be honest with yourself. If you find this characteristic, begin to ask yourself *why* you see males as more valuable than females. Look at your own upbringing to determine how the lie was established and reinforced. But most important, begin work on ridding yourself of it so that it cannot become woven into the fabric of your household interactions. Although it may seem obvious to some, it bears repeating: your daughter requires the affirming experiences of being valued and valuable. To deny her this can be as potentially dangerous to her mental health and self-esteem as more blatant forms of neglect and abuse.

So the next time a chore or responsibility is not urgent—take the opportunity to put off its completion in favor of a day spent with your little girl. You won't regret it. The next chapter will discuss some more activities and discussions that fathers and daughters can participate in together.

If the father of the little third-grade girl who felt her daddy didn't love her were made aware of her response, he would probably feel heartbroken, guilty, and sad. We can only hope he would do everything in his power to make her feel his love. But, alas, she will probably never tell him, and he will never know. Instead, she will go through life guarding a secret loneliness, a secret need, and despite the numbers of male admirers she may attract in her adult life, none of them will be able to fill that empty place. Only her daddy can do that.

SEEING YOURSELF AS OTHERS SEE YOU

Individuals come to think of themselves as others think of them. For the sake of simplicity, we will call these thoughts "unspoken messages," since they are behavioral as well as verbal. Also, even verbal messages contain unspoken messages if one reads between the lines. We will begin with the verbal.

This seems like an easy enough principle to incorporate into one's parenting style: reflect only positive statements back to your daughter and she will think highly of herself. Unfortunately, over-simplifications such as this often do more harm than good. We have all seen parents who only say "positive" things to their children; either the children become obnoxious boors who think they can do no wrong, or they come to think their parents are silly and superficial. (When one of my students brought home a bad report card, his mother came to parent-teacher conferences and brought her son with her. When she smiled vapidly and said, "His father and I just know he'll do better next time," her son replied with embarrassment, "Oh, my mom's just being 'positive' again.")

In reality, the business of reflecting a message to a child which says "You're OK" is a sophisticated and complex process. Mere lip service alone, without behavioral evidence to support it, will have very little impact on a child's sense of self-worth. In fact, lip service alone can be undermined quite effectively through subtle, negative interactions, which send an even more powerful message. Finally, there will be times when a child needs to hear the truth, which may not be positive.

Let us now turn to an example of how a behavior can undermine a child's feeling of adequacy and competence. It is an example of how actions speak more eloquently than words. In it, fathers are acting completely out of love, yet making momentous mistakes.

In a study by Jean Block, parents were observed helping their children solve a difficult puzzle.[8] Their interactions with their offspring were observed and recorded by a video camera. Later, under scrutiny by researchers, fathers (more than mothers) tended to treat their children differently based on the child's sex. With their sons, fathers emphasized the principles of problem solving and task mastery. With their daughters, they focused more on personal interaction, engaging in more playful behavior, i.e., joking, supporting, encouraging, rescuing, and protecting. Emphasis for boys was on performance. Emphasis for girls was on enjoying the game. They answered more task-oriented questions for boys. With daughters they were concerned with their degree of emotional comfort. Finally, they set higher standards for boys.

The most important facet of this study, however, and I want to emphasize this, was in the area of "rescuing." When interacting with daughters, fathers displayed a curious behavior which they did not display with sons. They would pick up the puzzle piece and put it in place for the daughter *before she requested help*. This type of behavior, obviously motivated by love and a desire to protect, has devastating effects. Ultimately, it produces a type of behavior called "learned helplessness."[9]

The theory of learned helplessness is aptly conveyed in the label itself. It states that given the right conditions, individuals learn to be helpless. In other words, the helplessness which many females exhibit is not a feminine trait, but rather one that has been taught and reinforced. One of the vehicles for teaching learned helplessness is *premature rescuing*.

If you stop and think about the unspoken message conveyed in the act of premature rescuing, you realize how insidious it is. In essence it says, "You are not capable of doing this by yourself. You need help." Females receive this message much more frequently than do males. With males, we allow them to experiment in order to build character and test their limitations. We do not offer females the same luxury. Instead, by rescuing them, we cripple them.

Unfortunately, in a father's overly zealous desire to protect his little girl from risk and the discomfort of anxiety-provoking situations, he tells her that she is incapable, incompetent, and in need of help. His behavior sends the message that that is what *he* thinks of her, so she comes to believe it herself.

Many fathers in my seminars react with extreme agitation over this bit of research, because (1) most of them have innocently engaged in it themselves and (2) they realize how its very subtlety contributes to its power. It is frightening to confront how potent parental behavior can be.

Other research shows that this sex-role stereotyping in the form of behavior toward a child begins in infancy, often as early as birth. In one study, newborns (both boys and girls) were closely matched in height and weight. They were randomly divided into two groups, each consisting of both boys and girls. One group was dressed in blue, and the other in pink. Fathers were asked to describe the babies of each group. The blue group was described as healthy, robust, strong, and alert, while the pink group was described as fragile, sweet, pretty, and dainty.[10] When fathers had only had visual contact with their newborns, without having held them, they rated their boys as better coordinated, more alert, stronger, hardier, and firmer, while daughters were rated as softer, weaker, less attentive, more delicate, and finer featured than sons.

These perceptions, which were not based on factual information but rather the beliefs and expectations of the fathers, may have profound consequences on paternal behavior toward a son or a daughter. A perception of a female as weaker and more inattentive than a male reinforces the belief that she is in need of protection. This in turn causes a father to rescue prematurely, thus creating inappropriate dependency, a vicious cycle endlessly perpetuated.

Still another study found that fathers play with firstborn sons more than firstborn daughters.[11] Furthermore, they play differently with boys and girls. Fathers are more physical with boys, engaging in activities like lifting and tossing. With their daughters they engage in more vocalization, once again reinforcing the fragility of females.

The great irony, of course, is that female newborns and infants are stronger and healthier than their male counterparts. The infant mortality rate is higher for males, though they are slightly heavier and longer, if only by a few centimeters, than females at birth.

Soon thereafter society intervenes to reinforce the learned helplessness in a multitude of ways. Teachers ask boys rather than girls to lift heavy books even in junior high school where the physical maturity and strength of the girls is significantly more developed than the boys'. Girls are rescued from changing tires or dealing with machinery. In some marriages, wives are "spared" the anxiety of dealing with budgets and bills. In most marriages the principal breadwinner of the family is dad, who has primary responsibility. Boys are encouraged to use computer labs more than girls. Boys are freer to explore their physical environment. Boys are encouraged to take risks. The list goes on and on. In the end, this treatment teaches girls to be inappropriately dependent and helpless, and then society labels that as feminine.

Imagine a girl's confusion when, on the one hand, she is verbally encouraged to take risks and test her mettle, and on the other hand, she is given the insidious unspoken message of helplessness inherent in premature rescuing! What happens is that she receives a double message. The verbal encouragement she receives is clearly undermined by the unspoken messages that emerge from the way she is treated.

Shirley Muldowney, seventeen-time National Hot-Rod Association (NHRA) national champion and three-time world champion, was not given a double message by her father.

"When I was about six or seven, right on up through junior high school, I had a problem in school. I was a mouthy kid, and I was the skinniest and scrawniest. I attended school in a bad section of the city, and I would get chased home from school more often than not.

"Anyway, I would complain to my dad that I was having to endure this just to go to school. His reaction was, 'Don't run. Turn around and kick their butts.' " Laughter interrupts her words, "I turned into quite a scrapper in my early years, and my dad actually pushed that along.

"See, he was a heavyweight fighter, the Vermont State Champion. He wanted to go on to professional fighting, but his health held him back. I think when I learned to be a fighter, he was proud that I took after him.

"I don't think he was trying to make a tomboy out of me; he just wanted me to be able to physically protect myself and hold up under the strain. He taught me a lot."

Obviously, Shirley learned to hold up under the strain. Her career is proof of that. She also learned not to be a helpless little victim. She learned to take responsibility for her own safety. Since there was no one to rescue her on those long walks home from school, she learned to take care of herself.

If you recall rule number 1 in all effective parenting, that actions speak louder than words, you will avoid sending a double message—like the father who refused to buy his daughter a new dress for her initiation into the National Honor Society, but happily forked out $175 three days later for a new cheerleading uniform. (Or as a close friend of mine is fond of saying, "It's not enough to talk the talk, you gotta walk the walk.") Instead, you will endeavor to back up your verbal encouragement with the kind of behavior that says the following to your daughter:

> I believe you are perfectly capable of handling any situation that arises. I am here if you need me, but I will rely on *your* judgment, rather than my own, to determine if and when my help is needed. I will not jump in prematurely to rescue you and diminish your achievement.

> I know there will be times when you will feel frustrated and anxious, lonely and scared as you cope with the hardships that will be unique unto whatever path you choose to walk. I will love and support you as you walk your path, but I will not save you from its lessons. I will not trespass on your right to grow, to make mistakes, and to learn the lessons inherent in them. I will not trespass on your right to autonomy.

Another form of premature rescuing is probably as old as parenting itself. It goes something like this: Dad becomes impatient with a child who is trying to accomplish a task, whether it be tying shoes or zipping up a winter parka. His impatience grows until finally, out of desperation, he interferes in the child's effort to complete a task with the accompanying statement, "Here, let me do that for you." Whether he has helped the child because he believes she needs rescuing or because he is in a hurry and out of patience, the message is the same, "You can't do this alone. You need my help."

Always wait until your daughter requests help. Even then, you may decide it is in her best interest to withhold assistance a little longer. (Try not to get carried away here. Remember, she is a child, and in learning something new, she may need some guidance along the way. But guidance and doing it for her are two different things.) Never, never give help before it is requested. Stop and think, "How many times in my adult life has anyone barged in to rescue me before I requested it?" Indeed, "How many times have they rescued me even after I *did* request it?" Since it is adult life you are preparing her for, the answer is self-evident.

Unless it is an emergency situation, pause and ask yourself, "Would I rescue her from this situation if she were a boy?" "If this were my son, would I do this for him?" If your answer is yes, then go ahead and rescue. You are probably just being a concerned father. *But* if you would not rescue a boy from a particular situation, do not rescue a girl. It is as simple as that.

Third, if you hear yourself saying, "Here, let me do that for you," stop dead in your tracks and examine what you are doing and why. After taking a moment to examine your behavior, you should be able to determine more accurately whether your "help" is necessary. If you decide you were too hasty, simply say, "Nope, I was wrong. I see you can do that for yourself. Sorry for butting in like that!"

Barbara Grogan tells the story of the revelation of her own degree of learned helplessness and how the acceptance of the fact that she must rescue herself was the catalyst which enabled her to overcome it.

"There were times after my divorce when I thought, oh, certainly, somebody's going to come along and love me and save me from having to work and figure all this out.

"One night I was writing a check for my children's tuition and I thought, 'I'm going to marry somebody wealthy because I want to keep my children in their school. They've had enough trauma already, they shouldn't have to change schools.'

"Suddenly, I went [she gasped] when I heard myself say that. I thought, 'That's indentured servitude!' and I literally started the company within a week.

"If I choose to get married again, it will be because I love him and because he loves me. I will figure out a way, thank you, to keep my children in that school myself. It was a very clear decision," she said quite seriously, "I was highly motivated."

We talked about why the revelation doesn't happen for all women, about why some continue to depend on men to take care of them.

She replied, "My heart aches for those people. I do a lot of public speaking to women's groups, and I think it's real important for them to know I'm not Superwoman. I have had all the fears, the gutwrenching, the sleepless nights."

"Still," I persisted, "you didn't knuckle under to the temptation to be helpless." Her reply was interesting.

"I wasn't allowed to," she laughed, "I didn't have the time. I had hocked my house, I hocked my whole soul, almost, to start this company. I didn't have the luxury of sitting around worrying about if it was going to fail. I had to make it.

"The metamorphosis came," she continued, "when I finally decided that I was in charge of my life. While I was sitting around waiting for my white knight, while I was hating my life, nobody was fixing it. If I allowed somebody else to fix my life for me, there would always be that underlying instability based on dependence. *I* wanted to be the underlying stability.

"Whatever happens in the world, my boat is going to stay afloat."

This is the kind of attitude you are working to build in your daughter. Actually it is more than an attitude; it is a confidence and a willingness as well, but the attitude comes first. When the confidence and the willingness to take control of her life are there, the refusal to wait for someone else to "fix" her will follow. If you prematurely rescue her, you will teach her that she can *expect* someone to come along, as daddy always did, to make everything better. It is a deadly way to live.

As Dr. Resnick says, "I taught Judy that *she* would have to earn whatever she got, that nothing would be presented to her on a silver platter, and not to expect anything to be handed out."

Another businesswoman said, "My dad taught me a girl has to make it on her own. He said, 'Honey, I'm going to tell you right now, it's a struggle to the grave. You might as well get used to the idea.' "

Another type of unspoken message can be seen in the way in which some fathers choose to discipline. Unfortunately, just as some fathers confuse pressure with encouragement (Chapter 3), others confuse punishment with discipline.

The word "discipline" comes from the Latin *disciplina*, which means "instruction" or "knowledge." Let us use *this* meaning of the word so that we do not mistakenly discourage our daughters when we should be disciplining (teaching) them instead. In other words, discipline should be seen as an opportunity to instruct, build character, and teach responsibility, not as an opportunity to inflict punishment, discourage a child, or destroy self-esteem.

All human beings make mistakes, not just children. When your daughter makes an error in judgment, acts out petty emotions, goofs off, sasses you, irritates you, breaks things, or becomes rebellious and unruly, your job as her parent must be to teach her a better way, a way to function more responsibly and intelligently. Put-downs do not teach a child a better way, they only belittle and degrade. Ultimately, they are cruel.

This may seem self-evident, yet countless times I have heard parents, in the so-called act of disciplining, say to a child, "What's the matter with you?" or "What is your problem?" or "Can't you do anything right?" or "How could you have been so stupid?" or some other variation on this theme.

As a father who dreams of having a successful daughter, you cannot afford to use phrases such as these. They reflect your appraisal that something is "wrong" with her, that she is unable to function adequately, or that she has a "problem." Given that individuals make decisions about themselves based on the way others see them, this kind of discipline is risky.

Obviously, this advice applies to raising sons as well, but if you recall the results of studies on attribution theory, you will remember that females have a strong tendency toward self-blame anyway, toward accepting responsibility for their failures but not their successes, and toward attributing failure to lack of ability rather than lack of support. Given this propensity, incorporating the instructive rather than the punitive (and often humiliating) approach to discipline is all the more important for your daughter.

In Chapters 7 and 8, some real-life dialogues are presented to show how to incorporate instructive discipline into your parental repertoire, since many of you will be requiring something more concrete when your little darling spills grape soda on your new vanilla-cream car upholstery. Contemplating infanticide will render you just about incapable of being a good, instructive disciplinarian. These examples will be provided to give you something to hang on to when you have been pushed beyond your limits. Good luck!

PRIORITIZATION OF TRAITS

In the process of learning what behavior is appropriate to their sex (gender identification), children learn that both femininity and masculinity are defined by strict codes of behavior. The young female will naturally try to emulate the behavior that is socially sanctioned for females. Furthermore, she will hierarchically order the feminine traits so that some are more important than others.

A perusal of the list of feminine adjectives appearing in Chapter 3 shows that feminine behavior can be classified into three basic categories: giving service, developing a nonthreatening personality, and cultivating beauty and sex appeal. These are the categories your daughter will hierarchically order as she seeks to incorporate femininity into her self-image. Both her parents, but particularly her father, will encourage this ordering as shown in the study below.

In one study, 2,000 mothers and fathers were asked, "What kind of person would you want your son or daughter to become?"[12] While both parents were shown to give responses which indicated higher career expectations for sons than for daughters, fathers demonstrated this attitude more frequently than mothers. Twice as many parents listed hardworking and ambitious as traits they wished for their sons as listed it for their daughters. Other traits parents indicated as desirable for their sons were self-reliant, responsible, intelligent, and strong-willed. For daughters the traits listed as desirable were attractive, kind, well-mannered, loving, and unselfish (for daughters they also indicated it was important to have a good marriage and be a good parent). While both sets of parents were shown to indicate these sex-stereotyped preferences, fathers did so more frequently than mothers.

I have no quarrel with the care-giving aspect of the feminine list. As a matter of fact I find the dearth of nurturing traits in the masculine list to be a pitiful statement on the American perception of masculinity. The only adjective in the masculine list that comes close to nurturing is "protective," while the feminine list contains at least ten: nurturing, caring, sensitive, sweet, understanding, flexible, compassionate, self-sacrificing, gentle, and warm.

Frankly, it is the other two categories that cause the self-esteem and achievement problems. In the case of beauty, many females are taught to feel that their entire self-worth is based on whether they are attractive to males. For some females, it is the central focus of their lives. This is what we hope to avoid with your daughter. Second, the development of a passive, nonthreatening (feminine) personality often stands in the way of achievement. We will examine each one separately and discuss ways fathers can minimize the impact of these requirements of femininity.

Beauty, the Beast

"You have to suffer to be beautiful," my mother said as I squirmed, whined, and complained during the ordeal of my first permanent. At age five, I don't think I really cared whether I was beautiful, but it was important that I be taught to care. Therefore, my mother, like a million mothers before her, was trying her best to instill in me an understanding of the world as she saw it, namely: Life is easier for a beautiful female. I was to hear this homily about suffering and beauty many times as I grew up, as did many of the women whom I interviewed. (Were any of you men given this particular bit of advice?)

Then there was my beautiful aunt. Actually, she wasn't beautiful, but she was skilled in the art of deception and was able to create the silhouette, the image, the illusion of beauty. Wherever she perceived a flaw, she set about camouflaging it. I remember watching her at her dressing table spending literally hours (I'm not exaggerating) with foundation makeup, powders, shadows, and creams. It all seemed *very* important, since she spent so much time at it. To add to the allure, this beautiful aunt seemed to have all the good things in life: gorgeous clothes, glamorous nights on the town, and, best of all, boyfriends!

A few years later in school I observed that the most popular girls were also the cutest. It didn't take long for the ideas planted by my mother and aunt to take root and grow. And so it is for most females. My story is not unusual.

Today, in spite of all our liberated talk about the importance of inner qualities, about an egalitarian society, about tearing down barriers to females, the major issues of time, money, and self-esteem are intimately linked to beauty and sex appeal for many females. Unfortunately, many men still continue to evaluate a female's worth based on her physical appearance. *Young* males do so with a vengeance. None of this will escape your daughters' awareness.

The importance of physical appearance may become even more intense if we can judge by the increase in its importance in the years since television arrived in the American living room. If one aspires to be the anchorperson for a national news broadcast, for example; it is not enough to be well-educated, experienced, articulate, insightful, white, and male. Now, even the *males* have to be good-looking! Furthermore, good looks have come to have an extraordinarily homogenous definition. The basic structure of the northern European face combined with the American look: small nose, straight teeth, blond hair, and thin, thin, thin, are the requirements for beauty in this country, and with alarming frequency, other countries as well.

You will find that your daughter will show an awareness of these issues at a very tender age. You may be surprised at just how early this awareness surfaces. Fathers in my workshop report little girls at the tender ages of four and five becoming upset if their hair "looks funny" or their clothes aren't color-coordinated.

It is unquestionably a more serious issue for females than males. Granted, males are becoming more aware of their appearance, but it is still not a requirement of masculinity to be attractive and sexy. How many males for example (other than those with media aspirations) actually believe that they must be handsome in order to achieve their goals? This seems ridiculous, yet many females feel the pressure to be beautiful as well as educated and competent.

This is confirmed in the comments you read earlier by the children of Dr. Papageorgiou's survey.

Such statements suggest that both boys and girls feel it is imperative that a female do everything she can to be attractive. . . . In addition, both boys and girls recognize that a male's appearance is relatively unimportant. Several boys emphasized that if they had to be female, the only way they could tolerate the change would be if they could be particularly beautiful. On the other hand, not a single girl said that if she had to be male, she wanted to be particularly handsome.[13]

Given the emphasis on good looks in contemporary culture, how are we to convince our daughters that there are more important traits to nurture and develop than one's physical appearance? How are we to convince them that while a pleasing appearance is important and grooming shows consideration for others, the endless hours some females spend in front of the mirror and the thousands of dollars they spend on cosmetics, clothes, makeovers and exercise equipment are excessive?

To make matters worse, we have said that it is important to

reassure your daughter that she is attractive and pretty so that she feels confident in her beauty. How does a father do this without seeming to be emphasizing appearance over achievement?

First, it is important to express love and approval for your daughter *exactly as she is*, regardless of whether she measures up to your personal standard of beauty. This means giving compliments and flattery unconditionally, not after hinting that she should fix her hair or lose some weight. It is even more important if she happens to have a beautiful mother, which can be very hard on a girl, particularly if she has not inherited her mother's good looks.

Second, avoid the kind of fatherly advice shown below. All these statements have been reported by my interviewees. While I'm sure their fathers had what they thought was their daughter's best interest at heart, it is indeed questionable if these warnings were helpful.

"You'll never get a boyfriend if you look like that."

"You better fix yourself up, or no guy will ask you out."

"You need to lose some weight if you want the boys to like you."

"You want the boys to like you, don't you?"

These kinds of statements give your validation to a male's right to pass judgment on your daughter, to determine if she measures up to *his* standards. Your goal should be to develop your daughter's self-esteem to the point where she is more concerned that he measure up to *her* standards.

Third, teach the importance of grooming and cleanliness but avoid comments about physical attributes or liabilities. Especially avoid remarks about your daughter's weight. We will discuss this in greater depth in Chapters 10 and 11.

Fourth, be aware of whether your compliments to your daughter revolve around her accomplishments, her behavior, or her appearance. Praising performance and deed above all else will help (though not eradicate) her perception of the importance of beauty.

The last point I would like to make is a bit ironic given all I have said above. Remember, the girl who is already beautiful often has a very casual attitude toward her looks. She can afford to. *She* may feel less confident about her personality or her intellect. On the other hand, the girl who is plain or unattractive needs more reinforcement that she is beautiful just as she is and for whom she is. The message here is to be sensitive to your daughter's particular needs, which are sure to be quite individualistic and may change from daughter to daughter.

Being a "Good Girl"

Another trait on which your daughter may place a high priority as she attempts to incorporate femininity into her self-image is the development of a feminine personality, one which is sweet, polite, inoffensive, and above all nonthreatening. If you look at the list of feminine traits, you will see it contains at least fourteen adjectives which indicate deference to others, awareness of their feelings, and compliance with their wishes—to wit: understanding, caring, sensitive, nurturing, sweet, refined, flexible, compassionate, gentle, warm, subtle, self-sacrificing, passive, and submissive! (The masculine list, on the other hand, which exemplifies the assertive behavior synonymous with achievement in our culture, contains not even one!)

Being a good girl, therefore, often means taking orders, deferring to the wishes of others, and cultivating a nonthreatening demeanor, even at the cost of one's own integrity and self-esteem. As you know, this type of behavior is not congruent with the behavior required to meet the demands of achievement, to handle the harsher realities of the business and professional worlds, which are often neither very tactful nor civilized.

This desire to please, to be polite and inoffensive (feminine), is at the root of many problems that females encounter because our culture expects bosses, executives, and entrepreneurs to be made of sterner stuff. Whether it is for fear of being labeled a castrating bitch or a genuine inability to risk hurting others, many females are undermined by their reluctance to get tough.

At this point, I can just feel the pained indignation of those gentle folk who object to females practicing the tactics of "winning by intimidation." They feel that the so-called feminine traits of deference and consideration represent our last glimmer of hope for engineering a society which cares about the rights and feelings of others. I agree, and for this reason, I wish to encourage any human being, male or female, to develop the capacity for mediation, compromise, consensus, and compassion—those traits for which females are so famous.

The problem is that deferring to others is not a cultural value for *all* members of the culture; consequently, when only one segment defers, the opportunity is created for the other segment to exploit, and thus the inequality is endlessly perpetuated. (Teaching young males to be considerate, nurturing, and deferential is, of course, the answer to this problem. But that's another book.) Given this cultural reality, it is counterproductive to the goal of achievement to fail to teach your daughter assertiveness skills or hesitate to develop her capacity for firm and decisive action simply due to a fear of her appearing to be unfemininely aggressive or threatening.

One issue concerning females and aggressive behavior has been raised many times in my seminars and deserves to be addressed. A father will inevitably ask, "Isn't it true that males are naturally more aggressive than females? Doesn't testosterone make men more aggressive?"

This is another version of the nature-nurture debate. Most experts in the field of sex roles and human behavior are loath to take an either-or position due to the danger of oversimplifying a very complex question. Two issues should be kept in mind, however.

First, the validity of the argument that males are naturally more aggressive hinges on the researchers' definition of aggression. If one defines aggression as a *physical* act, then yes, males do seem to exhibit physical aggression more often than females. On the other hand, if one defines aggression as "behavior with the intent to harm another" (a broader definition of the behavior), then the boundaries become blurred.

For example, let's take a look at your average fourth-grade class at recess on the playground. The males are into fighting at this stage of childhood development. The boys are out there "dukin' it out," as one fourth-grader put it. But what are the girls up to?

They are busily ostracizing one of their clique members due to some real or imagined infraction of the group's standards. These cliques have very strictly defined codes of behavior. Any member found guilty of a transgression is swiftly and often brutally dispatched. Furthermore, the blackballing techniques used by the group to ostracize or punish a member can become quite vicious. Rumors, lies, and innuendos abound.

If one accepts the second definition of aggression offered above (behavior with the intent to harm another), then it becomes obvious that the girls are just as hostile and aggressive as the boys. The difference is that it is not socially acceptable for girls to physically fight one another; it is not feminine. Consequently, then, we can see how girls simply learn to display their aggression in ways which are socially sanctioned.

Second, the issue of "natural" behavior becomes very difficult to pin down and define when discussing human beings, since the higher the organism on the evolutionary scale, the more important becomes learning and the less important becomes instinct. Indeed, many researchers postulate that there are *no* instincts left in human beings. (Even the sucking response of infants is more reflex than instinct.) Therefore, given the importance of learning in human lives, one is on precarious ground when attempting to justify aggressive behavior as more natural to one sex than the other.

The conflict between the need to defer to others in order to be feminine and the need to be mastery-oriented in order to succeed is aptly illustrated in the conflicting parental advice received by Clé Cervi, noted Denver publisher of *Cervi's Journal*, a Denver-based weekly business publication founded by her father, Eugene Cervi. She is currently the editor of *Parent* magazine in Denver.

"In high school, my mother kept saying to me, 'Will you please learn to keep your mouth shut? The boys won't like you if you talk so much and if you seem* smarter than they are. Will you please not do that?'

"On the other hand, the message coming from my father was exactly the opposite. He would say, 'So what? So you're smarter than they are. Go right ahead and be smarter than they are.'

"Probably because I identified so much with him as I was growing up, I decided to go with his advice and ignore hers.

"I think now that he very definitely has been a large factor in my life. He was a writer, he was a thinker, he was a philosopher. He was instrumental in shaping my thinking.

"I did not lead my life—particularly in those formative years, well, even into my thirties—I did not lead my life according to what was taught to me by my mother. If anything, I rebelled against that because my father presented a more exciting alternative."

Clé's mother, concerned only with femininity and popularity, did little to develop what her father realized was Clé's potential to lead.

"At one point, I was in New York and I had been basically partying for ten years." She laughs. "I must admit, I had a marvelous time. I traveled, had my hair done, went to Southampton

*I find it interesting that this mother used the verb "seem." In all probability, Clé actually was smarter than most of her male classmates, yet her mother very subtly undermined her self-confidence. Her mother was also careful to note that a female who talks and expresses her opinion is not popular with males.

in the summer, the New Jersey shore, Fire Island, party-to-party, suntans. . . .

"Daddy was getting wild with my job jumping and my absolute decision not to work at any of my jobs, so he says to me, 'Clé, you don't have a husband. You don't have children. I can just see what's going to happen. You're going to spend your life in New York accomplishing nothing. So, I'm going to give you a newspaper.' Give me a newspaper! Can you imagine?

"As I slowly began to take over the paper, which I did before he died, there would be times when I would say, 'Dad, I think we really ought to do this or that' and he would say, 'If you think so, go ahead and do it.' ''

Had Clé listened to her mother's advice to defer to others and keep her mouth shut in order to be liked, she never could have done what was required to run a successful publication. Her father, on the other hand, supported her assertiveness all the way.

"Once he made up his mind to give me the paper, he certainly let me run it. One time we had this very competent reporter, English, very stylized, who was absolutely incapable of accepting me as the person in charge.

"Daddy's advice was, 'Either you're running the paper or you're not running the paper. You'll just have to fire him.'

"Basically, my mother's viewpoint was a very narrow one. My father, on the other hand, left all the doors open. His viewpoint represented an adventure, a challenge."

Many females do, in fact, overcome their tendency to be too "nice," but why create a personal style your daughter must overcome? Why not smooth the way by avoiding the expectation that she be stereotypically feminine, malleable, and compliant in the first place? Without the kind of male support that gives your daughter permission to pursue her talents and goals, to be constructively selfish, she may never do so. It begins with you.

When you teach your daughter to be polite and considerate, teach her also how and when to be assertive and defend her rights. Teach her the difference between flexibility and submission, between compromise and self-sacrifice. Granted, these are judgment calls and will vary from person to person. The moral, however, is to be aware of a woman's propensity for becoming so sensitized to the feelings of others that she fails to act in her own best interest. As a father attempting to create a daughter capable of achieving her goals, it is better to err on the side of constructive selfishness. Furthermore, since she will be bombarded from every quarter with the expectation of feminine compliance, your instruction in constructive selfishness will provide the necessary counterbalance.

You can begin by allowing her to be assertive with *you*. You can abandon the requirement to please daddy. You can help her discern when it is appropriate and practical to challenge authority. You can allow her to challenge *your* authority.

Clé Cervi's father was a good example of a dominant figure who allowed his daughter to question his authority.

Says Clé, "He spoke with authority and he carried himself with authority, but he was not an authoritarian. He never said, 'By God, there's only one way to do it in this house, and you'll do it my way.' Absolutely not. He was too open to new ideas to behave like that. He was constantly exploring, searching, bringing in new thoughts, encouraging me to use *my* mind. He was an authority figure, no question about it, but he was not an authoritarian."

You can show your daughter when she is sacrificing herself needlessly. If your wife has been too thoroughly indoctrinated to be nice, and does so at her own expense, you should point these things out to her as well, particularly since she is the role model for your daughter.

Now, here comes the hard part: You have to be ready for the consequences of your actions. That may mean living in a household with females who talk back, stand up for themselves, and have minds of their own.

Whoops! There goes some of your motivation! You guys know as well as I do that it is a lot easier for you if the females in your lives (wives, daughters, secretaries, mothers, etc.) defer to the needs of others.

For those of you who secretly desire to maintain the comfortable status quo, your ability to rear a daughter capable of withstanding the demands of achievement is severely in question. (You just can't have it both ways.) For those of you who have realized that it is unjust, bravo! For those of you who have further realized that independent females (wives, daughters, secretaries, mothers, the same etc.) are more interesting and better companions for life on the planet, again bravo! For those of you who wish some practical applications, read on.

First, as I have said before, allow your daughter to challenge your authority. Second, do not admonish her when she is not behaving in a feminine manner by insisting on compliance and submission. Third, if your daughter comes home with a problem, do not necessarily advise her to passively endure a bad situation, but ask yourself, "If she were a boy, would I counsel her to stand up for herself?"

This is often a lot easier said than done, even when one thinks one is aware. A case in point involves a female student I once had. One day she had finally reached her limit with the obnoxious behavior of the classroom bully. He had knocked her books off her desk for the thousandth time. She sauntered over to him (he was seated), grabbed him by his shirt collar, and, looming above him, said in a loud voice, which the rest of the class could hear, "Knock it off." Then, still holding his shirt, she just stood and stared at him. Finally, she released him disgustedly and walked back to her seat.

My first response, which I did not act on (thank God) was to say, "That's not very ladylike, Kathy. Why don't you just ask him nicely?" I am not kidding. I almost said that. Luckily I realized in time that she had communicated with him far more effectively using the body language he understood. The point I am making here is that, even when one is extremely aware of gender behavior and making concerted efforts to teach children to respond appropriately to a situation regardless of their sex, it is easy to fall back on old habits and old behavior patterns.

Finally, remember the words of Dr. Papageorgiou: "Careers which involve giving orders, being in charge, and working independently are considered to be 'male.' Careers which involve following others' directions, serving or caring for others, and providing support are considered to be 'female.' "[14]

Therefore, give your daughter tasks and challenges which require her to give orders to others, work without supervision, and be the one in charge. It is the only way she will learn how to do it. Experiential learning is the only kind which is internally assimilated by the learner, thereby causing the integration that is necessary for a desired change in behavior (the definition of learning). All of which is just a fancy way of saying that life is not a spectator sport. Remember this and capitalize on every opportunity to give your daughter the experiences she needs to meet the challenges of her goals.

OBSERVING BEHAVIOR, CONSEQUENCES, AND OUTCOMES

This is one aspect of the formation of a self-concept (observing one's actions and the outcome) that is somewhat independent of outside influences. After all, if your daughter does well in math, she will see herself as someone who understands math, regardless of what others may say. If she can run faster than the little boy who lives next door, she must see herself as a faster runner than some boys.

The danger here is to allow this aspect of self-concept to give you a false sense of security. Remember that the tendency to prioritize traits (discussed earlier) may cause your daughter to place her feminine attributes above and to the detriment of her math skills and her running ability. Second, even observing one's behavior and its outcomes can go awry if mishandled, as we shall see in the next scenario.

Judy H. is a competent and ambitious young woman in her early thirties whom I met about a year ago on a very long train ride. When I told her of the book I was writing, she was eager to talk because she felt her father had made some mistakes that others could benefit from hearing. She loved him, but her emotions were ambivalent.

"My father was rigid, demanding, and critical of my accomplishments even when I brought home four A's and two B's on my report card. He criticized me for my 'failure' to get straight A's. He was very hard to please, and once he made up his mind, he was impossible. Also, he was always buried in work and it was hard to get his attention.

"There were times, however, when he did seem to soften a little, like whenever my mom used what has been popularly referred to as feminine wiles. If she would act helpless or burst into tears, she could get him to do anything. He would melt."

Judy learned quickly. She mimicked this behavior because it worked. It was modeled for her by her mother and reinforced by her father. Whenever she wanted something from him, she would go into her act. It became second nature. She continued this behavior as an adult, falsely assuming that it would work with all men. It backfired on her.

She had been using a variation of these tactics with her boss, rather successfully, for five years. Whenever she would play the role of a cute little girl, or alternatively, a coy lassie, she would get his attention. They both knew it was a harmless little game. Judy interpreted his attention as approval.

"At the end of four years, I decided it was time for a promotion and a pay increase. I had earned it. I knew it, and my boss knew it."

She got her act together, entered his office, and began the routine that had always worked in the past. Judy was in for a rude awakening.

"He politely put me off for several weeks. When I forced the issue, he informed me that he didn't think my style was appropriate for dealing with business people. He said I needed to grow up and act more maturely if I was to win the respect I needed in order to be promoted.

"When I cried, he comforted me but didn't give me the promotion. When I flirted, he returned the flirtation, but didn't give me the promotion.

"In a way, I blame my dad for this because he taught me that this was the way to behave with men. It took me a long time to figure out this behavior was inappropriate in a business setting.

"Years later, after having my consciousness raised, I realized that I had confused his male approval with his professional approval. They really are two different things. I was playing by the wrong rules, but it was the only script I had to go by. How could I possibly know that what had worked so well in the past would suddenly become ineffectual?"

The moral of this story is so obvious that I will not insult your intelligence by elaborating on it. Suffice it to say it happens with regularity in the business world.

Judy was basing her behavior on the fourth aspect of self-concept. She had observed her feminine behavior and its outcome many times with both her father and her boss. It had always worked. While her self-esteem may have been intact (prior to this encounter, anyway), the reality was that she had been taught to block her own progress.

This is why it is so very important to monitor your own behavior to determine what actions and outcomes you are reinforcing. If your daughter observes that feminine actions (i.e., tears, coy manipulation, or helpless dependency) result in the achievement of a desired goal, she will use them even in inappropriate situations. On the other hand, if she observes that assertive behavior *also* results in the achievement of a desired goal, she will have a broader repertoire available to her in any given circumstance and a stronger inclination to utilize it. Therefore, reward assertive behavior.

You may recall the advice offered in Chapter 2 in which we discussed the different fathering styles: the authoritarian, the protector, the softie, the pal. Softies and protectors can reinforce inappropriately feminine behavior even with good intentions and inadvertently create stumbling blocks for a daughter who wishes to be an achiever.

A father who is a pal will have nothing against being charmed or being protective (for that is part of friendship as well), but he will remain open to other behaviors his daughter may experiment with and explore. He will not be uncomfortable reinforcing assertive conduct, will not resist being swayed by his daughter's presentation of a logical argument (even if it opposes his), or be threatened by a display of independence (even when it makes him feel as if she no longer needs him).

Ultimately, he will realize that in the formation of her self-concept, it is crucial that she actually *observe* her independent and assertive actions as having a favorable outcome, and not just be *told* it is so. He will see to it that he reinforces this in the real world by his reactions to her behavior and by creating opportunities in which to do so.

One such pal-sy father-daughter relationship that still retained the expectation of achievement was that of Barbara Grogan and her father. Theirs was practically a textbook case. He seems to have done everything right and Barbara speaks of him with great affection and admiration.

"After you called," she says enthusiastically, "I realized how delighted I was that I get to talk about my father because it's a real testimony to him.

"He was my first prince, a very important person in my life. I always identified with him and whatever he was doing. Even as a small child, I have a vivid memory of waiting for him to come home and having him read me the newspaper.

"On Saturdays I would spend the day with him going to the hardware store or hanging around the basement watching him build. He had a workroom down there, where he built model cars or shelves or cabinets for the house, and I used to just love being with him, passing the time, and watching him build. Sitting there among all the nuts and bolts . . . Well, you know, I wasn't playing with dolls, I was following my dad around."

She laughs, "He never would have thought that what he was doing was creating a nontraditional female, because he was actually kind of a traditionalist in his view of women and their role, but absolutely, that's what happened. Just being able to closely identify with a male . . ." Her voice trails off at this point as she gazes into some past memory. Suddenly she says, "Still though, he never made me feel that the boys did this and the girls did that. We had a go-cart, and I would go out there and grab that go-cart just as fast as the boys. And it wasn't, 'Oh no, you don't want to do that, Barbara. You'll hurt yourself.' None of that. I just put my helmet on and went out there and rode 60 miles an hour.

"When I think about it now," she says, shaking her head, "I wonder how he let us do that. But there was never any, 'Oh no, that's too dangerous.' "

She muses about it now as a mother. "Speaking from the other side for a moment, I know it's real hard as a parent to let either sons or daughters take those risks. But I think in order to give them their sense of personal power, you have to.

"My father was really such an extraordinary person in my life, and I was certainly trying to live up to his expectations of me, which were to always do my best.

"If I could only have my Dad for a short time or somebody else for fifty years, I would pick my Dad because in the years I did have him, he gave me a lot. He was my best friend."

S U M M A R Y

To summarize, then, an enlightened father will use his knowledge of how self-concept is formed to provide the right kind of verbal responses in conjunction with appropriate activities to build his daughter's sense of competence and confidence. The following summary should help.

1. *Individuals assess their worth by comparing themselves with others.*
   Remember that one group your daughter will be comparing herself to is boys. Bear in mind the study quoted earlier which shows that her male peers will, in all likelihood, be denigrating female activities. Remember, therefore, to be the male strong voice countering these negative assessments of females. Furthermore, weaken her belief that it is better to be male by giving her the same opportunities, freedom, skills, and education that boys are given.

2. *Individuals learn to see themselves as others see them.*
   Back up your verbal encouragement with the kind of behavioral evidence that shows your daughter you believe her to be competent, intelligent, and trustworthy. Remember that lip service alone is shallow and superficial, that your behavior will be the true barometer of your beliefs.

3. *Individuals prioritize their personal traits so that some traits become more important than others for overall self-esteem.*

   Help your daughter gain perspective on the importance of beauty and sex appeal. Don't deny these things are important, but focus your attention (in the form of compliments, encouragement, and rewards) on her efforts, achievements, and performance.

4. *Individuals describe themselves by observing their behavior, its consequences and outcomes.*

   Give your daughter the kinds of experiences in the real world that force her to define herself as one who takes risks and masters situations, just as you would a son. Help her see any failure as a mistake and a learning experience. Don't rescue prematurely.

A New Concept in Self-Concept

Earlier in this chapter the statement was made that an individual's self-concept is in a constant state of flux and depends on the circumstances in which one finds oneself, the work one is doing in the world, and the current level of one's performance and reward. This is good news for fathering a successful daughter, since it means that self-concept is not static but can be changed and modulated.

A recent study by Dr. Kristen Yount at the University of Kentucky on women coal miners provides some interesting new insights along these lines. Women miners use the same adjectives to describe themselves as men miners.[15] Similarly, men in caregiving roles, like nursing and teaching, describe themselves using much the same adjectives as women in these fields. In other words, the self-images of adults (including their images of their own masculinity or femininity) are to some extent generated by their current work in the world.

What is provocative about this study is it literally reverses our old concepts of work and gender, which assumed that the sexual division of labor was due to the natural traits exhibited by men and women which both preceded and dictated the type of work they chose to do. This study postulates that the opposite may be equally true. Says Dr. Yount,

Women may be in human service occupations, not because they are naturally more warm and nurturant, but rather, they come to see themselves as warm and nurturant when they work in the service professions. Since their reproductive destiny has historically placed them in care-giving roles they have developed this self-concept and continued to work in the service professions.[16]

We can see this concept manifested in our everyday environment. The numerous articles and books appearing on the "new fathering craze" have men describing themselves as loving, warm, caring, and nurturant. This is a direct result of participating more actively in child care. When a father is required through the daily activity of child care to be warm and nurturant, he is forced into a new perception, a new evaluation, and ultimately a new definition of himself. It is difficult to imagine a father of the 1950s describing himself in these terms. Likewise, many career women, who by the nature of their work have been forced to emulate so-called masculine behavior, describe themselves quite differently from the traditional feminine stereotype.

What is useful about this study for our purposes is the notion that the activities in which individuals are currently engaged influence their self-concept. This means that self-concept is painted on a changing canvas. If you want your daughter to incorporate assertive behavior into her repertoire, you must provide her with experiences and activities in her play which require her to be strategic, strong, assertive, clever, and brave. Climbing trees, building forts, playing chess, making paper airplanes, wrestling, riding bikes, and engaging in competitive sports are all activities which build a self-image of courage, intelligence, vigor, and strength. Taking care of babies, preparing meals, and getting pretty are activities which build a self-image of a person who is nurturing and deferential and who meets the expectations of others.

Some little girls will readily take to both types of activities. Others will prefer one type over the other. Do not force your daughter to engage in activities she doesn't like. Don't be an authoritarian about her playtime. However, if your little girl is too focused on female activities, you can encourage her participation in activities which build courage and strategic thinking by participating in them with her, teaching her skills you may have reserved for your sons, and pointing out women as role models who engage in these types of activities. Encouraging her mother to participate in new, nontraditional activities is a good idea also.

Must She Choose? Not Either/Or but Both Together!

As we have seen, it is likely that your daughter will experience a conflict over achievement that will be based on a gut-level comprehension of what the world expects from females. She will see the demands of success clash with her role as a female in our society. Never mind that there is life after junior high school. Never mind that we are in a period of slow transition and that things are changing. Never mind that some boys get smarter as they get older and eventually come to appreciate an intelligent, independent female. By the time the junior high school experience is over, many females have already gone permanently underground. Their early choice to conform will have sealed their fate for many years to come.

Furthermore, the constant bombardment of our culture undermines your daughter's self-esteem and discourages her willingness to take risks. Then, there is the smugly superior posturing of young males whose attitudes demean females and their value to society. You and your wife may be ambivalent about raising a daughter whose behavior may be interpreted as masculine. Yet, in spite of these overwhelming influences, you do have the power to cultivate in your daughter the life skills, coping mechanisms, and positive self-esteem that are vital for her to prevail over opposition.

How? By accepting two premises: first, that the psychological processes which empower an individual to succeed remain the same, regardless of gender; and second, that successful people learn to adapt to circumstances.

To put it another way, when a situation calls for sensitivity and compassion, the adaptive, successful person, regardless of gender, responds appropriately. When a situation calls for action, aggression, power, and strategy, the successful person again responds appropriately, regardless of gender. The message is clear and inescapable: adaptive, appropriate, successful behavior is not dependent on gender. In other words, the key to your daughter's success is combining male and female characteristics in one.

If you accept this premise and you further accept that life is so supremely unconcerned with gender that it dumps everything on everybody, then you will embrace the idea of making a range of responses available to your daughter so that she learns how to respond appropriately regardless of the situation in which she finds herself. You will do this not just through verbal encouragement but by incorporating a wide variety of experiences into her life.

Imagine what it is like for the young female trying to meet the gender expectations of her society today. On the one hand, she is supposed to be the obedient daughter, serious scholar, and budding young career woman to please her parents and teachers, while on the other hand, she is supposed to be the sex kitten and "cute piece" to please males and attract their attention. No wonder she becomes confused!

Ultimately, then, your goal is to train your daughter to see *options*, to recognize that she has available to her a *range* of choices as well as the freedom to exhibit whatever type of behavior is most appropriate to a given situation. In this way, she will internalize the belief that feminine behavior and achievement-oriented behavior can peacefully co-exist. When it is appropriate to be flirtatious, sweet, and sexy or to be the nurturant caregiver, she will feel free to exhibit that kind of behavior. By the same token, when it is appropriate to ace her physics exam or annihilate the opposition on the debate team, she will feel free to do that as well. It will teach her that one type of behavior need not exist at the exclusion of another.

If we teach our daughters to adopt a wide range of behaviors in order to achieve, we must also teach them the difference between image and substance, for in my experience observing young females for the last eleven years, one of two things usually occurs. If they do not understand that the purpose of a range of behaviors is to provide *options*, they either reject the concept because they fear appearing masculine or, like some of their favorite rock stars, they adopt a superficial persona consisting of all image and no substance.

It is our responsibility to teach them that image alone is an empty shell with all the power and vitality of a department store mannequin. They need to understand that *behavior*, with all its demands on one's conduct and challenges to one's attitude, is infinitely more appropriate, adaptive, and rewarding.

In the words of a woman plumber fighting the good fight, "Being a pioneer is no picnic, but it's the most exciting part of my life. The excitement is the challenge. You can't be afraid to be different. What's important to me is I know the difference between being tough [image] and being strong [substance]. I never want to be tough, but I have to be strong every day."

CULTIVATING PERSONHOOD OVER FEMININITY

How do you ensure that your daughter does not confuse image and substance or forsake assertive behavior in favor of feminine behavior? By giving her *opportunities* to express a wide range of responses (that is, to *exhibit* flexible behavior); by providing occasions in which she must adapt to a situation rather than respond automatically with a sex-role stereotype; by reinforcing both the positive components of traditional femininity, such as caregiving and intuition, and the positive components of traditional masculinity, such as risk taking and assertive behavior; and by engaging her in both typically male and female activities. In other words, one does not learn how to ski by talking about skiing. One learns how to ski by skiing. Similarly, one does not learn how to take risks or master situations by talking about them.

As you will see, Chapter 8 is based on the premise that your daughter must develop a flexible self-image regarding her behavioral choices. Nearly all the recommendations and strategies offered will revolve around developing and cultivating her belief in her own ability to successfully negotiate risks and master any subject or situation which arises. These strategies, when combined with your approval of her femininity and your verbal expression of her physical attractiveness, will give her the winning edge—confidence in both masculine and feminine fields of expression as well as the ability to weather the storm of puberty with her self-esteem intact.

We will discuss the subject of risk taking as it applies to females, for it is a complicated and emotionally charged area, in Chapter 7.

CHAPTER 6

❦

Moms and Dads Together and Apart: Developing an Effective Team

So far, this book has concentrated on the role a father plays in his daughter's achievement potential, and indeed it is a critical one, but bear in mind that the suggestions given in this book do not apply to fathers only. They can and should be incorporated by mothers as well. Premature rescuing is just as dangerous a behavior for a mother to practice as a father; a girl can be just as crippled by an overprotective mother as an overprotective father. A mother, as well as a father, can send subtle and destructive unspoken messages which undermine a girl's self-esteem. A mother can be a risk taker and set an example of courage and determination as well.

A father does not work in a vacuum. His efforts and likelihood of success must be seen in a particular context; that is, he is part of a team. If he and his wife don't work well together, confusion and strife are generated.

Both parents must recognize this. It is the first awareness in building an effective team. Since no parent would purposely debilitate his daughter's capacity to achieve, we can be optimistic that parents will work out any conflicts they may have to arrive at a mutually satisfying teamwork approach. It may require nothing more than a simple discussion to express viewpoints and clarify goals in order to get themselves on the same wavelength. Once they understand how their behavior (both individually and as a couple) affects their daughter's potential, they can coordinate their tactics and be more consistent in the messages they send her and more uniform in their expectations of her performance. Thus, they create a harmonious influence which, by its complementary nature, is doubly effective.

For those times when this seems easier said than done, however, this chapter is provided to help you develop an effective team and resolve conflicts. It is divided into three parts. The first section discusses the impact that your relationship with your wife has on your daughter. The second section discusses different types of moms and what to do if you are running into parenting style conflicts. The last part contains suggestions for what to do as a couple. But first . . .

A Story of Mixed Messages

Little Ann Bernard's mother was a jazz musician. During the courtship of her parents, her father was dazzled by her mother's talent and celebrity. He even basked in the reflected glory. At every social gathering, he would insist that she play the piano for the assembled guests. He would encourage her to audition in local night spots and would faithfully go every weekend to listen to her play. It was common to hear him say, "My wife's a piano player. Come on, Honey, show 'em what you can do." Sounds like a supportive male if ever there was one, right? So what's the problem?

Unfortunately, a strange irony developed after they were married. The qualities that made his wife an outstanding performer and musician, in demand and highly paid, the very qualities that had attracted him in the first place, were unacceptable to him in a wife. They were incongruent with what he perceived as her role. On the weekends it was OK for her to be aggressive and independent so she could cope with the frustrating realities of the music business, but during the week she was supposed to be Donna Reed, vacuuming in her pearls and deferring to her husband.

These widely discrepant roles were impossible for her to manage, even though she tried. She was not a woman with a stage personality which she could shed after the gig was over. The traits of her stage persona—perfectionism, ego, creativity, and a slightly larger-than-life approach to things—were as evident at home as they were onstage. Her husband could never reconcile the two. He spent their married life trying to change her behavior from a dynamic stage personality into a timid, deferential little wife.

Essentially, he disapproved of her *as a person* because she didn't fit the acceptable feminine stereotype in existence at the time.

Why do I recount this story? Because it illustrates the central themes presented in this chapter. First, is that Ann's father violated rule number 1—he offered verbal encouragement but could not behave in a manner to support his words. Second, this contradictory situation had the predictable results we have already discussed. Little Ann Bernard learned it was not OK to be like her mother—independent, creative, and gutsy. It was unfeminine. She learned that these traits were not valued by men because they were not valued by her father—the only man whom she had the opportunity to observe at close range. Consequently, she stifled these traits in herself, and for many years tried to be the passive and quietly demure creature her father believed females should be.

To give him credit, her father's heart was in the right place. He wanted to be supportive of his wife's gift. In many ways he was. He continued to encourage her career and was always proud of her talent. But in his own home he created strife and contributed to an unnecessary conflict in his daughter. The lessons we can learn from Mr. Bernard are valuable.

What Your Treatment of Your Wife Tells Your Daughter

Your daughter will learn that certain types of behavior are valued by men and other types are not. Your wife will set the example of behavior, and your reaction to it will tell your daughter whether or not it is acceptable to males.

For example, if you respond negatively to independence, assertiveness, or leadership in your wife by withdrawing, showing rage, making fun of her, or openly criticizing her, your daughter will learn that this type of behavior is not valued in females and could be downright risky (even around her supposedly supportive father). If you show approval for assertive behavior by listening attentively, asking questions, bouncing ideas around, and enthusiastically supporting new ideas, you teach your daughter that it is safe to display independent behavior around men who love you.

In a California study, Marjorie Honzik found that fathers who exhibited a friendly attitude toward their wives had daughters who were more likely to succeed intellectually.[1] In other words, part of your daughter's self-esteem as a female may be tied to *your* attitude toward your wife and whether you show approval or disapproval of the way she conducts her life.

The idea that your treatment of your wife will have a rippling effect on your daughter's self-esteem is central enough to pursue further. The most effective way to form (or transform) your daughter's behavior is to give the verbal encouragement, love, and affection that are required and then to back them up *behaviorally* by demonstrating the same kind of valuing toward your wife or other females with whom you relate.

In other words, do not send contradictory messages. Do not support independence and risk taking in your daughter only to dissuade it in your wife. The easiest way to remember it is this: You do not encourage your daughter by discouraging your wife. That will only confuse your daughter and teach her that male support is superficial and limited to lip service only. It will teach her that one day, should she exhibit independence around a man she loves, she will risk losing his approval and perhaps even risk abandonment. In all likelihood it will increase the conflict at puberty and subtly encourage her to go underground.

When, on the other hand, you teach your daughter that assertive behavior in a female is attractive by responding positively to it in your wife, you teach your daughter that she can come to *expect* positive treatment from males. If she is reared in this kind of environment, it will not occur to her that her ideas may be inferior simply because she lacks a penis. Then, as she matures, she will be less likely to tolerate a sexist attitude from certain types of males and be less likely to choose a sexist man as a life mate.

The tables on pages 122 and 123 should be read carefully. They show how a man's treatment of his wife will have later consequences on his daughter's behavior.

This is no great revelation. Psychologists have known for years that children are strongly affected by the relationship of their parents. In this case, however, we are applying the concept specifically to the fathering of a successful daughter.

The first part of the chart represents the more traditional, stereotypical role—with father as the head of the household. It is called "Traditional, Nonvaluing Behavior" because the fundamental message is that a female's value is determined by her willingness to participate primarily in domestic duties and child care.[2]

The second part of the chart represents a more democratic relationship between husband and wife, one in which the wife's individuality, talents, opinions, attitudes, goals, and problem-solving skills are not only valued but sought after.

In the first male role (traditional, nonvaluing), a husband may say he values his wife's input, but if there were disagreement between them concerning a course of action, his word would be the final word. She would be expected to concede graciously and support him regardless of the degree to which she opposed his decision. (Her role as wife is to support her husband, but the reverse is not always true.) The message to the daughter observing this situation is that males make better decisions.

This can become particularly ridiculous if the wife shows better judgment than her husband. I know a couple where the wife is a better money handler than the husband, but because he believes that it is the husband's job to make the financial decisions in a family, she is expected to concede. Time and again he has made foolish financial moves and caused suffering and sacrifice to the entire family, while her suggestions, which went unheeded, turned out to be the sounder of the two. Unfortunately, his thinking, which says that men handle money better than women, continues to put the family in difficult and, on occasion, even untenable situations. It would be so much easier on everyone if he would just concede that his wife is more skilled in money matters than he.

In the second male role (nontraditional, valuing), a husband who disagrees with his wife endeavors to reach a compromise, a win-win situation in which neither party has to "surrender." This might require hours or even weeks of negotiations during which they might agree to disagree until they worked out their differences in as egalitarian a manner as possible. This type of relationship provides a daughter with direct and observable evidence that female ideas, talents, and goals are respected.

In reality, it is likely that most marriages fall somewhere in between or change depending on the issue at stake. The important thing to bear in mind with regard to your daughter, however, is the frequency with which she observes female input as a valuable commodity. Your attitude of consistent acceptance or rejection will lead her to believe that males routinely accept or reject female autonomy, and this will have an effect on her subsequent behavior. If you want her to believe that the ideas and talents of females are valuable, that independence is a trait for her to develop, then you must demonstrate this in your behavior toward the females with whom you associate.

Types of Moms

Now that we have examined how your relationship with your wife will affect your daughter's beliefs about acceptable feminine behavior, it is time to look at mothers themselves. Just as with dads, there is no such thing as a garden variety mom, and just as different kinds of dads produce different kinds of daughters, the same may be said for mothers.

Your wife will be helping you raise your daughter. She can facilitate your relationship with your daughter and support the work you are trying to do; refuse to interfere in any way, neither enhancing nor detracting from your effort; or, in extremely difficult cases, actually obstruct your path and block your efforts. Even in the last case, it is not necessarily conscious and purposeful. There may be a whole variety of reasons for negative behavior from a wife.

Sometimes a father in a seminar will raise a question concerning a conflict between his parenting style and his wife's. I remember one father articulated it quite well.

"What do I do if I'm training my daughter to be decisive and independent, but her mother refuses to model the behavior?"

Recognizing his problem as an important one which other fathers may be forced to deal with as well, I pressed him to elaborate further.

"Well, my wife absolutely refuses to make a decision. Even the littlest things. For example, I might say, 'Let's go to a movie tonight.' If she agrees, I say, 'What do you want to see?' and she will always say, 'I don't care. You decide.' Sometimes I don't feel like deciding. Sometimes I want her to decide.

"After listening to your information, I am beginning to think that her refusal to make a decision is not setting a good example for my daughter."

His honesty prompted another father to open up with his concerns.

"I have a similar problem. I don't think my wife really wants our daughter to be independent. She doesn't think it's feminine. Sometimes if I encourage my daughter to think for herself or be different or act on her decisions, my wife will say something like, 'She's not a boy, you know. What happens when she gets older? That independence you are cultivating is going to backfire. It's going to turn off the guys.' By the way, my wife is very beautiful and always had lots of boyfriends herself."

Earlier we discussed how some fathers send a chaotic message

Traditional, Nonvaluing Behavior

Behavior of Husband toward Wife	Unspoken Message to Daughter	Subsequent Behavior of Daughter
Husband makes all the major family decisions particularly in regard to money management and choice of living location.	Females make poor decisions. Females are incapable of decisions. Females do not have to take responsibility for actions. Females are powerless.	Panic and severe feelings of inadequacy. Low self-esteem. Financial dependence. Emotional dependence.
Supports division of labor by sex: (1) Household chores and child care are primarily female responsibilities. (2) Male siblings are exempted from participation in household chores. Families on limited budgets restrict educational opportunities to male siblings.	Male work is more important than female work. Intellectual and physical prowess are the exclusive domain of males. Female work is not achievement-oriented, nor is it rewarded. It is better to be male than female.	Girl lacks belief in her physical and intellectual abilities. Thinks achievement is masculine and gives up the risk-taking behavior necessary to achieve. Becomes fearful and won't try or gives up easily. Lacks career direction or job planning. Low self-esteem. Heavy dependency. Early marriage. Early pregnancy.
Says things which devalue the feminine: (1) Jokes and put-down humor which make women the butt of the joke through ridicule of their minds, bodies, and roles. (2) Expressions like, "That's women's work."	Females are inferior to males. It is better to be male than female.	Low self-esteem. Self-hatred. Panic and feelings of severe inadequacy. Early pregnancy.

Nontraditional, Valuing Behavior

Behavior of Husband toward Wife	Unspoken Message to Daughter	Subsequent Behavior of Daughter
Participates equally with wife in money management, particularly at the decision-making level.	Females can handle financial affairs. Females make good decisions.	High self-esteem. Independence. Autonomy.
Seeks out and acts upon wife's opinion and advice.	Females make good decisions. Females can solve problems. Females' ideas are valuable. Females are responsible for their actions.	Independence. Autonomy. Self-esteem.
Supports wife's plans and goals: (1) Gives verbal encouragement. (2) Frees woman of child-care and household responsibilities so she can pursue goals.	The lives of both participants in relationship are equally important. Females have ability. Females have rights. Female contributions are worthwhile.	Increased achievement orientation and motivation. Awareness of career planning, and job-related skills. High self-esteem.
Does not support division of labor by sex: Everyone participates equally in household responsibilities and child care.	All work is equally valued and valuable.	Daughter views both male and female contributions as worthwhile and meritorious. Self-esteem.

by verbally encouraging assertive behavior while undermining their efforts with premature rescuing, which reinforces learned helplessness. A similarly chaotic message emerges when a daughter is exposed to her father's encouragement to be daring, independent, and adventurous but consistently witnesses her own mother behave in dependent and helpless ways. It can become particularly confusing if mom vociferously defends these practices or encourages her daughter to behave in a helpless and dependent fashion.

First, a mother and father who find themselves with conflicting viewpoints must set aside time to discuss their differences (in private, so that their daughter does not witness any disagreements they may have). Until they have openly discussed their feelings and beliefs concerning the realities of female achievement, they may be working at cross-purposes. Below are some questions which will stimulate discussion of the issues:

1. How do each of you define femininity?

2. What do each of you want for your daughter's future?

3. What do each of you believe your daughter is capable of achieving?

4. How would each of you feel if your daughter rejected marriage and/or motherhood in favor of a career, perhaps indefinitely? (If the response is negative, give reasons.)

5. Who are the role models that each of you would like to see your daughter emulate and why?

6. What are Mom's best qualities that she would like to pass along to her daughter?

7. What are Dad's best qualities that he would like to pass along to his daughter?

Using these questions to stimulate discussion will reveal attitudes and beliefs that heretofore have probably never been examined by the two of you together. Once you are able to sort out the issues involved and your feelings about them, you can use your new insights to determine the degree of conflict you are facing and take appropriate measures.

The conflicts may be the result of different definitions of femininity, different perceptions of a daughter's abilities, or different goals for a daughter's future. Or they may involve a mother's desire to validate her own lifestyle or a lack of awareness on a mother's part concerning the nature of her influence on her daughter. They may indicate the type of conditioning a mother received concerning the nature of females as well as what options and opportunities she sees for her daughter in this society.

The following discussion of certain types of moms may help you understand your wife's behavior and the unspoken messages it carries (to you as well as your daughter). If you find the following descriptions and labels of different types of moms too narrow, disregard them. If, on the other hand, they can help you understand some of the more subtle complexities, use them.

THE MOMMA BEAR

One very sensitive issue is if Mom doesn't *want* Dad to get involved in child care. Frankly, this is not usually a problem. Most mothers would give anything if their husbands would become more involved with child care, especially with their daughters, but for the occasional mother who feels threatened by Dad's involvement, it can be a very painful experience for all parties concerned. The reasons are varied.

If your wife's only sphere of influence and authority is in her role as a parent, she may be reluctant (and understandably so) to relinquish her one opportunity to express adult authority and exercise control in her life. Your decision to become more involved in child care may threaten her sense of limited influence, her feeling of importance, and her need to be needed. If her entire self-image rests on her role as a parent, then your increased involvement may seem like an attack on her very identity. Before she can gracefully relinquish some control as a mother, she will need to replace it with something else. Undoubtedly, this will require time and introspection on her part. Therefore, should this be the problem, your *patient* understanding is essential.

You should consider that she may not be acting defensively at all, but may be making a very valid point. If Dad is in control and in charge of everything else, then it is perfectly rational for her to feel annoyed when he attempts to impose his influence in yet another domain. After all, she is an adult, and like all adults, she enjoys exercising some measure of authority and being respected. If a wife is treated like a child or a second-class citizen, then being a mother may be her only opportunity to act like an adult.

The way to handle this is to give your wife more authority in decision making, more freedom to explore her earning and career potential, more respect for the contributions she makes which are unrelated to domestic tasks. By so doing, you will enhance her power and authority in areas other than parenting and proportionally reduce the likelihood that she will feel defensive or territorial about her sphere of influence.

I cannot resist pointing out two important things here. First, the obvious implication of the previous paragraph (obvious, that is, to the women reading this chapter but perhaps less so to the men) is that the husband is in the position to give his wife more freedom, power, and authority, which says he has it to give and she doesn't. Second, if you are an authoritarian type of male, you will be forced to deal with a wife who, by acquiring more power and authority, may be more willing to let you participate in the rearing of your daughter but less willing to display docility and obedience on other fronts. Once again, unless you want to be a tyrant (which I firmly believe you don't), you can't have it both ways.

Finally, a wife may feel threatened that she will lose that most precious commodity—time with her daughter—if Dad becomes more involved. Reassure her that you have no desire to intrude on precious mother-daughter time and that you recognize and respect the continued importance of their personal relationship separate from you.

THE MOM AS DAUGHTER

There are some women who prefer to remain children themselves. Most often these women find themselves married to authoritarians and protectors. It is perfectly natural that these two should be attracted. Her behavior allows him to fulfill the masculine role of taking charge, protecting, and defending, while his behavior allows her to avoid taking responsibility for her actions and remain forever a child.

If you have high expectations for your daughter, it is imperative to avoid this relationship. It reinforces all the wrong behavior patterns—those which undermine her ability to take risks, be responsible for her actions, and realize her goals. If you are already in this type of relationship, transform it. This bears repeating: the lessons that a daughter will learn about gender behavior from this combination are not in her best interests if she is to be achievement-oriented.

Some mothers, when they recognize and become sensitive to the kind of message that their ''little girl'' behavior sends to their daughters, will seek to change it. Others have a harder time acting on this knowledge, particularly if it has served them in the past or helped them attain their goals (which are usually security- and protection-oriented).

For the man who is attempting to change his behavior, but whose wife may be slow to change hers, there are a couple of things to be aware of and show empathy for.

First, your wife may be suffering, herself, from a poor self-image. Remember, she too is a product of a society which routinely taught that females were helpless and inferior, or, if not inferior, at least fragile and in need of protection. She may have been convinced of this and gone underground.

Using a gentle and nonjudgmental tone, you can make your daughter aware of this. It is not necessary to criticize your wife or point to her as a negative example, but rather help your daughter sympathize with the fact that her mother's potential may have been sidetracked or undermined by the times in which she lived. In this case, what is important is that your daughter be exposed to the idea that *she* lives in a different historical time and therefore has other choices open to her. Point out that your wife's decision to be dependent or helpless is *her* decision, but it does not have to be your daughter's decision as well. In this way, you reinforce your daughter's sense of individuality and right to choose the roles she wishes to play in her own life.

If you are uncomfortable with these suggestions or if you feel they are too critical of your wife, simply confine your statements to those about yourself and how *you* have handled fear or helplessness in your own life. Similarly, you can point out that different people (not just females) are fearful of different things and that some people (not just males) are fear*less*! By telling her about your experiences with fear and helplessness, you underscore the lesson that they are not the experiences of solely the female population. This somewhat alleviates the tendency to believe that women are fearful and men are fearless. (Don't forget to remind her of one of the most fearless acts all mothers have had the courage to face, regardless of how helpless they may appear—giving birth! If this doesn't prove women are fearless, I don't know what does.)

Emphasize that changing fearful, helpless behavior doesn't require a miracle, it simply requires that the individual make a new decision. Stress the importance of making a decision as an *individual* not as a member of a gender group, and remind her that decisions need not be made according to the society's gender expectations. Reassure her that when Mom is ready to make a change in her behavior, she will be perfectly capable of doing so.

If your wife is suffering from a poor self-image and you see her communicating that to your daughter, a little subversive action may be required. Enlist the help of your daughter to assist you in changing your wife's self-concept. The two of you can work together as a team. It will educate your daughter about the consequences of a negative self-concept and give your wife the kind of support she needs to change her self-image. And they can both be done simultaneously! Such a deal.

Perhaps as your daughter matures, she will then continue to practice the techniques you have used on *her* to help her mother become more independent, self-confident, and assertive.

THE FEMME FATALE AND THE BEAUTIFUL MOM

This category has been included because it may be a very difficult one for a daughter to handle maturely and it may have some grave consequences with regard to her self-esteem if handled improperly. It will require special sensitivity on your part.

First of all, if Mom is a beautiful femme fatale herself, she may not necessarily value independent and assertive behavior over the cultivation of beauty and sex appeal. Her concern is probably over whether her daughter will be able to attract potential suitors (like the beautiful mother mentioned by the father earlier in this chapter). In a case like this, inform your wife that there are men who find other qualities besides beauty in a woman highly attractive. Let her know you are one of them. (Are you?) Also, suggest that since the strictest stereotype of feminine beauty and sex appeal is adhered to by the *adolescent* male population, your daughter's independence may actually prevent an early marriage!

Second, make it clear you have no wish to transform your daughter into a pseudo-male, but rather to teach her the wide range of responses she has available and how to use them effectively to adapt to any situation in which she may find herself.

Make her aware that your wish is simply to provide a balance to counteract the extreme tendency in the culture to make her helpless and dependent.

Remind your wife of the infinite possibilities your daughter may have to confront, such as the experience of those women who found a male partner to take care of them "forever," only to be left alone through death or divorce. Discuss the fact that those who learn to be independent fare much better.

Talk over the numerous ways in which society already provides all the training (indoctrination?) your daughter will ever need in order to be feminine. Do not forget to reassure your wife that *her* example of femininity provides a fine model for your daughter to emulate. Remind her of her impact as a role model so that she feels secure that her daughter's femininity will remain intact.

Which leads me to a very sensitive issue. If a daughter is not as beautiful as her mother, she may feel inadequate or even ugly! It is up to you, as her father, to provide all the loving support and compliments you can, as long as they are sincere. Never pay a false compliment to your daughter. She will see right through it. Find the fine points in your daughter's appearance and behavior that you can compliment genuinely and capitalize on those. There will be more about your daughter's need for male approval of her physical appearance in Chapters 10 and 11. If your wife is beautiful and your daughter is not, *please read these chapters carefully* and make an extra effort to help your daughter cope with what can be a difficult situation.

THE ''NONTRADITIONAL, TRADITIONAL'' MOM

This type of mom does not necessarily pose problems but has, on occasion, been portrayed by others as posing problems. For example, *some* old-style feminists have portrayed the traditional mom as a poor role model for girls; you also may feel she is inadequate. It is my hope you will change your mind.

It isn't necessary to be Mrs. Cleaver or Aunt Bee to be a good traditional mother. In retrospect, it seems likely that the moms we all grew to love in those sitcoms of the fifties and sixties were rare creatures even then.

A mother I remember vividly from my childhood, Mrs. Larson, provides a good example of the nontraditional, traditional mother. She was traditional in that she stayed home, fixed lunches for her children, was there when her husband and children arrived home, and was generally a caregiver. That is where it stopped. Her conventionality was limited to these characteristics.

She began taking music lessons from my mother at the age of forty-six. When she wasn't practicing her piano, she was tinkering with an old crystal set from the twenties she had down in the basement along with the rest of her old radio collection, throwing pots on her potter's wheel (which often meant that the dishes sat dirty in the sink), or sticking colored pins in the world map she had stuck on the wall (I never did figure that one out).

All of us kids adored going over to her house because she didn't care if we messed things up. She understood the way messes spontaneously generate when the learning process is taking place. (My mother understood that, too. She used to say, "Life is messy.")

Both her daughters held positions in our high school traditionally held by males; the older was the class president, and the younger was the class clown (a nonelected post). Their mother's example of intelligence and involvement with a wide variety of nontraditional interests and her free, unfettered approach to motherhood produced daughters who were similarly intelligent, nontraditional, and unfettered by gender restraints.

The lesson we can learn from Mrs. Larson is that there is nothing wrong with exercising the option of being a traditional mother. It is not mandatory to become the CEO of a major corporation or a test pilot for Boeing in order to set a fine example for a daughter to follow. However, it is important to bear in mind that being a stay-at-home mom *is* a traditional choice and therefore more limiting as a role model to daughters who may be capable of larger-scale contributions.

By the same token, I feel compelled to note that most of the women whom I interviewed were daughters of "traditional" mothers. I use quotation marks because they were traditional much as Mrs. Larson was traditional—they stayed home and were caregivers. At the same time, almost without exception, the women I interviewed noted that their mothers didn't quite fit the stereotype (does anybody, really?): for example, one's mom was a part-time carpenter, and another's had her own business. In other words, one way or another, they managed to defy the stereotype, and this independence seems to have had a positive effect on their daughters.

This is a particularly cogent point for two reasons. First, it somewhat debunks the myth that the traditional mom is always a poor role model for a daughter who is a potential high achiever. At least it puts it into question. While it may be true that a traditional mom who is clinging, fearful, and helpless is a poor role model, a traditional mom who is strong, intelligent, energetic, and capable is a good role model. To put it another way, the role itself that mom chooses to play may be less important than the individuality, boldness, and uniqueness of vision that she brings to that role.

Second, it strongly suggests to moms who do not work outside the home that they make a conscious effort to regularly demonstrate any nonstereotypical behavior that is natural and comfortable for them. In this way, mothers can seize the opportunity to expose their daughters to a more varied, complete, and well-rounded picture of the nature and capabilities of women. For a daughter of high potential, who may have the capacity to achieve greatness, this is crucial. (*Note*: One very special type of mom—the single mom—has not been omitted. She appears in an upcoming section, "Moms and Dads Alone.")

"Perfect Parents": Creative Teamwork

PARTNERS AND PROJECTS

One successful woman I interviewed (single parent, university professor, and sky diver) remembers watching her mother fix up old houses with her father to sell for profit.

"I saw her tear out walls, lay foundations and tile floors, and do electrical wiring. It never occurred to me that she was helping my father. He could just as easily have been helping her! I just saw them as partners."

My own parents ran a nightclub together. My mother was just as responsible for all aspects of the business and its success or failure as my father.

The message here is that whenever you are working together on a project, do not present it to your children as "Mom helping Dad." Conscientiously present the "other" perspective occasionally: "I'm going to go downstairs and help your mother tile that floor (tear down that wall, wire that room, etc.)." Present your wife as the person in charge and making decisions.

If this bothers you or your wife, ask yourselves why. Is it threatening to present your wife in an authoritative position? If so, you may have an unbalanced relationship in which you appear to (or actually do) make all the decisions. At the very least, always present yourselves as equal partners in any project or endeavor. Let your daughter see both her father and her mother giving orders, making decisions, and being equal partners in all aspects of problem solving and labor.

For example, have you ever noticed that when families go out in the car together, Dad *always* drives? Mom wipes noses, ties shoes, mediates sibling squabbles, and *relies on Dad* to get the family where they are going. The symbolism is more than coincidental. Dad is "in the driver's seat," with all the authority that implies: decision making, goal setting, being in control and in charge. This may seem like a meaningless issue, but imagine the scene in reverse. Mom is now at the wheel, making decisions and being in charge. Dad is wiping noses, tying shoes, etc. Right away we get a clear sense of a contrasting message being communicated to the kids in the backseat. This is one small way in which fathers can demonstrate a willingness to submit to female decision making within the family. Try it sometime. Your daughter will benefit from the exposure to Mom and Dad in reversed roles.

Another traditional situation in which you can upset the applecart is the family gathering for the holiday meal. After the feast is over, suppose all the women retire to another room to talk, smoke, or watch television while the men clear the table, fill the dishwasher, or do the dishes. I actually mean that perhaps just once the women shouldn't participate in the cleanup *at all*. I realize full well that some family members will object to this vociferously. They may even use a crude but popular slang phrase suggesting that you are enslaved by your wife's female genitalia.

Another way to upset your daughter's unquestioning acceptance of gender identification is to trade chores for a day with your wife. If the labor at your house is divided by sex, switch roles. Some Saturday, you stay indoors. Do the laundry. Make the beds. Do the dishes. Prepare breakfast, lunch, and dinner. Manage the house. Your wife will be running to the dump, making small repairs, washing the car, and trimming the hedges.

The most common reaction to this suggestion is to say that it is too time-consuming. Everyone always says that the reason labor continues to be divided by sex in their home is because it is more efficient. You already know how to take care of the car, and she doesn't. She is used to managing a household, and you aren't, etc. This is a valid argument, one which I will not debate.

On the other hand, consider a different reason for trading chores. Suppose that the point of trading chores for one day is to gain a new perspective. In that case, efficiency becomes a secondary concern, while learning becomes the primary concern. Furthermore, your children will love it. If you use their sense of fun and play to make it a fun day for yourselves, you can turn it into a day of self-discovery rather than a bothersome ordeal.

If you and your wife agree not to ask each other for help during your Saturday experiment (since the tendency would be to fall back into the old patterns), you will discover many things about yourself, your spouse, and your children. If you take it one step further and have a family discussion at the breakfast table the next day, concerning what the day was like for all parties concerned, you turn it into a real learning experience.

You and your wife may discover how helpless you are at many tasks. You may realize how dependent you are on each other. You will have an internal experience of how important it is to learn to do many different things in case something happens to one of you. You will see how easy it is to become enslaved to gender-acceptable work. You will see how it is only an efficient method as long as there are the two of you. If one mate should leave, it is no longer efficient at all but debilitating. You will discover what life is like for your mate. Your children will learn *why* labor continues to be divided by sex. You and your wife's helplessness at some tasks will be witnessed by your children and teach them a valuable lesson about the importance of being skilled at many different tasks regardless of sex.

If you really get brave and adventurous, try it for longer periods of time until you each become more comfortable with the other's duties. Pretty soon your children will not even notice something unusual is going on.

MORE CREATIVE TEAMWORK: KID STUFF

Remember the mom I talked about earlier who tinkered with old radios, studied world maps, and threw pots? Well, her husband was as unusual as she. They were quite a team.

Together on Halloween they would create a most theatrical and exhilarating experience for the neighborhood kids. It began with Mr. and Mrs. Larson setting up the front yard with a huge, old cast-iron pot in which they would place dry ice. Under it they would situate spotlights so the smoke from the dry ice could be seen eerily rising from the cauldron in the night air. Then, as darkness approached, *Mr.* Larson would dress up like a witch, complete with black cape, pointed hat, warty nose, and blackened teeth. Positioning himself at the cauldron, he would slowly stir the evil brew, cackle maniacally, and quote Shakespeare:

Double, double, toil and trouble
Fire burn and cauldron bubble

terrorizing the littlest of the children. On a table located behind Mr. Larson were displayed scrumptious homemade candied apples made by Mrs. Larson—the most delicious apples in the world made sweeter by the taste of victory. Why? Because an apple was yours for the taking *if* you had the nerve to run by the witch and steal one.

The littlest kids would stand there in terror, dying for an apple, and trying to summon their courage. Older kids would fake bravery but in truth were just as terrified as the little kids. Even though they knew it was just Mr. Larson in that getup, he was so into his part that he was wholly transformed. Over the years the word spread, and eventually neighborhood parents began dropping by to watch the fun and join in the spirit of things.

Just telling this story gives me goose bumps; both in remembrance of trying to summon my courage to steal an apple from the witch *and* in my adult realization of the gift they gave us by being such creative parents. My adult conclusion is that my childhood evaluation of them as "cool" parents was accurate.

Unfortunately, when planning kids' activities, like birthday parties and such, it is usually the woman alone who gets into the spirit of play that is required. When Mom and Dad participate together, they create double the fun for their children, send the important message that creative play (kid stuff) is not just for women, and strengthen the sense of joy and creativity in their marriage.

When I was little, my mom would teach me a ballroom dance step like the fox-trot, waltz, jitterbug, or cha-cha. Then she would sit down at the piano and play an appropriate rhythm, and my father would dance with me in the living room to her music. When I had mastered a step, they would take me dancing with them. Sometimes I would dance with my father, and he would lead. Other times I would dance with my mother, and *I* would lead.

In this activity my father was not an outsider but an active participant. We had fun, we laughed, we played. The important thing to remember is the value of time spent together. In Chapter 8, you will find many more activities (for dads, moms, dads and moms together, whoever wants to participate), but remember this: not every activity must be "meaningful" or educational. Both Barbara Grogan and Shirley Muldowney remember most poignantly the casual times, just being pals with their dads. Time spent together, bumming around, goofing off, just enjoying each other's company, is the most meaningful of all.

Bear in mind the implications of the research on successful women which shows the strong correlation between achievement and a close father-daughter relationship. What this seems to suggest is that the bonds forged between a father and daughter (*if* he spends time with her and she comes to identify with him), as well as the lessons he can teach her in risk taking and competency, can help overcome the messages of helplessness, dependency, or manipulation that are often woven into the cultural definitions of femininity.

Moms and Dads Alone

SINGLE MOMS

I have included a section on single moms because they have problems peculiar to their situation, namely, no father around to provide male approval. Furthermore, your daughter may be living with a single mom if you are a divorced father. I hope this section will help you understand your ex-wife's situation and influence on your daughter as well as reinforce your understanding of the need for you to be a *present* and active influence in your daughter's life.

Single moms, like traditional moms, have sometimes been portrayed in a negative light. For example, *some* traditionalists have portrayed the single mom as a poor role model for girls. I hope that the discussion here will help you see that is not true.

Before we begin discussing in detail the problems that single moms face, I would like to tell you a story to illustrate the power of a mother's example on her daughter.

I was in the seventh grade before I knew it was unusual to have a mother who played gigs and came home at four o'clock in the morning.

One weekend I was making plans with a friend who said she would call me Sunday morning to firm up our arrangements. I said, "OK, but don't call before noon. You'll wake my mother."

"Your mother doesn't get up till noon?" she asked incredulously.

"Well, of course not," I replied. "She doesn't get to bed until four."

A look of horror crossed my friend's face, "What does your mother *do*?"

It was then that I realized I had an unusual mother. Once the realization dawned, I began to notice that my mother was unusual in many ways I had not noticed before. She was loud. She spoke her mind. She often disagreed with my stepfather politically and said so. She wasn't afraid to be out late at night alone or to be in front of large groups of people. In fact, she loved it!

There was more. On Sunday afternoons, bunches of musicians would pile into our house with their instruments and jam. In the summer, the neighbors would bring over lawn chairs and sit in the front yard for a free concert.

My mother liked rock and roll music. She liked almost anything new and innovative, as long as it was quality. While my friend's parents (and my stepfather) criticized the Beatles, my mother loved them.

She was a laugher, loud and long. She never covered her mouth to laugh in the demure way so many other women did. When she laughed, you could hear her.

She loved to dance and taught me how to lead as well as follow. (I still pride myself on the ability to whisk away a female friend for a spin around a dance floor in a mad jitterbug!) "The trick to leading," my mother used to say, "is to know where you are going. That's what 'leading' means. How can someone follow a person who doesn't know where she is going?" It wasn't until years later that I realized she was giving me a metaphor for life.

She could swear mightily, and she told off-color jokes (much to my stepfather's dismay). In the sixties, when I came home from college with stories of marijuana, she wasn't shocked. She had seen a lot of drugs in the music business, although she never partook.

When she was a young woman, she and my "real" father* bought a little two-bit bar in what was then a prairie, and turned it into Denver's premier nightclub in the 1940s complete with a bandstand, huge hardwood dance floor, and a bar which could accommodate four bartenders. She had her own all-female band called Maxine's Melodies.

I grew up hearing exciting nightclub stories of how my mother had to play the piano, handle the drunks, tend bar, and wait on customers. (My father, who was a musician as well, also did all these jobs.) When she wasn't entertaining customers, she was hiring and firing employees, auditioning musicians, keeping the books, talking to cantankerous creditors, ordering liquor and food, even cooking if the necessity arose. She was a full partner in the business in every sense of the word.

When my father died, she was forty years old, a new mother with her first baby and "a stack of medical bills that would choke a horse" as she loved to say. She told me stories of having to deal with the construction crew in the process of building my parents' dreamhouse; selling the nightclub to pay off medical debts; handling business negotiations and contracts; dealing with bankers, lawyers, and real estate agents; fending off the vultures who thought that a widow with her first baby was easy prey; plus handling all the other myriad details of closing down a booming business. At night she would rock her baby and cry.

But she got through it.

One day, I complimented her on this accomplishment. Gruffly she said, "What else was I supposed to do?"

"Well, you could have fallen apart at the seams," I replied.

"And rely on whom?" she said matter-of-factly. "Don't forget, I had a baby to take care of." She paused before continuing, "In a way I did fall apart. I was definitely around the bend. I was a little crazy with stress and grief. I made some poor decisions. It was bad enough to have lost my husband and the business and to be in such terrible debt, but I was also worried about being a mother for the first time with no one to help me."

---

*Referring to my biological father, who died when I was eight months old. I was raised by my stepfather, who was the only father I ever knew, so I called him my father, and my biological father my "real" father. She married my stepfather when I was a little over two.

"Mother," I pleaded, "what are you apologizing for? I think you are the bravest and most courageous woman I know."

"Well, life doesn't always give you a choice," she said philosophically. "You must be able to rely on yourself. Security isn't money. It isn't even a man. Real security is being confident in yourself to survive any situation.

"I hear my friends tell their daughters marrying well is the key to security, but I disagree with them. You will have to make up your own mind, but that's how I feel about it."

Yes, she was an unusual mother. Still is. Because of her example, I grew up taking it for granted that women took care of business. It never crossed my mind that women acted any differently than men when it came to managing their affairs and taking control of their lives because I never witnessed anything different in my own home. Because my mother set a standard of high expectations by her behavior, I learned to expect a lot from myself and other girls and women.

The moral of the story is that a mother is a daughter's role model, the most important player in a daughter's life concerning what women are like. It is from her mother that she will learn what females are capable of and what they can do. In spite of all the negative programming that may be fed to her via the media, her relatives, thoughtless boyfriends, or unenlightened peers, if she witnesses a mother possessed of spirit and strength, one who refuses to accept society's limited expectations of her, she will grow up knowing in her deepest self that women are capable of extraordinary deeds.

Furthermore, a mother doesn't have to be a Nobel prize winner, an astronaut, a research scientist, a coal miner, a race car driver, or an upper-level manager to set an example of strength, courage, energy, and determination for a daughter to observe and emulate. Whatever behavior a daughter witnesses from her mother on a regular basis will become the yardstick by which she measures the capabilities of women.

In the case of my mother, a widow, I learned that women are streetsmart, savvy, and gutsy. I was a child in the fifties, yet my own mother's example of determination and showmanship was sufficient to overcome even the rigid model of the fifties mom.

In most cases, a single mother who is a responsible adult is already setting an extraordinary example, spending eight hours a day at work; coming home to clean and cook; making mortgage payments; finagling every nickel and dime to make ends meet; worrying over financial planning, the orthodontist's bill, and her children's college education; getting tough with the car mechanic who is trying to convince her that the engine must be replaced; arguing, cajoling, and negotiating with bankers, lawyers, real estate agents and bosses; fixing her plumbing; putting up her storm windows; handling her ex-husband, loving her children, and dating men (not to mention the daily plotting and scheming she goes through to fight a predominantly white, male system which is basically hostile to her needs and values).

What more could she possibly do to set an example of courage and determination? Cure cancer? End the nuclear arms race? She is a warrior in the truest and most ancient tradition of service and struggle. It may not have been her choice, but she is doing it just the same. I, for one, admire her and so will her daughter once she is old enough to figure out what her mother has accomplished.

A single mom can rest assured (even when it seems her daughter hasn't the foggiest notion of her sacrifices, her emotional state, or her fatigue) that the example she sets just by keeping it all together will solidify her daughter's belief in the capable female. It will imprint the most indelible image on a daughter's psyche, one that far exceeds what society may tell her about the nature of females. When she hears they are weak or fragile or in constant need of protection, she will be forced to measure these ideas against the behavior she witnesses from her own mother.

Furthermore, since most single moms are working moms (or aspiring to be), they will be pleased to hear the following data. According to a study released at the American Psychological Association annual conference in 1986,[3] children of working mothers do better in school, both socially and academically, than children of nonworking mothers. They scored higher on IQ tests and were rated higher by teachers on academic achievement; they appeared to be better communicators, better at practical living skills, better behaved in school with fewer absences. The study said that children of intact families with a working mother do best of all, but even children from a single-parent household where Mom is employed do better than children with nonworking mothers.

Prior to this, studies had shown that a working mother had no negative effects on a child, but this study goes one step further to show they actually have a positive effect. Says Dr. Helen Cleminshaw, associate professor of child and family development at the University of Ohio at Akron, "We do see positive outcomes of maternal employment." Dr. Dominic Gullo, of Kent State University, who appeared on the panel with Cleminshaw, said, "It dispels the myth that working moms are bad."

So, to some extent, a mother who works can stop feeling guilty. It is not a foregone conclusion that because she works, her daughter will grow up to be Bonnie Parker (although she certainly was a nontraditional woman!). Like all parents, of course, she must stay alert and ensure that an adult is present to supervise her daughter's free time. Too much unsupervised time can lead to drug abuse and unwanted pregnancies, but, in all fairness, those things happen in families where Mom stays home, too.

I have included this section because I do not want to convey the false idea that if a daughter is without a father she is doomed to failure or obscurity. There are too many counter examples to prove that belief erroneous: Eleanor Roosevelt, Bella Abzug, Geraldine Ferraro, Gloria Steinem, Helen Gurley Brown, Isak Dinesen, Edna St. Vincent Millay, Anaïs Nin, George Sand, Susan Sontag, Anna Pavlova, Martina Navratilova, Gilda Radner, Carly Simon, Cicely Tyson, Sophia Loren, and Barbra Streisand are all highly accomplished, distinguished women of international fame and recognition who lost their fathers sometime between birth and eighteen. Obviously, a fatherless upbringing does not mean the end of achievement for a girl.

To minimize the negative effects of being fatherless and maximize a daughter's potential for achievement, a single mother must (1) remember her own importance as a role model and (2) enlist and train the men in her life to give the male attention and approval her daughter needs and craves.

In her book *Father Loss*, Elyce Wakerman studied high-achieving women who grew up fatherless. Says Wakerman,

> Among the 'high-achievers' in our study—women who earn more than twenty-five thousand dollars a year and/or received advanced degrees and/or married very successful men—an exalted image of father was very much in evidence. These women held their absent father in the highest regard and described him and their relationship as 'special.' These distinctly positive memories reinforce the significant connection between the sense of loss and the sense of striving. The impulse fueling ambition would seem to originate in a desire for restitution with a father whose presence was, or is imagined to have been, a great source of validation.[4]

Reread the last sentence from the above quote. It is most provocative in its implication not only that the impulse for achievement originates in the desire for the father figure, but that in most cases, the *imagined* special relationship was enough to motivate the striving. In other words, even an imagined source of male validation is better than no male validation.

In the case of daughters who must suffer the reality of being ignored by fathers who are alive and present, the fatherless daughter, in her opportunity to create an imagined relationship with Daddy, may be better off. She can identify with her dad in her imagination, if not in real life. It does not seem to be significant whether he was actually present, just that she believe if he had been, he would have been loving and supportive.

To some extent, my mother tried to instill this sense of identification with my real father. She wanted me to know him—what he was like, what he would have thought of me, how encouraging and demanding he would have been, how similar we were.

One day when I was about five, barely old enough to know what death was, my mother called me inside from playing. She said she had something important to tell me. I remember the conversation perfectly.

"You know your Daddy Al?" she said.

"Uh huh."

"You love him very much, don't you?"

"Yes."

"That's wonderful because he loves you very much, too."

"Uh huh."

"Well, Al is not your only father. You had another daddy before him. You don't remember him because he died when you were just a little baby. His name was Nick, and you were named after him. Do you understand?"

"Yes."

"Well, he would have loved you very much, too. He did love you very much when he was alive."

"Uh huh."

"Do you have any questions?"

"No."

"Well, you and I will talk about your Daddy Nick some more later. If you ever want to know anything, just ask. And remember, your Daddy Al loves you very much. He is your daddy now and always will be."

"OK."

There was no trauma, no shock. Being only five years old, I

just listened calmly to the information and went back outside to play. I absorbed the information in that matter-of-fact way that small children do, before they are taught they should be traumatized.

From that day forward, my mother would talk freely about this "other daddy." Whenever I would do exceptionally well at something, she would tell me how proud he would have been if he had lived. She also told me we were very much alike.

"You remind me so much of your father."

"You look just like Nick when you do that."

"You act just exactly like your father."

"Nick used to do that, too."

In all fairness to my stepfather, who loved me, raised me, and coped with the daily nitty-gritty hassles of fatherhood, I suppose it is debatable whether this was fair to him. Keeping alive the memory of my real father may have left him feeling like an outsider or a substitute. I cannot say, although he did hint at it a few times.

However, it didn't feel that way to me. It just seemed as though I had two daddies; one who loved me here on earth and another who loved me from far away. I knew my stepfather loved me, and I adored him back. There was no question in my mind who was the more important of the two. I never would have traded my flesh-and-blood daddy for a dream daddy. But I could create a special relationship with the daddy who passed away whenever I needed to feel special and validated.

Some psychologists believe that females avoid achievement because success implies the ultimate separation from the father. In the case of a fatherless daughter, some psychologists believe the opposite pattern may be in action. If she exhibits traditionally male traits, like ambition and determination, she can be just like him, identify with her lost father, restore him in her life, and thus prevent ever separating from him again. Indeed, many accomplished women who grew up fatherless have used his loss as the impetus to fuel their relentless drive and impressive productivity.

Ms. Wakerman, herself a fatherless daughter, writes,

The accomplished father-bereft daughter may have succeeded at turning deprivation to advantage. . . . Through single-minded dedication to a goal, the ambitious fatherless daughter may be trying to overwhelm powerlessness with

action, insecurity with accomplishment . . . to prove beyond the shadow of her doubt that she is lovable.[5]

To prove that she is lovable. To get that male approval. It is
indeed a tragic episode in a young girl's life if she loses the man
whose love and approval she so desperately wants, but it need not
be the end. There are many things a mother alone can do.

First, she can enlist the aid of men in her life to give the male
approval her daughter will want and need. Grandfathers, uncles,
next-door neighbors, male teachers, even older brothers (if they
are quite a bit older)—all are human resources that can be tapped
to help with this task.

Once a single mother has determined that a particular man has
made the transition from casual date to potentially serious relationship, she can begin his "training." She has every right, if she
has her daughter's well-being in mind, to make some demands
concerning his behavior around her daughter. Considering the
amount of time a mother's boyfriend spends in her daughter's life,
it is easy to recognize how important his behavior is. A mother
can teach him how to give approval appropriately and comfort-
ably.

She should make it clear that physical affection is not a necessity, as this may make either him or the daughter uncomfortable
until they know each other better. This is really a decision that
must be made on an individual basis, as each specific relationship
will be different. It is up to the mother to decide her degree of
comfort in the situation. If there are any doubts about a man's
behavior around the daughter in a sexual context, the relationship
must be severed and every precaution must be taken to ensure
that the daughter is not blamed for the demise of the relationship.
In this case the blame must be placed squarely where it lies—not
with an innocent girl, but with the adult male.

When a new man has passed the "tests," it is OK for a
mother to teach him what to say and when to say it. She needn't
be embarrassed to feed him lines until he gets the hang of it.
She should encourage him to compliment a daughter's new
haircut or outfit, attend her athletic events, show interest in her
grades, take her out for a day of errand running, or prepare
dinner together once in a while. She may have to teach him
that something as simple as making eye contact with her when
she speaks or telling her she is pretty will have a powerful
effect on her self-esteem.

It is unbelievable how many men do not know the most basic

principles of child rearing. Many of them, wishing to be good surrogate parents and operating on an old model taught to them by their fathers, begin disciplining a child before they ever establish a relationship with her. Then they wonder why the child becomes resentful, or worse—rebellious.

It may be necessary to teach a stepfather or boyfriend that rapport precedes discipline, that trust precedes criticism, that a daughter will respond more positively when she feels important to him in her own right, and not just because he is in love with her mother.

If he doesn't know how to spend time with her, a mother can suggest that he let *her* teach *him* how to do something. This puts her in the driver's seat and allows her the upper hand. By reversing the roles, she doesn't have to be on guard, because he is the vulnerable one. A day spent teaching him how to ski, skate, or what-have-you requires *him* to trust *her*. Children love to see adults in this position. (It must be very refreshing for them.) If he can let his guard down long enough to let himself have fun and be foolish, to laugh unselfconsciously at himself, the pathways to friendship will be forged forever. Then she will find it easier to be unselfconscious when he tries to teach her something.

Surprisingly, more men are capable of this than one might think. Using his behavior when he is with an adult woman to gauge his willingness to be foolish and childlike around children is not an accurate measure. Many a man who cannot indulge in foolish or "out of control" behavior in front of the woman he loves can be quite uproarious and unselfconsciously silly with a child.

If there is no romantic relationship with a man in a mother's life, she can recruit any man she thinks would be appropriate and willing. She may be hesitant due to the fear of sexual abuse. Her fears are founded on some harsh realities, and it is always wise to err on the side of safety, but if she knows a man or has brothers, uncles, or fathers whom she trusts completely, she can use them as a valuable resource.

Whatever man she is "training," she can give him this book to read, discuss it with him, and get his feelings. If he seems reluctant, she should try to ferret out the reason. If it is just a healthy fear of relating to a child, she can reassure him she will be there to help and give guidance. If it seems he just doesn't care for her daughter, then of course, she must withdraw her request.

SINGLE DADS

The purpose of this book is help you learn to relate to your daughter in a positive and constructive way to facilitate both your relationship with her and her potential to achieve. But what happens if your relationship with your daughter is being threatened or is already poisoned by the recriminations and bitter aftertaste of a less than amicable divorce?[6]

If you and your ex-wife are doing this to each other, *it is imperative that you stop and consider what you are doing to your children*. It is cruel and self-serving for adults to burden their children with their failures, try to force them to take a stand in order to validate one side of the story, or manipulate them to ''prove'' their love. It will make your children feel guilty and anxious. I am sorry to have to be so harsh, but this kind of childish behavior is harmful to kids.

It is completely immaterial, in terms of parenting, who is ''right.'' Your daughter won't care anyway; she just wants to feel the love of both her parents. Even if she must endure their separation, it will be less stressful if she knows they aren't going to kill each other. (Unfortunately, given the statistics, even this is not an exaggeration!)

Try to talk the problems over with your ex-wife. I know. You are already thinking it's impossible. You've tried. You may be right, but it certainly won't hurt to try again. Maybe a new approach will work. Here are some guidelines:

1. Most important, read steps 1 to 5 in the section entitled ''Delivering Difficult Communications'' beginning on page 184. You will have to modify the explanation slightly to fit the situation with your ex-wife, but the steps themselves are invaluable to help you deal with this potentially explosive discussion.

2. Next, read the section entitled '' 'I' versus 'You' Messages'' on page 176. Be sure you understand it. In other words, the purpose of your discussion with your wife is *not* to try to prove, once again, who is right or to try to promote your own side of the story. The purpose is to express yourself in as nonthreatening a manner as possible in order to make life easier for your daughter. Do not try to have a conversation like this off the top of your head. Prepare! Write down your ''I'' messages. Plan ahead how you will respond (in a nonthreatening

and nonaccusatory manner, of course!) to certain statements that you know your wife will make. Write down your ideas and practice them.

3. Begin by saying you wish to discuss something that is important to the well-being of your daughter.

4. State clearly that you realize you have been just as guilty as your wife of this polarizing behavior. Even if you don't feel this is true, accepting some of the responsibility is the adult thing to do (somebody has to start it!), it is probably more realistic, *and* it will help smooth the waters.

5. State that your goal is to find *solutions* to correct the behavior rather than to air old grudges one more time. Focus on the *future*. Contribute to her belief in your sincerity by stating what *you* are going to do. Do not try to tell your wife what *she* should do. Remember, you are only in control of yourself.

6. Further suggestions:

   a. Give her this section (or book) to read before having your talk.

   b. If you feel so much hatred toward your wife that you can't face talking to her even for the sake of your daughter, get some therapy. I know some of you will hate to hear that statement for a variety of reasons:

      (1) You don't have the problem, she does.
      (2) You can't afford it.
      (3) You feel like you're crazy if you go to a therapist.
      (4) You dislike sharing your innermost feelings with a stranger.
      (5) You don't even know *how* to share your feelings.
      (6) You don't want to share your feelings.

   These are all excuses. Your anger, hatred, and guilt will not just go away. Statistics show that men often turn to various kinds of substance abuse to dull these feelings. It doesn't work and only makes you more of a slave to your negative and debilitating emotions. It

is not a disgrace, a weakness, or an admission of guilt
or mental imbalance to get emotional help and support when (not *if*) you need it. Even if you feel your
wife is the one with the problem, you could probably
use some help in dealing with her, so don't hesitate.
You and your daughter will be happier in the long
run.

7. Finally, read Chapter 10, on puberty. There is a section
entitled "To the Weekend or Single Father," which contains some more suggestions. Use this and the rest of
the information in this book to help you build a wonderful relationship with your daughter in spite of the
problems that exist between you and your ex-wife. Remember, if you allow yourself to be defeated by these
problems, the biggest loser will be your daughter, so
keep trying. Good luck!

CHAPTER 7

❧

Risk Taking: Changing the Belief System

So far we have discussed Daddy as an almost mythical figure, one who possesses great powers to mold, shape, or change his little girl's self-concept. His approval of her, his willingness to show love and to respect her as a person are crucial determinants of his little girl's self-image, particularly as it relates to three things:

1. Her perception of femininity
2. Her feeling of value as a person
3. Her inclination to achieve

We have also discussed the paradoxical nature of fathering a daughter through contradictory circumstances (femininity versus mastery behavior, and risk taking versus safety) which must be resolved if she is to overcome the negative components of traditional feminine programming. We have discussed the importance of reassuring a daughter of her femininity and attractiveness and at the same time recognizing and developing her abilities.

Now we need to discuss increasing your daughter's inclination for risk taking in order to build self-esteem and to teach that adaptable behavior is required to handle oneself in different situations. The subject of risk taking is fraught with difficulties when related to females because of the concern over female vulnerability we have discussed before. Many fathers do not wish to encourage risk taking in their daughters for fear of consequences and out of a sense of responsibility to keep them safe from harm.

Some people question whether self-esteem precedes risk taking or vice versa. Some say females lack self-esteem and therefore do not take risks. Others say females do not take risks and therefore lack self-esteem. Our goal is not to determine, once and for all, which comes first, but rather to be aware that self-esteem and risk taking are irrevocably linked.

Some people also contend that females do indeed take risks; however, those risks are usually emotional, rather than financial, intellectual, or physical. Many females seek their thrills (for we all need a certain amount) by attaching to unavailable, dysfunctional, or otherwise inappropriate men, thereby satisfying a craving for adventure by taking emotional risks. Perhaps if they were encouraged to take other kinds of risks, their craving for adventure would be satisfied and they would no longer feel the need to hook up with inappropriate men.

Rather than sort out these variables, which are a complex interaction of influences and which might well require another book, we will limit ourselves to the connection between risk taking and self-esteem in general.

Perhaps the best way to understand this connection is to examine the reluctance to take risks. When an individual is confronted with the opportunity to take a risk and does not, it can be a decision against his or her "self." In other words, this decision communicates an insidious message to the self that the individual believes he or she is unequal to the task, eroding the very foundation upon which self-esteem is built. Every risk not taken can be interpreted as another negative assessment of one's ability to meet life head on and emerge victorious.

The opposite is also true. With every risk successfully negotiated comes an equal and proportional surge of confidence and vitality. Since the degree of risk can only be determined with accuracy by the individual involved, the experience of success is strictly a personal one, but the waves of energy and positive emotions that crest and break are potentially transforming. In a way, one is almost ensured of success whenever one takes a risk because the act of taking the risk in the first place is a positive self-assessment and a boost to self-esteem, even if one fails at the undertaking! *Not to try is the ultimate failure.*

Safety and security are dead ends. They do not foster personal growth, they do not encourage development of one's coping skills, they do not inspire one to push beyond one's comfort zone, and they do not provide what Robert Frost called, "the shocks and changes we need to keep us sane."[1] In short, safety and security are false gods.

Furthermore, as my wise mother used to say, "Real security lies not in money. It lies in trusting yourself to survive any situation." The only way to give your daughter that kind of unshakable faith in herself is to let her begin taking risks now, while she still has a relatively safe environment in which to test her wings and recuperate should she fall.

One of my interviewees, a woman of thirty-seven and a professor at a large state university, told of how her father taught her self-confidence and the courage to overcome fear through risk taking.

"When I was nine years old or so, my father taught me how to roughride. He had already taught me how to catch and saddle the horse, pull a plow, walk, lope, and canter.

"One day at my uncle's ranch, he had me tear across this pasture full of gopher holes," she reminisces. "I was scared, but I did it anyway. I learned how to lean back and jerk up on the reins. I learned to stop on a pinhead and spin my horse on her toenails. Basically, what I was learning was how to take control.

"Looking back, it was a fairly risky situation. All kinds of things could have gone wrong. On the other hand, there is really no safe way to learn rough riding. It's a rough and risky sport.

"Now I realize they were fairly masculine skills he was teaching. They built up my confidence by making me realize I could sit in the saddle and control the horse. When it came time to join a riding club, I was so far advanced, they didn't really have a place for me that was appropriate to my age."

It is possible to get hooked on risk taking and the high it produces. It is equally possible to get hooked on security. Unfortunately, the romantic myth of being taken care of is still prevalent enough to be desired by a large percentage of females, including those old enough to know better. As we have seen, many females get seduced into believing this is a viable option due to their upbringing.

Either extreme of the continuum between safety and risk can be dangerous, but given the effects of each on the individual, I would choose getting hooked on risk. The product of risk taking is a greater belief in oneself, even when one fails. Without periodic boosts to self-esteem, one can deteriorate into a fearful, timid, and withdrawn nonparticipant in life. We have all encountered adults who have let fear and insecurity, symptoms of a lack of belief in the self, transmogrify them into pale ghosts who fade away without distinction.

Unfortunately, no matter how vigilant you are, the truth is: your ability to protect your daughter only goes so far. Children can be snatched from their own front porches. Young women have been abducted from their own driveways in broad daylight. The truth, the one no one wants to hear, is this: *there is no safety*. As long as a heart is beating, it is vulnerable. In our most lucid moments we all know this. The great irony is that it is this awareness that gives the intense appreciation for life and a profound respect for the moment. We must not protect our daughters from this great truth, for it is shielding them from real life.

Deep down, you already know this. You know your ability to protect your daughter only goes so far. This is a bitter pill to swallow. Since you cannot predict what her life will bring, and your protection only extends so far, you must prepare *her* to handle whatever life places before her. Anything less is a disservice to her. By rescuing her or overprotecting her, you proportionally limit her capacity to control her personal destiny and teach her to rely on others for the safety and success of her life.

It is vitally important for you, as her father, to make a distinction between protecting your daughter from the truly dangerous aspects of life and overprotecting her in general, as well as recognizing when the time has come for her to learn to protect herself. Much as we hate to admit it, girls must be allowed to take the risks that will develop self-confidence and courage, just as boys are allowed to do.

Please do not misinterpret this advice. I am not advocating allowing your daughter to take risks that are sure to endanger her life. I am merely asking you to look at your own behavior to determine when you have carried protection too far and by so doing, have inadvertently taught your daughter to be helpless. In the section on safety, we will discuss this further.

Can a Victim Be a Risk Taker?

I met a father recently at a party. After discussing the subject of my book, I asked him to tell me what his idea of a successful daughter was. Since we were not in a classroom and he had had a few drinks, his answer was refreshingly candid compared to the ones I'm used to. He said, "I see a successful daughter as one who faces the world, balls out, to go after whatever she wants."

Isn't that great? I couldn't resist including it. While I'm sure the irony of his statement hasn't escaped you, I include it to emphasize a commonly held misconception—that bravery and testicles are related, that risk taking is a masculine trait. This brings me to the second major issue I told you you would have to confront.

However one defines success, whether it is defying capitalistic materialism to paint watercolors in an attic or being responsible for corporate decisions affecting thousands, there is a common thread running through any successful undertaking. It is the element of risk. The degree to which one is able to risk is the degree to which one is able to succeed.

But how do we socialize our female children? Due to the dreadful statistics of sexual abuse, kidnapping, rape, and murder, we train girls to be aware of their victim status. Unfortunately, but predictably, individuals who feel like potential victims develop personalities that are fearful, timid, dependent, and overly cautious.

The question is: Can a female who has been socialized to feel like a potential victim be a risk taker? Can she face the world, "balls out," or does her perception of herself as a victim preclude her predisposition to take a risk? By training females to be ever vigilant, cautious, and careful, do we instill a self-image that sabotages future efforts to be bold and adventurous? In essence, is the training that we hope will keep them safe destined to give birth to the very self-image we wish to avoid?

This paradox of trying to make your daughter aware of her vulnerability without creating a victim mentality must be understood if you are to raise a daughter capable of the great risks required to achieve the great heights. In a following chapter we will discuss ways to do this. For now, simply pondering the paradoxical nature of your task may be an enlightening experience.

As you can see, the challenges facing you as the father of a potentially successful daughter are broad and complex. They require a heightened degree of awareness and a willingness to play quite a new role in your daughter's life.

This would be a good time to take a breather and review the nature of the challenges facing you.

The first involves the discrepancy between femininity and achievement. You must make your daughter feel feminine and pretty so that she believes she is attractive enough to attract boys *at the same time* that you develop in her the traits that contribute to achievement, *even though* they may be in stark contrast to the stereotypical portrait of femininity required to attract adolescent males. Whew! Even writing it down in a coherent manner is a challenge, much less doing it! But that's still only half the story.

The second issue is the enormous complication of making your daughter aware of her status as a potential victim without creating the kind of mentality that makes her feel like a victim!

This is sort of like living with bees in your head. You may feel like throwing up your hands in surrender to the society that created these problems and relinquishing your talented, intelligent, unique daughter to the formidable forces that will shape her. Remember, in so doing, you increase the likelihood that she will not reach her potential, will not make the contribution of which she is capable.

And Speaking of Risk Takers . . .

"I can kick tail with the best of 'em." She laughs. "In all my forty-six years, I have never changed, although I've mellowed somewhat. I've done basically everything I've wanted to do in my sport. When it comes down to making it happen, to winning the race, I guarantee you, I am always dead serious about what's going to happen.

"You have to be serious. We're running 270-mile-an-hour cars here. . . . It's not a kid's game.

"Besides, I like to be thought of as a racer who wins."

Shirley Muldowney has nothing to prove anymore. Besides having won the National Hot-Rod Association Championship seventeen times, she has won the World Championship three times. (Actually, she is a four-time world champ but does not take credit for the 1981 championship because it involved an organization which she considers "softball.") She has pitted herself against the best in a sport which is perhaps the most dangerous in the world of sports and has emerged victorious.

Obviously, this is a woman who takes her sport seriously. She credits her father with giving her the attitude of a winner.

"There are some women driving cars who use what I call 'the women's edge.' They compete but they aren't real winners. That's the difference. My dad taught me how to be a winner.

"If I had to pick one thing my dad taught me, the most important was to be a fighter. I grew up as a street kid in an inner city, and I didn't have a lot going for me.

"He taught me to think of myself as a winner. He taught me

about backbone and how to stand up to a lot of people who were not my fans, not my friends, people who certainly were not for me. People who weren't thinking about what *I* wanted.

"Support is the main thing that I think girls need from their dads. When you're young and you're a dad, you tend to do your own thing. And even though my dad did that too, when it came down to the nitty-gritty of it, you know, he was there. He stuck with me. I went to him for support, and I got that support.

"He would leave whatever he was doing, whether it was a construction job or driving a taxi or even a card game down in the local coffee shop if I needed him. He came over to my side, my way of thinking, and he fought for me.

"Like when I was thirteen, I got into some trouble. By today's standards it wouldn't be trouble, but I just got crazy. I was a hellraiser like my father.

"They wanted to send me away. Not to a home for wayward girls or anything like that; I'm talking about a place that would stabilize me. I was headed, well, I'm not sure what direction." She chuckles. "I didn't know what I wanted. I was having a hard time.

"Anyway my dad wanted me at home with him. He fought to keep me there. I never forgot that. That kind of support meant a lot to me, even then. I went on to straighten up my act, stopped skipping school, stopped hitchhiking, stopped raising hell."

Support can come in a lot of ways. With Shirley and her dad, an attitude of mutual fun together was the cement which bound them together.

"My dad and I used to spend a lot of time together. I was close to him in my earliest years.

"When I was real young, starting at five or six years old, I would go up on my uncle's dairy farm on an island in northern Vermont with my dad. He would run me up and back and usually my mother wasn't around, so my dad would get away with things like driving real fast." She laughs warmly with the memory. "We had a lot of wild rides together.

"Also, he was a construction worker, and back then he would have to go out and light the lanterns for the road construction crew. On Sundays, he would put me on the back of a truck, and I would get to sit on the back and drop the lanterns. As I said, we used to spend a lot of time together. . . .

"When I got older, and I had a day off from work or I just wanted to get out, I would take a ride to his construction site and seek him out and we would go out together.

"It was great. We'd sit in my little Corvette, and I'd have to put the top down for his head so he could get inside the car." She laughs again before continuing. "We'd go up and down the main street, the new stretch of pavement, brand new cement, no rubber on it at all, and we would just peel rubber all up and down the highway and have the greatest time.

"He loved it. You know, showing off. 'My daughter, the race car driver.' "

At this point, her voice trails off and she becomes wistful.

"I wish I still had my dad. I really do. When I see my friends doing something with their fathers, or if I see a girl who is very close to her dad, I still feel quite envious. It was such a crushing thing when I lost him."

We pause in our conversation as I tell her that I too lost my father and continue to long for him. We commiserate at the level in which we have a strong commonality—as two daughters.

I ask her what she personally gets out of being such a risk taker. Her answer is characteristically forthright and confident (another legacy from her father, no doubt). "I make it happen. I drive the car and I pay the bills. I have to generate the money that makes it happen.

"After my people do their work, get the car to the track, qualify it, and do whatever there is to do—and believe me, they make me look good—it's all up to me. When they tell me to go to the starting line, it's in my hands.

"I like that—having the final say."

And have the final say, she does. This courageous, daring woman is living proof that females can take the risks that land them in the big time. All they need is some male support and a little encouragement to test their abilities. A willing and available father couldn't be more perfectly positioned. He is there to provide both.

On the Rocks

Since I am encouraging you to allow your daughter to begin taking some risks, the most effective way I know how is to relate my personal experience with Outward Bound, a survival school which encourages adventure as a medium of self-discovery.

Ever since I had first heard of Outward Bound when I was in college, I had been attracted to its philosophy. I was intrigued with the idea of adventure as a medium of self-discovery, of finding out who I was by casting my fate to the wind, so to speak. It is no accident that I phrase this in such romantic terms, for that was my picture of the Outward Bound experience.

Finally, last summer, as I sat writing about females and risk taking, I realized that my time had come. I had to do it. I could not play the hypocrite any longer. I could not write about risk taking while staying safe and snug in my little house. Oh sure, I had taken other risks—financial risks, emotional risks, professional risks—but Outward Bound seemed like the ultimate risk. I knew I would have to face technical rock climbing and a three-day solo experience in the wilderness, as well as a variety of other challenges and discomforts.

I signed my name on the dotted line. By doing so, I released Outward Bound School from any liability in case of injury or death. It was a sobering thought.

On the fifth day, after many harrowing escapades, I was experiencing my most frightening moment thus far. I had climbed about 100 feet up a steep, smooth outcropping of rock that offered few hand- or toeholds. I was approximately half way up when I realized I had come to a point where there was absolutely nowhere to go. The rock jutted *out* from where I stood rather than sloping away from me. There were no finger holds or toeholds. One would have to be a human fly to get past this section of the rock. I reasoned that this meant I would either be allowed to climb down or be pulled up by means of my belay rope.

"There is nowhere to go," I yelled down to my instructor.

"Look around," she yelled back.

I thought this was a stupid answer, but I obliged her anyway and looked around. Still nowhere to go.

"Nope. I can't see anything," I yelled. There was a pause followed by more silence. "Can I come down now?" I said timidly.

"No."

"But there is nowhere to go. Honest! If there were, I would go there." I was starting to get annoyed. "Do you think I enjoy standing here on this stupid rock?"

Then came the coup de grace. "If it takes you two minutes or two days to figure out that no one is going to get you off that rock but *you*, we will be glad to wait. We have all the time you need." She then resumed her conversation with someone waiting below.

I was infuriated that she took this all so casually. Why wasn't she watching me carefully with an expression of grave concern?

Couldn't she see I was nervous and scared? Or worse, didn't she care? She acted as if this was no big deal!

I stood there contemplating what she had just said, all my weight on one teensy, tiny little patch of my big toe. My knees were trembling from nerves and fatigue. I stood there a long time.

"She has no right to put me through this," I thought to myself. "Can't she see there is nowhere to go? Who does she think she is anyway? Hasn't she got any feelings? Can't she see I'm in trouble? I'm sure her superiors would like to hear about this!"

I continued this "productive" line of thought as I vacillated between conjuring up mean, petty things I could say to her and thinking poor-little-me thoughts. At this point, I failed to notice that I was still stuck at the same place on the rock.

My next line of defense (against having to climb the rock) was to direct my anger at myself. "How could I have been so stupid to get myself into this situation in the first place? I could be sitting home on my patio sipping a cool iced tea with fresh mint and gazing at my flowers. Or talking on the phone. Or just about anything." Once again, I failed to notice that I was still stuck at the same place on the rock.

The next ploy, since there was no one left to be mad at, was to take out my frustration out on the rock itself. "Stupid, frigging rock," I thought to myself. "Why isn't there anywhere to go?" And yes, I was still stuck at the same place on the rock.

Eventually, it occurred to me (perhaps I am a slow learner) that I had been standing in the same place for about twenty minutes and that ultimately darkness would fall. I realized that all the energy I had devoted to blaming first my instructor, then myself, and then the rock hadn't helped one bit to solve my problem. I was still stuck in the same place.

When I finally accepted there would be no rescuers, I did so reluctantly and bitterly, *but* I began to climb anyway, at first hesitantly, then gradually with more confidence. Yes, I was terrified. Yes, the rock was still smooth and impossible. But I found pathways up that rock that didn't exist before. If you asked me today how I got up that rock, I could not give you an answer. I have absolutely no idea. I do remember my instructor saying, "Just place your foot and trust yourself." All I know is that once I stopped hoping against hope to be rescued or blaming others for my predicament, I overcame my terror and made it up the rock.

The metaphor is obvious. Females can waste an incredible amount of time being angry or depressed that no one is there to rescue them, particularly if they have been raised to expect it. All the emotional displays in the world do not change the fact that, as an adult, there are situations which demand that one take action oneself, or stay stranded on a rock through a very long and terrifying night. At some point in time, we all have to place our foot and trust ourselves.

I also learned that what has been given is enough. No matter how scant one's resources or how rigid or limiting one's environment, if that is all one has to work with, then work with it one must. Wasting time and energy expecting to be rescued is futile.

Through the "no rescuing" philosophy of Outward Bound, I learned that I could do what I thought I could not do. My self-esteem soared, and I acquired greater serenity about meeting life's challenges. In spite of daily terror and feelings of inadequacy, in spite of my firm belief that I would be the weak link in the chain, I did whatever was required of me at whatever time it was required. Mainly because I had no choice. It was kind of like boot camp.

I learned that my tendency toward constant "futuring" kept me in a state of perpetual anxiety. I was so busy worrying about the next challenge that I did not allow myself to savor my victories until I felt safe at last, on the bus riding home. Had I had the confidence that I would do whatever was required, because it was required, I could have actually enjoyed some of my experiences instead of being terrified of them.

Basically, that is a lesson in present-time thinking. Present-time thinking requires a good deal of self-confidence. We females who doubt our ability to handle whatever life may dish out spend a good deal of time worrying about and fretting over the future and what we will do if such and such happens. Since females are often made to feel weak, fragile, inadequate, and in need of protection, they are more likely to spend their time worrying about the future, instead of enjoying the present.

When you give your daughter the opportunity to take a risk and test her limitations, I guarantee she will find they are much further out than she thought they were. Since her achievements will be determined by what she believes are her limitations, the best you can do for her is to weaken her belief in those limitations. One of the best vehicles for this is risk taking.

When your daughter says, "I can't," realize that she is arguing for her limitations and tell her so. Tell her you are there to argue for her abilities and that's why you believe she can. When she says, "I'm scared," be kind and understanding and relate how you get scared sometimes too, but that is no excuse for not meeting the challenge. One can be scared and still do the deed. Just think of Sigourney Weaver in *Aliens*!

Finally, all this will teach her that waiting to be rescued is useless. She will learn that the only viable alternative is to analyze her situation objectively and act on her analysis. These gifts of confidence and self-reliance are the most precious gifts you could give her.

Safety

"Once, when I was twenty-one, I had this job as a waitress at a really high-class restaurant. I worked the night shift between five o'clock and midnight. I made a lot of tips because of the dinner hour, but I hated the shift because I had to come out into a dark, isolated parking lot to get to my car. Even with our upper-crust clientele, it made me nervous to come into that parking lot alone. Even today, I am still anxious in parking lots, even in the middle of the day in a shopping mall."

The woman whose story you are about to hear is a tiny woman (5 feet tall and 100 pounds) who was forced to defend herself against an attacker. She is testimony to the fact that size is not an accurate measure of threat.

"Anyway, one night I was on my way to my car when I spied a shadowy figure approaching from the side. He was crouched down low, moving swiftly and approaching at an angle that would eventually converge at the exact spot I was headed for—my car. In a panic I looked around for someone to help me, but I realized I was utterly alone.

"I got a bolt of adrenaline that left my knees trembling and my stomach nauseated. I realized that a physical confrontation was about to ensue. As I saw it, I had no choice but to be brave.

"The first thing I did was to throw down my purse. I didn't need that extra baggage. Then I took a defensive stance, with my feet apart, weight evenly distributed, and fists up.

"I decided to take the role of the aggressor. You know, try to throw him off balance psychologically? I knew that he saw *me* as the victim and himself as the aggressor and I wanted to change his perception," she says cagily. "Of course, all this was unconscious at the time.

"I said, 'Look buddy, I don't know what you want or why you're here, but *I'm* here to tell *you*, it ain't gonna be easy. I'm gonna fight you every step of the way.'

"We just stood there looking at each other, me poised to defend myself. After a while, he started to back up. He wouldn't even turn his back on me. That made me feel like maybe I had the upper hand, but I was still terrified. He just backed up and when he got far enough away, he turned and ran.

"I jumped in my car and drove home. I immediately called the restaurant to inform them some weirdo was lurking around in their parking lot and I thought he was dangerous. They called the police and, sure enough, he was still out there. Waiting for a timid woman he could victimize more easily, no doubt."

Although Ginny's size was hardly formidable, her attitude, her body language, and her verbal threats were enough to make a potential attacker think twice. Luckily, due to her upbringing, she had not learned to be helpless. She had developed some "masculine" behavior, and she was able to call it forth when she needed it, was able to confront the situation more effectively than most women.

As the second child, who was expected to be a boy, she became the companion her father had wanted in a son. She helped him rebuild engines in their garage, arm wrestled with him, went camping and hunting with him. Because she identified with her father and had some practice at masculine behavior, she was able to call on it in order to save herself.

This story was told not to activate all your darkest fears but to introduce you to a very important concept necessary to the proper understanding of this book—that a female trained to be ladylike will lack the skill, the practice, or the inclination to become aggressive and even hostile if need be. A girl who has been raised to be stereotypically feminine will not be able to spontaneously abandon the set of feminine behaviors she has learned, even in order to defend herself regardless of how urgent that need may be.

In the foregoing scenario, Ginny might have become a victim if her early training had never prepared her to act aggressively. Unfortunately, aggression is something heartily discouraged in females; it is not ladylike. In our culture, it is considered extremely unfeminine, and therefore unattractive, so we do not cultivate it in our female children.

The typical female has had little to no experience with defending herself against a hostile opponent. Most have never doubled-up their fists and struck anyone in their adult lives. Perhaps their entire lives. When seriously threatened, many freeze. They can't even scream. This reaction turns them into precisely the kind of frozen victim the aggressor is looking for, and he is ready.

This chapter postulates that within the range of possibilities that life offers, there may be occasion for even the most extreme behavior. We cannot predict what events may be foisted upon your daughter. If you train her only to act within a narrow set of behavior patterns, to always be a good girl or a feminine female, you limit her capacity to handle extreme situations where her life may be in danger. Furthermore, since you cannot always be there to protect her, you must teach her how to handle herself and give her opportunities to practice.

I will recommend two things: (1) self-defense courses (or at least practice in the backyard with Dad or the chance to wrestle with her brothers) and (2) the emphasis of safety over vulnerability.

Let us first examine the issue of self-defense courses for girls. There are two lines of thought on this. One says any training in self-defense is positive. The other says a little knowledge is a dangerous thing, giving a girl a false sense of security and causing her to take foolish risks. There is some truth to this outlook, but I would like to postulate a different perspective.

In his book entitled *Crime Free*,[2] author Michael Castleman cites a study in which researchers videotaped pedestrians in New York City; no one in particular, just your average people on the street. Then the tapes were shown to prisoners, who consistently picked the same people to mug. They were not necessarily the people whom the researchers had postulated would be picked (like ''little old ladies'') but rather a cross section of the population.

When pressed for explanation, the prisoners cited those people whose body language sent a message of frailty, distraction, or uncertainty. According to the convicts, these people looked like easy targets; they sent a message of vulnerability.

To some extent, therefore, a confident demeanor, an attitude of assurance and poise, builds a psychological wall of protection around a person because the potential assailant pegs the individual as a difficult mark. They would much rather wait for the timid, unsure victim who will not give them any trouble.

I am not suggesting that confident body language is an adequate deterrent to all crime and victimization, but it worked with my friend Ginny. Her aggressor was not in the mood for a battle. He had too much to lose. Her confidence, her boldness, her ability to be aggressive fended off what was sure to be an attack. For that reason, classes in self-defense which give your daughter a sense of confidence as well as the skills she needs to fend off an aggressor are better than having no idea what to do in case of an emergency.

I also suggested wrestling with her brothers. I have seen parents admonish a brother to leave his sister alone because he might hurt her. True. On the other hand, what does she do when they are not there? She probably learns to take care of herself. In the long run (and as long as her brother is not psychotic), it may do her more good to learn to handle herself physically. Remember Shirley Muldowney's dad, who told her not to run and cry, but to "turn around and kick their butts"?

Emphasize safety and competence over vulnerability when talking with your daughter. The following example will show you how to accentuate her awareness of safety measures and feeling of competence and minimize her belief in victimization. It will show you both what *not* to do, in terms of fostering a victim mentality, and what *to* do, in terms of fostering a sense of competence.

Finally, as you will see, it also exploits a rare opportunity—the chance to find out exactly how your daughter thinks, how aware she is of danger, and how willing she is to be responsible for her own safety. It opens up communication between parent and child and gives you a glimpse into the workings of your daughter's mind. Then it is much easier for you to determine if she is as ready to handle risk taking as she thinks she is.

THE BICYCLE TRIP*
(A Play)

MARY: Dad, Kathy and I want to go on a bike ride to Boulder next Saturday.

DAD: Absolutely not. (I better squelch this right now.)

MARY: Why???!!!

DAD: Because there are too many dangerous people out   5 there who rape and kill young girls. (There, that should scare her.)

MARY: You let Dan go when he was my age.

DAD: That's different. (Oh yeah, I forgot about that.)

---

*Special note to readers: In parentheses, following the lines spoken by the characters, is the subtext of what Dad and Mary are really saying; it is reading between the lines, if you will.

MARY:	Why?	10
DAD:	Because he's a boy. (Boys aren't victimized like girls are.)	
MARY:	So? What's that got to do with it?	
DAD:	I already told you. He's a boy. (Doesn't this girl know anything?)	15
MARY:	So what you're saying is that because I'm a girl, I can't do anything. It's not fair. I'm just supposed to stay home and do nothing with my life.	
DAD:	Don't exaggerate. Nobody said any such thing. (Author's note: Oh, yes, he did.)	20
MARY:	Yeah, but what's the difference? I want to go do something my brother was allowed to do but just because I am a girl, I can't. It's not fair. (I refuse to accept my victim status without a fight.)	
DAD:	Maybe not, but life is not fair. You just have to learn to accept some things. Girls do not get to do all the things boys get to do because they are more vulnerable. The world is not a safe place for young girls out by themselves, and I would never forgive myself if anything happened to you.	25 / 30
MARY:	Could you have lived with yourself if something had happened to Dan? (Now I've got him.)	
DAD:	(Who knows he's been had) Now look, I'm not going to argue about this anymore. I said no, and that's what I mean. Consider the subject closed.	35
MARY:	But . . .	
DAD:	No "buts" about it. That's it. I'm not going to discuss it any further.	
MARY:	But . . .	
DAD:	Mary, I'm warning you. . . .	40
MARY:	(Screaming as she storms from the room) *It's not fair!!!!*	

I have asked scores of participants in my seminars if they think this is a realistic dialogue. Every father of a daughter over the age of ten has admitted to similar conversations. One father said, "I had this one before I came here this morning. Were you following me with a tape recorder?" The fact is that this is a true story told to me by a gifted girl in one of my classes.

Now, let's analyze the scenario. Dad's intentions were good. His heart was in the right place. What parent doesn't sympathize with his fears? Furthermore, he is right—the world is *not* a safe place.

But, inadvertently, Dad weakened Mary's self-esteem, and more important, he undermined her courage. He reinforced her victim status as a female and thereby increased her vulnerability. But what could he do?

First, Dad might have looked at the situation more realistically to begin with. Boys get kidnapped and sexually abused just as girls do. The sick people who prey upon children do not discriminate between genders. This is perhaps the bitterest of all pills for parents to swallow. It is, nevertheless, true.

Dad could have better served Mary by teaching her how to take care of herself than by making her fearful of the world. One day, Mary will leave home, and the world, complete with all its dangers, will be there waiting for her. Teaching her how to be responsible for her own safety ultimately makes her less vulnerable than preventing her from participating in what the world has to offer.

Let us examine some of the key mistakes Dad made in his interaction with Mary, and then follow this analysis with an alternative dialogue which communicates the same need for safety but does so by emphasizing *competence* rather than *vulnerability*.

Dad's first mistake occurs in line 3. Taking a hard line before he has even heard any details immediately sets up an adversarial situation. He has taken an either/or position, and by so doing, has fired the first shot in what is sure to be a battle. This occurs because he, like many fathers, continues to operate out of an anachronistic model, a belief that if he "lays down the law" his daughter will simply obey, will not question or debate the word of the master.

It is a puzzle why fathers continue to do this. It seems to be an unwillingness to accept, even after numerous examples to the contrary, that children do not just simply obey. They always want to know why not. Unquestioning obedience went the way of Oliver Twist and "Children should be seen and not heard."

Like it or not, approve or not, that is the way it is. In the long run it is more effective to outsmart your kids than to engage in endless, futile battles attempting to prove who is in control. This is particularly true as kids approach the teenage years, when they will begin to wage these power struggles in deadly earnest. Because their developmental task is to break away from parental control in order to grow up, they will nearly always have more energy for the battle and commitment to it than you do.

Whenever I see a parent locked into a power struggle with a child, I wonder what is the parent's first priority; is it the child's welfare or the protection of the parent's own ego? Granted, I will be the first to admit that there are cases when a child is testing parental limits and actually wants boundaries set. But in the case cited above, Dad has jumped to conclusions too quickly, laid down the law too rapidly, and gotten involved in an unnecessary battle.

Finally, as a father, it is wise to avoid power struggles with your daughter (or any of your children) for any reason because so many ugly and hurtful things can be said in the throes of these kinds of arguments. Many times wounds are inflicted which never heal. Circumventing the issue of who is in control helps to maintain an open and friendly relationship between father and daughter and minimizes any possibility of authoritarianism and the inevitable rebellion that will follow.

The next mistake occurs in lines 5 and 6. In essence Dad has said, "Because you are a girl, you are a victim." This is the message he *wants* to communicate. He believes, as do many of you reading this right now, that it is the only way to make her aware. In reality, it does not make her more aware, it just makes her more frightened.

Many of you are thinking, "That's OK. I don't want her to be frightened, but if it keeps her safe, it's a price I'm willing to pay." Remember, a victim mentality results in a victim pose, a type of body language which can act as a signal of the easy mark to potential attackers. For that reason, utilizing a different approach to heighten her awareness (which you will see in the next dialogue) is a potentially safer tactic.

The next few lines that Dad speaks are fairly self-explanatory, except to say he simply reinforces over and over the victim status a female must accept as part of her lot in life.

The next major mistake occurs in line 19, where Dad is heavily into denial. While it is true that his daughter, in classic adolescent fashion, has exaggerated what her father said, it is also true that her perception of being severely restricted in life (and not just this particular situation) is an accurate one. A better response might have been, "You are right, I did give that impression. Now that I look back on it, I probably shouldn't have let Dan go either." This may have totally prevented Mary's response in lines 21 to 23.

Dad's responses in lines 25 to 30 are deadly. He has told her to simply accept her victim status and learn to live with the terror of living in an unsafe world. A better response might have been, "Well, it's true that life is unfair. What this means is that you have to think about how to keep yourself safe and what to do if and when you find yourself in danger. When I hear that you think about keeping yourself safe and that you have learned to take responsibility for your own safety, maybe I will be more open to your request. I should have done that with Dan as well." By responding in this way, Dad could have avoided the pièce de résistance of Mary's argument.

Mary's remark, "Could you have lived with yourself if something had happened to Dan?" is a perfect example of the wisdom of kids and their ability to cut through adult subterfuge to get to the heart of a matter. As I said earlier, this dialogue actually took place, and when Mary told me of her remark, I was instantly sympathetic to her father, who certainly must have clutched when she said this.

He replies in the fashion of someone who knows there is no reply—he refuses to discuss it any further. At this point he has dug himself in so far that he is forced to resort to authoritarianism to win the battle with his daughter.

The following alternative represents a completely different approach to Mary's request to take a risk. As you will see, it too communicates the need for safety, but does so via a different route. It emphasizes developing Mary's competence so that she will learn to take care of herself, and it does so without reinforcing her helplessness as a victim.

MARY: Dad, Kathy and I want to go on a bike ride to Boulder next week.
DAD: Boy, that makes me nervous. I don't think so. (Here, Dad has used an "I" message instead of a "you" message. More about these later.)
MARY: We'll be all right, honest.
DAD: I'm afraid that doesn't make me feel any better. How do I know you'll be all right?
MARY: Oh, Dad, we can take care of ourselves.
DAD: OK, give me some examples. (Dad has seized a golden opportunity to actually find out, directly from Mary herself, just how seriously she takes her responsibility to keep herself safe.)
MARY: What do you mean?

DAD: Tell me specifically how you will take care of yourself. (Furthermore, he now has her concentrating on the subject of safety and competence, which fosters her sense of control rather than her sense of impending doom.)

MARY: Well, let's see. I'll make sure my bike is in good working condition.

DAD: What if something breaks down along the way?

MARY: I'll take my repair kit, tools, air pump, and manual.

DAD: OK, what else?

MARY: We will lay out a route for you so you'll know exactly the route we'll be taking. If we don't get there, you'll at least know where to look.

DAD: OK, what else?

MARY: We'll call you the minute we get there.

DAD: OK, what else?

MARY: Oh, Dad . . .

DAD: You can "Oh, Dad" me all you want, I still need to hear more about how you will take care of yourself.

MARY: How about if more of us go? A group is safer than just two.

DAD: That sounds good. How many?

MARY: As many as I can get. What's the minimum?

DAD: Four or five.

MARY: Oh, Dad . . .

DAD: Four or five.

MARY: You're so paranoid.
(This is OK because Mary has now identified the paranoia as her father's problem and has not begun to own it as her own.)

DAD: I know. I don't deny it. What else?

MARY: We'll take a first-aid kit in case anybody gets hurt.

DAD: This is helping. Got any more ideas?

MARY: How about if I take Mom's Mace? Plus a change of clothes in case the weather turns bad?

DAD: You know, you're a pretty smart kid.

MARY: I told you I could take care of myself.

DAD: Come on, be honest. Did you really think of all those things before we had this talk?

MARY: (Grinning guiltily) Of course.

DAD: Well, I'm still not ready to make a final decision, but I do feel better about it. Give me a couple of days to think it over and I'll let you know.

MARY: Dad, come on, I have to know *now*.

DAD: Sorry.

MARY: Pleeeeease.

DAD: I said I would let you know in two days. Talk to me then.

My purpose is not to advise you to let Mary go on the bike trip. That is a decision you have to make depending on your own comfort level, but as you can see, the father in the second scenario has a good deal more information to work with, a much greater awareness of his daughter's maturity level and ability to cope, than the father of the first scenario. At least he can base his decision on something real, rather than the imagined state of his daughter's mind.

What do you do if your daughter, when questioned about keeping herself safe, replies, "I don't know"? (This is quite possible, since it is the standard reply of an adolescent when attempting to avoid the distasteful act of thinking.)

Simply reply back, "Well, if you don't know, you are obviously not ready to go. You can think about it for a few days and if you come up with any ideas, just let me know." If she doesn't come back with ideas, she didn't want to go very badly. If she does, you are back in the driver's seat with the opportunity to listen. If she has only one or two ideas, send her back to the drawing board, but don't allow her to trick *you* into coming up with all the answers. (Children can be absolute geniuses at this. They exploit a parent's sense of responsibility by manipulating them into foreseeing all the possibilities.)

Instead, give your daughter the gift of self-reliance by shifting the responsibility for anticipating the possibilities on to her shoulders. Besides, it is the only way she will learn.

It is important to emphasize that refusing to rescue and encouraging risk taking can be overdone, just like anything else. Each situation is unique, as is each individual girl. Some girls will be able to handle risk much better than others. Make your decisions based on your knowledge of your particular daughter, her ability to handle emergencies, her degree of self-confidence, and her level of maturity. That way you will avoid either overprotection on the one hand, or benign neglect on the other.

Finally, I have saved the most important recommendation for

last. If you refuse to rescue, make every effort to do so lovingly. Bear in mind that refusing to rescue can have an element of cruelty in it, so remember to be kind. Help your daughter overcome her fears by showing your love and concern, by being gentle, reassuring, and humane.

The biggest mistake fathers make is that they fail to show love and affection when encouraging a daughter to take a risk. I once watched a father trying to talk his daughter down an expert ski slope she had inadvertently landed on. Instead of saying things like, "Honey, I know you feel scared. Standing up there looking down can be scary. Just remember to keep your eyes right in front of your skis, not at the bottom of the mountain. I will be right here to help coach you down," he was saying things like, "Hurry up. I'm not going to stand here all day waiting for you to make up your mind. Let's go!"

Part of a humane approach in encouraging risk taking is patience, being aware that it takes time for an individual to summon courage. Rushing your daughter will only add to her anxiety, so make certain you have the time to wait and to gently encourage her. Sometimes, just patient silence will work.

Here, then, are some basics to keep in mind when coaxing your daughter to take a risk.

1. Use endearing names of affection like "honey," "sweetie," or any pet name you may call your daughter.
2. Speak slowly and softly. Never shout.
3. If she says, "I'm scared," acknowledge her expression of her feelings and indicate that you understand how she feels because you have felt fear too.
4. Be patient.
5. Share with her any tips or psychological tricks that you have used to summon your own courage through a frightening ordeal.

C H A P T E R 8

❦

*Strategies, Techniques,
and Activities*

Up to now, this book has concentrated primarily on what to do, with occasional forays into how to do it. There will be more about "what to do" following this chapter, but for now, it is time to concentrate on "how."

This chapter is divided into three sections. The first section, entitled "How to Discourage," is a rundown on what *not* to do. You will recognize many of these strategies as ones you have already tried or ones that were tried on you, and that, quite simply, do not work.

The second section, entitled "How to Encourage," offers a variety of techniques and strategies for opening communication with your daughter and establishing an overall positive climate in which your relationship can thrive and flourish.

The third section, entitled simply "Activities," provides some very specific information and suggestions for things to do and discussions to have with your daughter. New ideas are presented as well as a review of activities that have already been suggested elsewhere in the book.

It is my hope that this chapter gives you the tools you need, in terms of strategies and activities, and that it supports and reinforces the concepts already offered. Remember, the companionship and love of your daughter can only be enhanced and appreciated by interacting with her in an active and conscious way. Good luck. I hope the two of you have fun!

How to Discourage

Very few parents intend to discourage their children, yet, speaking as an ex-teacher with eleven years' experience, I can say that quite a few manage to do just that. Their intentions may be good, but a lack of parenting skills or secret hostilities can produce a child who feels inadequate, unsure of herself, and less than a valued member of her family. We have already discussed some methods of discouragement throughout this book. The ones presented here are new.

KILLER STATEMENTS

The term "killer statements" needs little explanation. Because we have all experienced them, we know what they are. Suffice it to say they destroy self-confidence. They are often made in anger or frustration. The two most common are, "What's the matter with you?" and "Can't you do anything right?" Other killer statements to avoid are shown below:

1. Where did you get a crazy idea like that?

2. What is your problem?

3. That is the dumbest thing I've ever heard.

4. That's impossible.

5. That's not practical.

6. If you do that, you're going to (fall down, get hurt, break a leg, lose your job, get in trouble with the teacher, etc.).

7. You have to think about your security.

8. Here, I better do that.

9. Here, let me do that for you . . . , followed by:
   a. You always take too long, are too careless, etc.
   b. You never get it right, check your work, do as I say, etc.
   c. Look at the mess you made, the places you missed, etc.
   d. You're going to drop that, break that, ruin that, etc.
   e. Look at all your misspelled words, messy papers, etc.

     f. You're going to get hurt.

  10. Negative "what ifs":
     a. What if the teacher gets mad?
     b. What if you lose?
     c. What if the boys don't like that?
     d. What if the girls don't like that?

  11. You can't fight city hall.

  12. You just have to accept some things.

DISCOUNTING

Discounting is the act of refusing to accept another person's statement of feelings or state of mind and body. It is a dangerous practice for two reasons. First, it undermines your daughter's self-confidence by teaching her to doubt her own perceptions and her ability to make sound judgments. Second, it is a subtle type of devaluing which sends the message that she is unable to define her own state of being. The following examples are some common "discounts," presented with some suggestions for alternative responses.

As you can see, the better responses are those which accomplish four things:

1. They acknowledge your daughter's ability to identify and articulate her inner experience.

2. They respect your daughter's right to have feelings (including negative ones) and to express them.

3. They recognize that all emotions are valid simply by virtue of the fact they exist.

4. They recognize your daughter's verbal articulation of these emotions as a sign she wants to communicate.

PREMATURE RESCUING

This practice was covered at length in the chapter on self-concept but bears reviewing here.

First, let it be said that rescuing per se is not necessarily bad. There are times when an individual genuinely needs a helping hand. However, there is a difference between lending a helping hand and either doing it *for* your daughter or rescuing her before

Statement of Being	Discount	Better Response
I'm scared.	That's silly. You have no reason to be scared.	I understand. Trying something new can be scary, but that's an even better reason for trying: to help you overcome your fear.
I'm confused.	You're just not trying hard enough.	Yes, math (or whatever) can be confusing. Sometimes putting in more time or writing down questions helps me. Do you think that would work for you?
I'm bored.	No you're not; you're just lazy.	I know what you mean. Life is full of boring tasks. When I get bored, I try to think of ways to make the task more interesting. Would that work for you?
I'm mad.	No you're not; you're just frustrated, selfish, hurt, tired, confused, etc.	I understand how you feel. What happened?
I hate . . .	You don't hate anybody. It's not nice.	That's a pretty strong emotion. What happened to make you feel so strongly?
Any expression of a negative emotion.	You don't know what you're saying.	Do you want to talk about it?

she asks for help. (It goes without saying that emergencies are a different situation.)

Remember, premature rescuing teaches helplessness. Helplessness becomes hopelessness. When that occurs, your daughter's chances of achievement are greatly, perhaps irrevocably, damaged. In order to avoid this most damaging practice, remember two things. First, if you would not rescue a boy in the same situation, do not rescue your daughter. Second, if you hear yourself saying, "Here, let me do that for you," stop and rethink your behavior.

OVERDOING YOUR INVOLVEMENT AND ENTHUSIASM

If your daughter comes up with a great brainstorm one day or gets involved in a major project, keep your fingers out of the pie. Sometimes parents get so enthusiastic about their child's idea, they get overinvolved and end up taking over the project by contributing too much. I have seen kids completely lose interest in an idea because their moms or dads got so involved that the children felt the project no longer belonged to them. Remember, if your daughter gets involved in a project or develops an idea, allow *her* to own it.

Some of you may feel slightly defensive at this or think I am splitting hairs at such a request. The truth is one day in class I overheard a girl tell her friend about winning a gymnastics competition. I said to her, "Boy, I'll bet your parents are proud of you." She kind of glared at me and then said, "I didn't do it for them. I did it for me." In typical adolescent (that is, brutal) fashion she taught me an important lesson. I am passing it along to you.

When your daughter comes home from school with a happy announcement concerning an accomplishment, resist the temptation to say, "I am proud of you," or, "That makes me very happy." Although this is a sincere statement and one made totally out of love, it carries a subtle, negative impact, a nuance that implies she did it for you.

Even though it does make you happy and proud, a better way to express the same feeling is, "That's neat! I'll bet that makes you feel very happy," or, "That's terrific. If I had done that I would sure be proud of myself." In this way, you send the reflected appraisal (unspoken message) that *she* has total ownership rights to both the deed and the wonderful feelings associated with it. You don't take away her glory by acting as though it were done for your benefit.

This does not mean you can't discuss it with her, brainstorm ideas together, or show interest and give help. It does mean to hesitate when you are tempted to take over. Let your daughter develop her idea in her own way and in her own time. That way, *she* can take credit for it when it is completed instead of feeling like an impostor because Dad really did all the work.

Finally, if you recall attribution theory, you will remember it shows that females tend to own their failures but not their successes. This chapter will present more strategies and techniques to "trick" your daughter into owning her achievements, but for now, one way to help her learn to take credit for her accomplishments is to let them be *her* accomplishments.

DISCIPLINE AS PUNISHMENT

In an earlier chapter I discussed the difference between discipline and discouragement. In that chapter I promised to give some examples of the positive, instructive approach to discipline. That will be done in the next section entitled, "How to Encourage." To do so now, however, would be premature because before one can fully understand an instructive approach to discipline, it is necessary to examine the current, popular approach more carefully.

Discipline is one of those parental necessities that can become discouraging to your daughter if handled improperly. One improper view of discipline is as punishment for wrongdoing. This view of discipline should be limited to convicts and felons. For children, it is an inappropriate response, a negative mind-set which can degenerate into practices which destroy self-esteem and even, in extreme cases, do physical harm.

It is unwise to discipline when angry, for that is when there is the greatest chance of doing actual harm, either physical or emotional. It is better to wait until your anger has subsided before taking a course of action. There is an ancient Chinese proverb which says it better than I: "Hesitate in a moment of anger and prevent a year of grief."

Let your daughter know you are displeased with her behavior and that you will deal with the problem more completely when you have thought it over. Simply say, "I am so angry right now that I don't want to discuss it in this state of mind." When your anger has subsided, you will be better able to evaluate the situation objectively.

Though children sometimes engage in what seem to be purposely malicious acts and though it may be sorely tempting to "punish" them, even these occasions should not be used to make a child feel unworthy or "bad." With the proper attitude toward the *purpose* of discipline, a parent can transform even these negative behaviors into growth experiences.

The key is to realize what the *purpose* of discipline is. It is meant not only to ensure that the child discontinue a certain activity, but also to ensure that the child not engage in it *even when there is no authority figure around*! Punitive forms of discipline ensure only that the child will not engage in the activity when there is a chance of getting caught. The positive, instructive approach to discipline, when substituted for the punitive approach, will cultivate a more mature attitude in your child, as you will see in the next section when we discuss discipline as instruction.

For now, memorize this phrase: "Discipline is not something you *do* to a child, it is something you *teach* a child."

How to Encourage

UNSPOKEN MESSAGES

Our earlier discussion of unspoken messages, those subtle but powerful communications that reside just below the surface of words and actions, was perhaps the most valuable for clarifying ways to encourage your daughter. Bear in mind that individuals come to see themselves as *others* see them, so the content of your unspoken messages must be supportive and encouraging. Review the chapters on success (Chapter 3) and self-concept (Chapter 5) if you wish to be reminded of specific ways to send positive unspoken messages to your daughter concerning her abilities and talents.

"I" VERSUS "YOU" MESSAGES

One surefire way to discourage your daughter and make her resentful of your authority (which can later lead to rebellion) is to present a problem as though it were entirely her fault. This is accomplished by expressing the problem using the pronoun "you" over and over again.

Think about it: when someone says, "You do this," or, "You do that," it makes you feel like you are being poked in the chest with an index finger by someone wielding it like a weapon. Your reaction would likely be either to become defensive and fight back or to become withdrawn and closed—the old fight-or-flight response at work.

A better way to express a problem is to use the pronoun "I." Instead of, "You never clean up your room," say, "I get upset when your room is messy." Instead of, "You never start your homework until it's too late to finish it and then you get upset because you don't have time," say, "I hate to see you get so upset about your homework. Is there some way we could work something out?" Instead of, "You talk back too much, and I'm going to kick your butt if you keep it up," say, "You know, it really hurts my feelings when you talk back to me, but it's hard for me to admit it so I get mad instead."

Now, some of you will find this entirely too wimpy to suit you. Admitting that your children have the power to hurt your feelings completely destroys the image of the authoritarian, "in control" father. Here is the point: do you want your daughter to stop whatever she is doing, or do you want to maintain your image? Do you want to encourage her to listen to your point of view, or do you want to engage in endless, repetitive battles?

When I first taught school, I thought the way to deal with recalcitrant students was to haul out the big guns. I would threaten to send them out of the classroom, suspend them, call the vice principal, call their parents, etc. It never really worked. Either the argument would escalate because I had publicly challenged the students, or the students would temporarily back off, only to resurface later with even more venom.

One day, a student said something particularly obnoxious. I was tired of the battle. I just put down my chalk and said, "You know that really hurt." It was miraculous. The boy, who had been a troublemaker from day one, turned bright red and looked mortified. He said not another word that class period. He came up to me at the end of class and said, "Miss Marone, I'm sorry about what I said. I didn't mean to hurt your feelings." Furthermore, other kids came up to apologize *for* him. He never made any more trouble for me after that day. As a matter of fact, we became quite friendly.

The moral of the story is that when we show our children our human side, they are surprisingly reciprocal. If it is not even necessary to be an authority figure with junior high kids, then it is not necessary with anyone! It is more important to be human. When we back kids into corners, make accusations, threaten, intimidate, and control, they react as any human being with dignity would—they refuse to take it. When we simply express how we feel, without an accusatory "you" message, we encourage them to see us as human beings also, even if we are adults!

For this reason, if you are having trouble with your daughter, tell her how you feel. If you are unused to this approach, you may have to give it some thought in order to identify your feelings.

Once identified, communicate it in an "I" message. You will be surprised at how effective it is.

DISCIPLINE AS INSTRUCTION

Let us return to the phrase, "Discipline is not something you *do* to a child, it is something you *teach* a child." I cannot stress enough the importance of this phrase. Unfortunately, in our culture, we do not discipline properly; consequently, many children do not learn *internal* control and restraint, and instead function only according to external threats.

If the purpose of discipline is not to punish, what is it? As was mentioned earlier in this book, the origin of the word is from the Latin *disciplina*, which means "knowledge." Using this definition gives us a clearer picture concerning what we are about when we discipline children. It means we *teach* them, not *punish* them.

In other words, discipline correctly applied transfers control from outside the individual to inside the individual. It cultivates internal control, rather than using external threats. The problem with many children I encountered when teaching was that they only monitored their behavior when there existed the threat of reprisals meted out by an adult authority figure. Many children had no internal authority.

If you want your daughter to be a successful individual, it is paramount that you teach her the kind of discipline that comes from inside, that is not motivated by external circumstances alone. One way to do this is to teach her to bear the consequences of her actions, that is, to take responsibility for whatever results from her behavior.

I had to learn the hard way, after numerous errors in disciplining junior high students. But I did learn. An example from my years as a teacher illustrates the point.

I had a girl in my class with whom I was having great difficulty. She was hostile, sullen, and sarcastic. She could not stand me, and I wasn't too crazy about her either. One day, I walked in my room after school and caught her gouging out *the* four-letter word on my closet door. This was the last straw in a series of events. I was blind with fury.

My first impulse, honest to God, was to grab her and shake her as hard as I could. Obviously, I stifled this impulse. (Thank goodness for laws against corporal punishment in the schools. I mean that. Being forced by law to control one's anger at a youngster is a good thing.) My next impulse was to scream something like,

"You worthless piece of garbage. There's just no getting through to you, is there?"

Instead, I paused to gather my thoughts and consider the purpose of my discipline. We just stood there and looked at each other for a moment, me with a face flushed with anger, and her with a face flushed with fear. I said, "I'm so angry I can't even talk. You're going to have to wait while I compose my thoughts." She got big tears in her eyes. After some consideration I opened with the only thing I could think of that would be a "neutral" introduction to the talk we obviously needed to have.

ME: You've ruined my door.

HER: *(Silence.)*

ME: I guess the reason I am so mad is because I don't understand why you hate me so much. We are going to have to talk about it, because I don't want to try 5 to continue to function as your teacher when there is so much animosity. Until then, however, other people besides me are going to have to look at that door, too.

HER: *(Silence.)* 10

ME: Right?

HER: *(Sullenly.)* I don't know.

ME: You don't know? *(I am perilously close to losing it again, but I manage to get control.)* Well, obviously, they will. So, how are you going to solve your prob- 15 lem?

HER: I don't have a problem, you do.

ME: *(Barely in control of myself.)* Oh really? What's that?

HER: I don't know.

ME: We'll have to talk about that later. In the meantime, 20 what are you going to do about that door?

HER: I don't know.

ME: Well, I've got plenty of time. I have to grade papers anyway, so I'll just sit here and work until you come up with some solutions. *(A few minutes of silence.)* 25

HER: *(Barely audible.)* I could stay after school.

ME: Well, that's a start. Unfortunately it doesn't really take care of the door problem, does it? I mean, people still have to look at that door. *(More silence while I pretend to grade papers.)* 30

HER: I could paint the door.

ME: That's an idea, except that all the doors in this school
       are natural wood, and one painted door wouldn't
       look very good. You could ask the principal though.
       Maybe he will let you. Shall I call him for you?   35

HER: No. *(A few more minutes of agonizing silence.)* How
       am I supposed to get that off of there then?

ME: That didn't seem to bother you as long as it was
       someone else's problem, did it? *(She glowers at me.)*
       I think there is a tool called a sander that would   40
       work.

HER: Oh yeah, my dad has one.

ME: Uh huh. You will also need other tools and supplies.

HER: Where am I going to get them?

ME: That's what I mean when I say you have a problem   45
       to solve.

HER: The janitors?

ME: Yes, they probably have some. Of course, you'll have
       to talk to them about cost.

HER: You mean I have to pay them for them?   50

ME: Of course. They didn't plan your little escapade into
       their budget this year.

HER: Can I call my father?

ME: OK, but I would like to speak with him first.*

At this point, I was able to convince her father that the most
important thing that he could do was not to rescue *or* punish his
daughter. Rescuing her would save her from the consequences of
her actions. Punishment should come in the form of forcing her
to solve her own problem, down to the last detail, just as adults
must do. Eventually, we determined that he would "rent" her his
sander and that she would have to buy brushes and varnish, all of
which she would do by using her baby-sitting money. Finally,
there was the little problem of time.

ME: You know, I don't want to have to look at that on my   55
       door for the next two or three weeks while you get
       the money together. So that's one last problem you
       need to solve.

HER: *(Breaks down crying at this point and screams at
       me.)* Well, what am I supposed to do?!   60

* Note: You may have noticed some mistakes on my part so far, but bear with me.

ME: I know you think I'm being callous, but the truth is it's not my problem. You created it, so you will have to solve it. *(I pause to give this a chance to sink in.)* I understand you are frustrated, but I am not going to solve your problem for you. It's all yours. *(By now,*   65 *she is glaring at me with hate in her eyes.)* However, I don't mind giving you a suggestion if you want to hear it.

HER: *(Tearfully.)* OK.

ME: You can borrow the money from your father or the   70 school, but if you receive a loan, you will have to pay interest on it.

HER: What's interest?

ME: It's money lenders charge you to use their money.

HER: You mean I have to pay back more than I borrow?   75

ME: That's right.

HER: That's not fair!

ME: I know how you feel. That's what I feel like when the bank charges me interest, but that's how it is. Besides, would it be fair for me or your father to   80 have to borrow the money when we didn't do the deed?

HER: *(Barely audible.)* No.

ME: One more thing. After this problem is solved, let's get together and talk about our problems, OK?   85

HER: OK.

As you can see, in my anger, it was very difficult for me to avoid putting her down and making her feel bad about herself, but except for a couple of sarcastic remarks in lines 38–39 and 51–52, I basically succeeded.

The point to remember is that a misbehaving child is usually a discouraged child. Furthermore, the act she was engaged in, carving obscenities on my closet door, was a powerful message that something was strongly amiss in our relationship. A girl who felt secure and confident in my classroom would not be carving obscenities on my door.

In "disciplining" this child, I wanted to punish her, more out of a sense of anger and revenge than true concern for her welfare. You may be thinking that she had no concern for my welfare, but our duty as adults is to be more mature than children are.

For that reason, I made a valiant effort to *teach* her something about the consequences of her actions, in an adult world, rather than concentrating on meting out punishment.

In the long run, however, by requiring her to solve her problem, by forcing her to spend her own money and time, by teaching her that her actions bore consequences, she was "disciplined." I believe she learned a lot more than if I had screamed and yelled at her about what a rotten person she was and had suspended her from school. This just would have given her another opportunity to affirm that I was, indeed, a bitch, that school was unfair, and that her stockpile of hatred for me and the system was justified. She could have continued to avoid looking at her own behavior as an important factor in the overall problem.

Teaching children to bear responsibility for their actions is the key to developing the kind of internal discipline that prevents them from engaging in dangerous or antisocial acts, even when there is no authority figure around. It is this internal locus of control that you should be cultivating in a daughter for whom you have high hopes.

One last example of an instructive approach to discipline begs to be included because it is so common a complaint among parents. When two parents are working, they expect the children to pitch in and do their part around the house. Very often, kids get sidetracked with their own concerns like watching television, talking on the telephone, doing homework, goofing around with their friends, dancing to the radio, fiddling with their hair, etc., and they "forget" to straighten the house, do the laundry, and vacuum. Parents rant and rave, scream and holler, but often to no avail. Here is a suggestion:

DAD: Listen, sweetie, we have a problem.
SUSAN: We do?
DAD: Yes. Actually there are two problems, ours and yours. Our problem is that your mother and I like a clean house, and we expect you to do your chores. When you don't, we get mad. Your problem is that we yell at you and ground you. The result is an almost daily argument which nobody likes.
SUSAN: Right.
DAD: So your mother and I have figured out a way to solve *our* problem. It is up to you to solve yours.
SUSAN: What do you mean?

DAD:	Well, *someone* has to do the laundry and vacuuming. Your mother and I are too busy doing the cleaning, the shopping, paying the bills, and taking care of household repairs and maintenance. Therefore, we have decided to have someone come in once a week to take care of your duties.
SUSAN:	Great!
DAD:	Unfortunately, it will cost money. So, we are taking your allowance to help defray the cost. We know you won't mind, since you don't have the time to do it yourself.
SUSAN:	That's not fair!
DAD:	Why not?
SUSAN:	Because I don't have time either!
DAD:	Well, it's a matter of choices.
SUSAN:	What do you mean?
DAD:	I'm not telling you you can't talk on the phone with your friends or watch television. I'm just saying you have to make a choice, just as we do. You can do those chores yourself and retain your income and standard of living, or you can have the time to watch television and talk on the phone and pay someone else to do the work. It's up to you.
SUSAN:	But . . .
DAD:	Look, I don't like having to give my money to a housekeeper any more than you do. I would much rather go to dinner and a movie with your mother. But we can only spend a dollar in one place, so we have to make choices. So do you. *Our* problem is solved. You may do whatever you choose.
SUSAN:	But Dad, I don't have time either.
DAD:	I understand how you feel, but it is not my problem. I have solved my problem. Now you must solve yours. Everyone must make choices between time and money. So do you. It's a lousy fact of life. No one likes it. Your choice is to either find the time to do it yourself or pay for the luxury of free time as everybody else does.

The key to instructive and constructive discipline is shown in the above dialogue. First, it is a lesson in real life, given without rancor. Second, it avoids making the child's problem the parents' problem. Mom and Dad have solved their problem and leave it up to their daughter to solve hers. Third, it provides a choice, albeit rather limited, which helps children feel less helpless. Fourth, the facts are presented in an objective and straightforward manner, without a lot of accusations and anger.

Therefore, when you are having a problem with your daughter, take the time to sit down and really analyze what *your* problem is, not hers. In the example shown above, Dad's problem was that there was work to be done that was not being done. In order to ensure the work would be done, he needed to come up with some money. He solved his problem. He controlled his part of the world rather than trying to control his daughter. Now his daughter must solve her own problem and control her part of the world.

Granted, this kind of discipline requires creativity and higher-level thinking skills on the part of the parent, but it is so much more effective, with less wear and tear on the nervous system. Furthermore, when you recognize that you are actually teaching your daughter some important lessons about life, rather than functioning as a sort of low-level executioner, you will feel better about yourself as a father. (Besides, it is fun to outsmart your kids!)

DELIVERING DIFFICULT COMMUNICATIONS

In my workshops I have discovered that fathers of daughters age seven or over often feel that they may have already done some damage and would like the opportunity to undo it. Take heart!

Children are the most resilient creatures on earth. Because they genuinely want to please us (in order to be loved by us), they will nearly always give us one more chance. Also, there are techniques which can, when practiced with sincerity, overcome even the most "closed" relationship, where communication has been severely lacking or even nonexistent.

The technique that will be presented shortly offers the opportunity to be honest, communicate difficult messages, and engage in self-disclosure. There is one catch, however. When you use a communication technique, your daughter may learn it from you and then you may be forced to hear *her* difficult communications. On the other hand, your daughter will have certain feelings, thoughts, and opinions regardless of whether you allow her to express them. Just because your daughter is not allowed to express certain thoughts about you doesn't mean she doesn't have them. (Don't you have thoughts and opinions about your parents?) Therefore, isn't it better to get them out in the open?

A word of warning is imperative here. If you set an example of openness and honesty with your child and then blow up when the child is open and honest in return, you slam the door for any future negotiations. Your daughter will doubt your sincerity and fear reprisals. Therefore, you must not set out to practice the following technique until you feel ready to handle the consequences.

Many times children understand their parents in deeper and more complex ways than parents understand themselves. To be sure, you may be unsettled by your daughter's keen and perspicacious insight into your habits, character, and personality. I would go so far as to recommend professional counseling if you doubt your capacity to handle your daughter's potential criticism of you. To be honest, this potential criticism may never emerge. But you must be ready to handle it properly if it does. Once the emotions have subsided and the healing process is over, the relationship will be on sounder footing, in equality, in sincerity, and in the expression of love.

Another important aspect to bear in mind is that "difficult communications" can be positive as well as negative. For example, many of us have experienced that sense of regret and helplessness when we lose a loved one to whom we never made the effort to say "I love you." We vow never to let it happen again. Yet we do. For many of us, men in particular, making positive emotional statements is as difficult as making negative ones.

Perhaps just sitting down with your daughter and saying, "You know, I've never told you how much I admire you. I watch the way you handle your life and I am proud of the positive and intelligent choices you make. I wasn't that smart when I was your age. For that reason, I have faith in you. I just wanted to let you know how much I admire and respect you. Ya got style, kid."

Can you imagine a child's sense of esteem at a revelation like this? Particularly from a father to a daughter? Imagine how you would have felt if your own father had done it for you. Your daughter will treasure it till her dying day. Don't delay. Time does run out.

Finally, the following technique should be used to clear up any "old business" with your daughter that may have been based on ignorance or lack of communication. It is best to clear away this old business in order to demonstrate that your efforts are sincere.

Remember the warnings, however. You must be brave. When you open the possibility for truth, honesty, and self-disclosure, you simultaneously open the floodgates of suppressed feelings and emotions. You must be brave enough to prepare for tears—yours as well as hers! The experts say that men, for all their risk-taking behavior, are emotional sissies. They say men back away from emotional confrontation. Prove them wrong. Take the risk. Be an emotional gambler. Your relationships will improve, and your life will be richer for it. Good luck!

The Technique*

Purpose:
For both parties in a relationship to clear away old business and get "complete" in order to re-create the relationship.

Steps:

1. *Ask if this is a good time; if not, set up a mutually agreed upon time. Repeat this step when communications begin to ensure that it is a good time for a talk.*
   Checking with your daughter to find out if it is a good time to talk sends two important unspoken messages: (1) that you respect the events which make up her life as being as significant as your own—that is, if she has had a bad day, you don't expect her to be at your beck and call—and (2) that you consider her important enough to make an "appointment" with.

   The admonition to check again on the day of the appointment again acknowledges that she may have had another bad day and not be in the mood for a heart-to-heart. This says you respect your daughter as an individual, one who has her own life and an identity separate from her role as your obedient daughter.

2. *Tell her the magnitude of what you are going to say (your greatest fears).*
   Maybe you are afraid she will cry. Or maybe you are afraid you will cry. Or maybe you are just embarrassed to say something emotionally revealing. At any rate, when you explain your greatest fears, you explain your tardiness and your reluctance. This willingness to be

---

*Reprinted with permission from Judy Wardell, founder and author of *Thin Within*. I have adapted this somewhat to fit the subject matter of fathers and daughters specifically. The steps themselves are the design of Judy Wardell, but my explanations represent the attempt to make them more relevant for the father-daughter relationship in particular.

emotionally vulnerable sets the tone for whatever comes next.

3. *Explain what you want from her ideally.*

   Obviously, you may not get what you want. On the other hand, a person can sometimes give you what you want, if they just know what it is. The trick is: don't *expect* a particular reaction. A good rule of thumb: don't expect it, just express it.

4. *Tell the truth. Keep delivering the message until it is received.*

   How can you tell when the message is received? Have your daughter tell you *in her own words* what she thinks you said. Listen carefully to determine if she received the message as you want it received. If not, tell her again, not louder this time (a common mistake when we are not understood the first time!) but using different words or stories to convey the same message.

5. *Acknowledge her feelings and accept whatever response she gives.*

   This may be the hard part. As I said before, if you feel unable to do this, it is best not even to start. One father in my workshop said, "I don't think that's right. I shouldn't have to accept whatever my daughter says."

   I responded that he didn't have to agree with or condone her remarks, simply accept them as a valid expression of how she feels. Whether we agree or disagree with how a person feels is irrelevant, for it doesn't change how they feel. Men, in general, need to learn that *all* feelings are valid, just by virtue of the fact they exist. In reality, it is impossible to "disagree" with the way another person *feels*. It is not a matter that is up for debate; it simply is.

   Trying to "disagree" with another's emotions is a form of emotional tyranny. The message is, "You must feel as I say you can feel. Any other response is either wrong, disloyal, or stupid."

   Furthermore, not accepting your daughter's response, even if you don't like it, is a form of discounting. As we learned earlier, discounting sends a deadly unspoken message to your daughter that she must distrust her feelings and doubt her perceptions, all of which contributes to an overall sense of self-doubt and inadequacy—hardly the kind of beliefs you want to instill in a future achiever.

Activities

The remainder of this chapter is a compilation of six new strategies and activities which have not been previously mentioned. It is followed by a review of the twenty-nine other suggestions which have been offered thus far. Use these ideas to build your daughter's self-esteem and to develop her inclination to take risks and master the world around her.

DINNER TABLE TALK

The evening meal is when many families are finally able to spend time together. In most households, it is the only time families sit down as a unit to discuss the day, share experiences, frustrations, and joys. It is an excellent time to provide relaxation, support, and nurturing for each family member, especially since the sharing of food, an almost universal gesture of love, is involved.

Unfortunately, many families get into the habit of using the time destructively by focusing on everything bad that has happened during the day. (To be perfectly fair, they are hardly to blame, because our culture establishes this mind-set. Just look at our favorite comedians—Joan Rivers and Rodney Dangerfield, the put-down queen and the no-respect court jester. Their humor focuses almost entirely on what an awful place the world is, how crummy life is, and how suspicious we should be of everyone around us. If we try to forget, they remind us.)

This tendency to focus on the negative side of life, particularly during what should be a relaxing meal, increases anxiety and contributes to tension in the family. Why not institute a new form of dinner table talk? Why not set aside this one hour of the day, the dinner hour, to talk of nothing but accomplishments and successes of the day?

Oh, I know what you are thinking. Most days, there are no real successes, just the relentless procession of meaningless tasks and mediocre relationships. Besides, "finding the good in every day" is just the recommendation of a bunch of Pollyanna types who refuse to see reality and furthermore, you hate Dr. Feelgood.

See? That is exactly what we do and we teach our children to do it too. No one is asking you to be Pollyanna, to put on your plastic smile, and proceed through life with blind optimism. But what is wrong with declaring one little hour of the day ''sacred,'' when no negative thinking, self-deprecation, or blaming of others is permitted? Can that really be so bad? There are twenty-three other hours that can be used for ''realistic thinking'' if you insist. (Personally, I think I'll pass.)

Here is how it works. Everyone, and that means *everyone* at the table, must list at least one success or accomplishment for the day. Sure there will be many days when you have to really stretch for a success, but consider this. What about those days when just dragging yourself out of bed in the morning and hauling yourself to work is a major accomplishment? Why not claim it, for God's sake? You have become so accustomed to it, it no longer seems like an accomplishment, but it is. Remember, there are people who *don't*—so say it proudly and give yourself credit.

No one is allowed to pass, no matter how much they protest that the day was without a success. For example, playing this game with my friends over coffee one day, I absolutely couldn't come up with an accomplishment. I hemmed and hawed. I protested that this was truly one day without a success. Then I remembered it! Success for me that day was not eating that third french fry. It may seem like small potatoes (pardon the pun) to some, but if they could look into my past and see the mountains of french fries I used to consume, they would realize what a great victory it was!

You see, when we don't teach our daughters how to claim the little achievements, they begin to think that ''success'' is limited to curing cancer or winning a seat in the senate, that only the great and noble deeds qualify. They don't realize that success is a *process*, the result of small, consistent, and daily efforts that eventually amount to a steady accumulation of little victories, of getting up in the morning and going to work.

This philosophy has particular relevance to females. Remember the discussion of attribution theory in Chapter 3? Research has shown that females, even successful ones, have a tendency to disown their achievements but claim responsibility for failures (while males do exactly the opposite). Females attribute success to external forces such as luck, assistance, or ease of task. They attribute failure to internal forces such as lack of ability, drive, or intelligence.

It is for that reason you must begin training your daughter early to claim her achievements as her own. These dinner table discussions are the perfect vehicle to teach her how and also to make her comfortable with her achievements. (They won't hurt your wife any either.) Give her lots of practice, for she will need all the help she can get to overcome society's message of her second-class status and to see herself as a winner. Save the "humble lessons" for your son.

ATHLETICS

One of the most positive results of the fitness movement has been the acceptance of female sweat. No kidding. Back in the fifties and sixties, females were not allowed to sweat or have muscles. Now, not only are they allowed, they are encouraged. Female muscles and sweat are even considered sexy.

Encourage your daughter to participate actively in sports. Individual sports such as running, cycling, weight lifting, skateboarding, surfing (one rarely sees a female participating in the last two activities), hiking, tennis, swimming, racquetball, gymnastics, track and field, and dancing (not a sport, but definitely a fitness activity) are terrific. The team sports of basketball, soccer, volleyball, and softball will teach her all the skills and challenges to one's attitude that males learn.

Terrie Ann McLaughlin, the top-ranked cadet of 1986 whom we met earlier, credits athletics with teaching her social skills and cementing her relationship with her father.

"More than anything else, my involvement with sports brought my father and me closer together. My dad was real involved, because I played basketball in high school and he had played basketball also.

"He took time with me. He was always helping me out and trying to tell me what I could do better next time. Since then, we've just become continually closer."

As an afterthought she adds, "I would also like to say that getting involved in sports gave me leadership skills, too. Learning how to take control on the court when you need to, that sort of thing."

Let us not forget another female who learned leadership skills on the old basketball court—5-foot industrial contractor Barbara Grogan—where she was, in her words, "running my fannie off, by damn, and playing basketball."

Developing athletic skills and a strong body, participating in sports, be it team or individual, will give your daughter that special brand of confidence, that aura of personal power that one acquires when one is confident in one's body. We are not talking appearance here but rather the physical skills of strength, endurance, speed, and coordination, those skills that are developed through consistent effort in an athletic endeavor. Just as males learn the value of pushing themselves beyond their comfort zone, so will females. This confidence will be communicated via body language and will teach others to take your daughter seriously. More important, it will teach her to take herself seriously.

Particularly encouraging is the evidence from some new studies which show that females are eminently "coachable." In a survey of 127 coaches, John Anderson, director of the counseling center at the U.S. Air Force Academy, reports that female athletes rate high on "mental toughness," determination, sensitivity, motivation, body awareness, physical endurance, persistence, concentration, and realistic goal setting.[1]

When you are encouraging your daughter in athletics, it is important to be physically present at her games or meets. In my school district the football stands and gym bleachers would be full whenever there was a male-dominated sporting event. Standing-room only. When the girls teams were playing, however, a paltry few would show up.

When I asked Terrie Ann if her father came to her games, she responded with great enthusiasm. "Oh, yes," she said proudly, "every single one. That's the thing I remember more than anything else."

If your daughter has a boyfriend, encourage him to go as well. Let him know you expect it. Little hints like, "You're going to be at Lori's game on Saturday, aren't you? I'll pick you up if you need a ride," will be enough to get the point across. If she has a brother with whom she has a close relationship, it wouldn't hurt him to attend as well to support her belief that her athletic endeavors are important.

One word of warning about females and sports. Eating disorders, which are discussed at great length in Chapter 11, have a disconcerting way of showing up in female athletes. In a recent study conducted at Michigan State University, 182 female athletes were surveyed. Thirty-two percent admitted to strategies of weight control that are symptomatic of eating disorders. Among the strategies used were diet pills (amphetamines and over-the-counter pills), laxatives, diuretics, and self-induced vomiting. Binging and purging (the behavior of bulimics and about half of all anorexics) was most prevalent among gymnasts.[2] Compulsive exercise (especially among runners) is another method of weight control that can become dangerous. Another area of activity which tends to produce females with eating disorders is ballet. Anorexia is the most common among ballerinas, but bulimia is also reported.

Be aware of the symptoms and behaviors of eating disorders, for they can become life-threatening. Do not assume that if your daughter does not *appear* to have a weight problem, she has been spared. Be aware that many girls are quite successful at hiding their problem from their parents for months, even years. Read Chapter 11 carefully and learn to recognize the signs.

TELEVISION GAMES

Watching television does not have to be a total waste of time. In fact, it can be a golden opportunity to discuss how *not* to live life. In other words, television can be used as a tool for instruction even when it is bad. Remember it is the passive, noncritical viewing and absorption of television that is so deadly.

Watching television with your daughter (particularly the commercials rife with sexist attitudes) can provide the right moment to let your daughter hear your beliefs about females as well as the chance to make her aware of the subtleties of sexism and how saturated our culture is with it. First, it will train your daughter to become aware of sexism and make her a critical viewer, which is essential if you want to prevent her absorption of sexism like a sponge. Second, it provides an opportunity for you to express your feelings in a fairly natural way, by simply commenting on what you are viewing. This way, it doesn't seem quite so contrived.

When you notice something sexist on television, never sit passively by and not express your disapproval. For example, the other day I watched a commercial in which the all-American family had just been through the ordeal of "moving day." Dad's shirt was all smelly and needed to be laundered. Cut to next shot of Dad sitting on the couch with the kids in his freshly laundered shirt, and Mom saying, "You're going to have to sleep in it if I don't find your pajamas!" I thought to myself, "Why does *she* have to find his pajamas? He's a grown man. He ought to be able to find his own pajamas."

In another commercial, members of a family were all suffering from a variety of minor injuries, and Dad was getting babied just like the children. Mom was busily tending to everyone. A father could make the simple comment, "Have you ever noticed how it is always the woman tending and nurturing everyone? How come no one ever tends to Mom?'' or ''Can you imagine what this commercial would look like if it were Mom acting like a baby with her hurt finger and Dad cooing over her as if she were five years old?''

You may not think these are major issues, but the cumulative effect of these little sexist episodes is devastating over time. Likewise, the cumulative effect of hearing an enlightened opinion on the subject will educate your daughter about nonpassive viewing and help block the negative effects of the sexist programming to which she will inevitably be exposed.

Of course, the key is that you first have to learn to see sexism for yourself before you can make appropriate comments to your daughter. Unfortunately, most of us are so accustomed to seeing women and men in their assigned roles that unless it is blatantly sexist, we don't even notice. For that reason, turn it into a game while the commercials are on. Whoever sees the greatest number of examples of sexism gets to be served their favorite snack. (At first, let your daughter win sometimes, so that *you* can serve *her* the snack.) Make a rule that particularly subtle examples get double points!

Another fun game is to imagine the commercial with men doing what the women are doing and vice versa. I and a friend of mine howled with laughter one night at the mental picture of a man reclining on his carpet, giving sensuous glances to the camera while lovingly caressing this beloved carpet with the palm of his hand and talking about his ''relationship'' with the carpet.

A sad commentary on this game is that, after you have played it awhile, you will notice that having women play the men's roles seems fine, but having the men play the women's roles strikes us as hilarious. There are two reasons for this. First, women are so often portrayed doing silly things, we don't even notice how silly they appear until we put a man in that position. Second, as a society we devalue the activities of women, and this becomes painfully clear when you put a man in that role. This will all become quite obvious when you play this little game with your daughter during family television watching. When that happens, you can seize the opportunity for another enlightening discussion.

There is yet another activity for which television can be exploited. Suppose you have just finished watching some detective show, or cop show, or something involving an adventure. At the exciting moments or the turning point of the plot, ask your daughter what *she* would have done in that situation. Ask her if she thinks the actions taken by the main character were clever or stupid, wise or dangerous, and if she can think of other ways the situation could have been handled. This works especially well with VCRs. Simply stop the action at the moment before the main character has begun to take steps to solve the problem and ask your daughter what she would do if she found herself in a similar situation.

One father of two daughters and a son tried this with his family. He called me several weeks after the workshop to tell me it had become a favorite pastime of his family. They would rent a mystery or detective movie and stop it periodically so the whole family could debate what they would do if they were the famous detective, cop, etc. Everyone was allowed his or her say individually. They would also stop it to discuss the clues in the case and see who could solve it the fastest. He said even after a few weeks he could see a change in his daughters. They were viewing television more critically, thinking independently about their own actions in a given situation, and just generally acting more confident about expressing their opinions.

The main character needn't be a female. In fact, asking her to think about what she would do in a situation which is normally reserved for males helps her see herself as capable of expressing the range of behavioral choices we talked about earlier. Imagining herself as one who may possibly be in that situation, she begins to think about the proper action to take rather than about who is going to rescue her.

A final word about old movies (whether you rent them or see them in a revival). Some old movies are very sexist, particularly those of the fifties. Certainly many are very enjoyable and worthwhile; however, if you notice sexist views being presented (and keep an eye out for the subtle ones), be sure to discuss them with your daughter both before and after the movie.

Recently a friend and I went to see *Lady and the Tramp*. It was a charming and heartwarming movie, but my friend, a male, made the remark that it should have had a PG rating (parental guidance suggested) due to its very sexist nature. I thought his point was well taken, and so I pass it along to you.

Finally, many movie heroines of the thirties and forties, à la Bacall, Crawford, Stanwyck, and Davis, make great role models for girls. They often portrayed women who were assertive, street-smart, wise-cracking dames who didn't take a lot of lip from anyone. Consider these the next time you go to the movie store. (For teenage girls, you may want to then rent a Doris Day or

Gidget movie from the fifties and compare the heroines in a family discussion. Sounds like so much fun, I wish I could be there!)

S E R V I N G

One of the expectations society has of females that your daughter will learn is to serve. She will observe females serving others in a variety of circumstances—teaching, nursing, "secretarying," mothering—all serving and caring for others.

In order to change her belief that it is her duty as a female to serve others, she is going to need more than just verbal support. She will have to actually observe others (forget this euphemism; the "others" I am referring to are males) in the role of serving as well. Furthermore, you must teach her that females, as well as males, deserve the right and the privilege of being served on occasion.

For this reason, I recommend that males in the household take their turn not just preparing dinner, but also serving it and cleaning up afterward. During the males' serving night, the females may do whatever they choose, watch television, talk on the phone, sleep. They should be totally freed from kitchen responsibilities when it is not their turn. This privilege must be granted without any guilt or obligation attached to it.

In this way, you inculcate in your daughter the expectation that she, as well as the male population, deserves to be served once in a while. Let's face it, everybody deserves to be served once in a while. Since many males out there are still being raised with the expectation that they will be served, your daughter is very likely to fall in with one some day. If you want her to assert her rights when the time comes, you must start now; otherwise, she will fall into the same old trap most women fall into. Instead of spending her time writing her Ph.D. or studying for the bar exam, she will be preparing meals or feeling guilty if she's not.

By witnessing her father serving her mother, or her brothers serving the family, your daughter will have behavioral evidence that her family is truly egalitarian and democratic. Furthermore, she will acquire certain expectations of a future husband, the kind of expectations that will ensure she picks a true helpmate rather than a kingly type who expects to be served and cares not if it interferes with her goals and aspirations.

To illustrate how unusual it still is to observe a man in a serving role (unless he is a waiter), I would like to relate a rather uneventful but telling little scene that I recently witnessed. It took me completely by surprise.

I went to visit a friend I had not seen in quite some time. I had met her husband only briefly. When I first arrived, it was her husband who asked me if I would like something to drink. It was a refreshing surprise because it was the first time in my experience that a husband had offered hospitality *even though his wife was around to do it for him.* Later, as my female friend and I sat and talked in another room, he came in to ask if he could make us sandwiches. I declined. My friend said yes she would like one. Once again I was astonished when a few minutes later he came in with a sandwich on toast, halved diagonally, complete with apple slices, a few grapes, and a frosty drink. He set it down on the table with a napkin and asked her if there was anything else she would like! I know women who would kill for this man and not because they are castrating bitches who want to dominate in a relationship, but because they receive so few acts of gentle kindness and consideration such as this.

Let your daughter observe this kind of behavior from you so that she learns that men also know how to nurture and give care. If she feels it is natural, as she surely will if she observes it at home, she will come to expect this from the males in her life and thus be more likely to choose a mate who will treat her with the same kind of care and respect she observed her father give her mother. Anything less is second best.

CONTROLLED IMAGINATION

The Soviets have used it in the training of their athletes with remarkable success. Americans, from salespeople to executive officers, from dieters to athletes, are discovering its power to change lives and achieve goals. "It" has been given a variety of names, from "mind over matter" to "controlled imagination," but regardless of the label we choose, it is a potent and easily accessible tool. Visualizations are but one of the many tools of our imaginations available to change our beliefs about ourselves and others.

Visualizations work because they utilize both sides of the brain; educational research has shown that students learn more and retain information longer if they utilize both hemispheres of the brain. Vsualizations are also powerful tools to alter self-concept and establish a healthy self-image. You can apply the same strategies used by athletes and successful salespeople to help your daughter overcome the debilitating effects that sexism has on her self-esteem.

Visualizations for our purposes work best as a type of bedtime story activity, taking the place of the more traditional bedtime story. First, they will get your daughter in the mood for sleep by allowing her to relax and use her imagination. Second, they will linger in her mind as she drifts off to sleep, perhaps influencing her night dreams in a positive way. Third, they give your daughter a chance to experience the warmth of your undivided attention. (Remember, there is no need to be self-conscious. Your daughter is not a *New York Times* critic. She will be too busy basking in the undivided attention she is receiving from the most important man in her life to criticize your stories!) Most significantly, they will begin to establish a new image of herself that your daughter can access at will and utilize to her benefit as the years (and challenges) go by.

It is not necessary to do them every night. One or two per week could make a tremendous difference when added to the other activities and recommendations made elsewhere in this book.

While I have provided visualizations for you to use, it is also quite fun to make them up on your own. This has several advantages. First, it provides the opportunity to "tailor-make" the visualization story to meet the individual needs of your particular daughter, and second, it gives you the opportunity to sharpen your own creativity. Some of you may even discover heretofore unrecognized genius as storytellers. Perhaps whole new careers in novels or screenwriting await you! Don't laugh. That is exactly how Richard Adams, author of *Watership Down*, got started (not to mention Lewis Carroll and the "Alice" books).

For those of you with a natural flair for inventing plots and developing characters, it will be easy to find the time to create your stories. You already realize that they can be created anywhere, anytime. For those of you less familiar with the active use of your imagination, it will require a little more conscious effort. How about on your way home from work? Whether you are driving your own car or using public transportation, the ride home from work is a perfect time to let your mind wander and a great way to release from the day's tensions.

Simply allow your mind to wander off on a fanciful journey, an adventure you have always dreamed of, or a cherished goal you have nursed over the years. Feel free to embellish, elaborate, weave intricate subplots. Go heavy on adventure and risk, dragon slaying (figurative or literal), and windmill tilting. When your story is exactly the way you want it, substitute your daughter as the main character, the hero.

The purpose is to change your daughter's belief about herself as a helpless victim or fragile creature in need of protection which society may have fostered. When she learns to *see* and *experience* herself as a brave and daring figure in the visualizations you create for her, she begins to see herself as a brave and daring figure in real life. This new self-image will be the foundation from which she acquires the persistence, fortitude, and courage she will need to face the risks, the rigors, and the obstacles that are an inevitable part of high-level achievement.

The following pages present some possible story ideas to get you going.* They are designated by age level and behavior you wish to target. There are different stories for different purposes, as you will see. Use them as a jumping-off place for your own ideas. Be loose. Have fun. Play.

Basic Directions for Any Bedtime Story Visualization

Begin by having the child lie down, close her eyes, and relax. Be sure to use a quiet, soothing tone of voice. Talk slowly, and give her time to visualize the scenes you suggest.

First, have your daughter just concentrate on breathing in and breathing out. Give directions. "Inhale, fill up your lungs. (Pause.) Now exhale. (Pause.) Inhale. (Pause.) Exhale." Allow this concentrated breathing for about a minute, as she relaxes and clears her mind. Talk her through her body and teach her to start with her toes and relax all the way to her head.

When she is relaxed, tell your daughter to imagine there is a movie screen on her eyelids, where she can see pictures just like in the movies. Explain to her that the pictures she will see will come from the story you are about to tell her.

Visualization 1
Ages: 4 to 6
Targeted behavior: Competition and self-esteem

Tonight we are going to have fun! Close you eyes and pretend you are looking at a big movie screen. On that screen is *you*! You look so happy. See that big smile on your face? You are running and

---

*If any of the visualizations bother you, from the point of view of physical danger, ask yourself "Would this bother me for a son?" If your answer is yes, then you are being a concerned parent. If your answer is no, you are being (sorry to have to say it) sexist.

playing with all your friends. (Pause.) See, there is _____ and _____. (Use names of child's playmates.) Everyone decides to have a race. You can hardly wait. You like to run as fast as you can. You feel good. You are ready. (Pause.) You *know* you can win. (Pause.) See yourself line up with your friends at the starting line. Someone yells, "On your mark." You feel happy and excited. Then you hear, "Get set." Your whole body can hardly wait to spring off the starting line and run as fast as the wind. Finally you hear, "Go!" and you are off! You are running right beside all your friends. Everyone is smiling and having a great time. So are you. (Pause.) The sun is warm and the sky is blue. (Pause.) You run as fast as you can. There is no one in front of you! (Pause.) Now you really pour on the steam. Your body does what you tell it to do and is fast and light. (Pause.) The wind blowing your hair back feels good on your face. (Pause.) Before you know it you are across the finish line! You are first! You won! (Pause.) You are so happy. It feels so good to run fast. You are laughing and smiling. (Pause.) Your friends come up and shake your hand and tell you what a great race you ran. You thank them. (Pause.) You feel happy and proud. Running fast is fun. You like your body. (Pause.) You love to win races, too.

Visualization 2
Ages: 4 to 6
Targeted behavior: Safety

Tonight you are going to learn what to do if someone you don't know talks to you. Someone you don't know is called a "stranger." You are not scared though, because you are smart and you know what to do.

See yourself playing with your friends or walking to school. (Name specific children your child spends time with.) You are having fun. You are all laughing and talking. A car drives up. There is a stranger in it. A stranger is a person you do not know, a person you have not seen before. (Pause.) The stranger asks you to get in the car. You do *not* get in the car. It doesn't matter if the stranger is a man or a woman. You do *not* go. (Pause.) Tell your friends that you should all leave. (Pause.) The stranger tries to tell you that something has happened to Mommy or Daddy. The stranger says we are hurt and we told the stranger to come and get you. (Pause.) You still do not go. (Pause.) *You know that no matter what, we would never send a stranger to come and get you.* (Pause.) See yourself walking quickly away. You know the stranger is not telling the truth. You are too smart to be fooled. (Pause.) You keep on walking (or running) to the nearest safe place. You get your playmates to come with you. If they do not come, you go anyway. See yourself walking away. (Pause.) No matter *what* the stranger tries to tell you, you don't listen. You don't feel afraid, you just know not to listen to the person. (Pause.) Remember, it doesn't matter if it is a man or a woman. If you don't know the person, don't talk to him or her. (Pause.) If Mommy and Daddy are not home, go to _____'s house. (Give the name of a trusted neighbor.) Tell us or _____ exactly what the stranger said and what he or she looked like. You do not feel afraid because you are safe. (Pause.) You are safe because you were so smart and so brave. (Pause.) Smart and brave. (Pause.) You feel happy to be safe. You are glad you are smart. You are happy to see us. Being brave feels good, too.

(*Note:* For an older child, it is wise to suggest during the visualization that she get license-plate numbers, car color, physical description, etc.)

Visualization 3
Ages: 4 to 6
Targeted behavior: Risk taking

You are outside playing with friends. It is a nice, warm day. Can you see what you are wearing? One of the little boys says to you, "I'll bet you can't jump as far as I can." You say, "OK. Let's see."

Now all the kids are real excited. Some think he can jump farther than you can. Others think you can jump farther.

Someone draws a starting line. He backs up from the line, takes a run at it, and you watch as he sails far into the air. (Pause.) When he lands, someone marks the spot. You go over and look at it. It's pretty far. You are not sure if you can jump that far, but you are excited to try. (Pause.)

You back up from the starting line. It is a little scary because he has jumped so far. (Pause.) You are a little worried that maybe you will fall trying to jump that far, but you are not afraid. (Pause.)

You keep your eye right on a spot just beyond where he landed. You aim for that spot with your whole body. (Pause.) You take a big, deep breath and run as fast as you can. When your foot hits the starting line, you push off and leap into the air as far as you can. Feel your whole body stretch toward that point. (Pause.) Feel light as a feather as you sail through the air. That was easy! That was fun! You land and slide on the dirt, skinning your knee, but it doesn't hurt because you had so much fun in the jump. (Pause.) When you slid in the dirt, it messed up the mark someone had made on his landing spot, so there is no way to tell who won. You don't care. You had so much fun trying to beat him. (Pause.) That was the fun part. (Pause.) It also felt great flying through the air like that! (Pause.) It was so much fun trying to beat him that next time you bet *him* he can't jump as far as *you*!

Visualization 4
Ages: 7 to 9
Targeted behavior: Adventure, risk taking, self-esteem

Tonight's story will star you as an astronaut assigned to a great adventure—a space walk outside the capsule! First, I want you to see yourself inside the space vehicle. (Pause.) What does it look like around you? See the dials, gauges, and three-dimensional computer graphics on video screens? All around you is information-gathering and retrieval-system hardware. You understand what it all means. You are a highly trained professional. (Pause.) Even though your living quarters are cramped, you are used to it after your many months of rigorous training. Watch yourself as you program the computers, read computer printouts, and take notes from the information appearing on the video screens. (Pause.)

It is almost time for your space walk. Mission control back on earth OK's the operation, saying all systems are ''go.'' The commander of this flight, Dr. Mary-Beth Pennington, advises you it is time to put on the special suit. You can feel the excitement building inside you. (Pause.) Even a highly trained test pilot like yourself feels excited and anxious to participate in such a unique experience. It makes you feel proud to know you were chosen out of many who were considered for this special honor. (Pause.) Some of your colleagues help you get in the awkward suit you must wear. How does it feel? (Pause.) Just stand there for a moment and feel the excitement building. (Pause.)

At last you are ready. The hatch is opened and you squeeze your body through, feet first. You let go with your hands and feel your weightless body float gently out into the great, vast darkness of interstellar space. (Pause.) There is no sound. (Pause.) You do not feel afraid. You feel completely confident, relaxed, and alert. (Pause.) As you float beside the spacecraft, which is to the right of you, you think of it as your little home in outer space. (Pause.) Feel a great, big smile come over your face as you savor the beauty and tranquility of this exquisite moment. Even though the space around you is boundless and black, quiet and empty, you do not feel alone or afraid. (Pause.) You feel serene, quiet, happy, and secure as you experience the weightless float and effortless movement of your body through space. (Pause.) The view of Earth itself has been blocked by the spacecraft until this moment. Suddenly, you see it. (Pause.) You feel a lump in your throat as you observe the incomparable beauty of this lovely blue marble floating quietly in the darkness. (Pause.) You realize how fragile and precious is this little blue jewel we call Earth as it drifts silently through the millennia. (Pause.) You vow to use your scientific knowledge to protect this priceless gem and all the millions of tiny lives it supports. (Pause.) Now just allow yourself to drift along, delighting in this lovely experience as you float serenely off to sleep.

Visualization 5
Ages: 7 to 9
Targeted behavior: Risk taking, adventure, self-esteem

You are in a dense jungle. It is steaming hot. You are wearing shorts with lots of pockets, a short-sleeve shirt, also with lots of pockets, socks, hiking boots, and a hat with netting to keep the insects off your face. You have a pack on your back, and are carrying a knife to clear away jungle growth on the path. Your clothes are all stuck to your skin because it is so hot and sticky.

You are leading a group of archaeologists to an ancient Indian civilization site in Peru. You are their guide. Both men and women are relying on you to get them there safely.

You are on a narrow ledge on the side of a steep hill. The jungle is so thick here that you have to clear it off the ledge as you go. There once was a path here, but it is now so overgrown, it cannot be seen. In order to avoid getting lost, you stop the group while you consult your map and compass.

You realize that the group has veered slightly off course, so you get your bearings by hiking to a little ledge where you can look more carefully at the terrain around you. Suddenly, you hear a scream.

You run back to the group and discover someone lost his footing and fell off the ledge. You yell down to him and discover he is OK but has broken his leg. He is unable to walk on it.

Everyone turns to you for their instructions. You tie a technical knot using climbing rope, set your anchor points, and rappel down to get him. Once there, you do a quick examination of his injury. At least there are no compound fractures, you think with relief. At that point, you tie a splint to his leg and tie him to a rope, which the group will use to pull him up. Your main goal is to get him up to the group, where there is a doctor who can set the leg and you can radio for a rescue team.

Everything goes pretty smoothly except that he is in a lot of pain. You talk to him quietly and gently, soothing his nerves and relaxing him. You climb up after him.

Once the mission is accomplished, the doctor takes over. Everyone is so grateful to you for having gotten him to safety. You say thank you, but deep down you think to yourself, "It's all in a day's work!"

Visualization 6
Ages: 10 to 11
Targeted behavior: Self-esteem, nonstereotypical aspirations

Tonight, as you close your eyes, I want you to imagine a great concert hall. Hanging from the ceiling are huge and glorious crystal chandeliers which catch the light and throw multicolored rainbows on the wall. The seats are made of plush red velvet and all the wood and bannisters are hand-carved. (Pause.) Now I want you to see the audience waiting for the concert to begin. They are all dressed up in their finest clothes and jewelry, reading programs, talking quietly, and waiting for the concert to begin. (Pause.) The orchestra is already on stage, dressed in traditional black, tuning their instruments, and practicing difficult passages in the evening's program. (Pause.) The house lights dim, and the conductor walks onstage. *It is you!* (Pause.) See what you are wearing. (Pause.) See yourself clearly. You are onstage. Hear the audience applaud. (Pause.) Look out into the audience. All you can see are the bright globes of the stage lights and the people in the first three rows. Feel the heat from the stage lights. (Pause.) You can tell by the applause that it is a sold-out crowd. Nod to the audience and indicate your appreciation. Hear the audience gradually quiet down. Turn around and step up to the platform in front of the orchestra. (Pause.) See all your musicians straighten up and move their instruments into playing position. Smile at them. (Pause.) Enjoy the moment. (Pause.) Raise your arms in readiness, hold the pose, and begin to conduct the orchestra. (Pause.) Feel the musicians respond as you direct them through the music. (Pause.) See the musicians playing their instruments and concentrating. *Your* instrument is the orchestra itself. Feel it as you "play" the orchestra. (Pause.) Do not forget to keep hearing the music. Feel the music build in volume as you reach the end of the piece. See yourself bring your arms up as you bring the orchestra to the final, majestic chord. (Pause.) Suddenly, from behind you, comes a burst of applause. Turn around. See the audience standing up, applauding wildly, smiling and shouting. (Pause.) Turn around to your musicians and have them take a bow. See them all smiling at you, too. (Pause.) Bow. Bow again. Leave the stage. Hear the audience continue to applaud. Come back onstage. (Pause.) Feel the love the audience sends you in gratitude for the performance and the pleasure you and the orchestra have just given them. (Pause.) Accept that you are a hard worker, capable of putting in long hours of rehearsal to reach this goal. (Pause.) Relish the sense of fulfillment that you feel for a job well done.

Visualization 7
Ages: 10 to 12
Targeted behavior: Self-concept and body awareness

Tonight as you close your eyes, I want you to see a bright, sunny day. You are jogging. It is fall. (Pause.) The sun is warm on your back, while the crisp autumn air cools your skin. Smell the musty aroma of burning leaves. Let your eyes drink the gold and flame-colored leaves. As you jog along, look up at the bright sky, blue and inviting. (Pause.) Feel your feet pounding the ground as you run. Heel, toe. Heel, toe. Heel, toe. (Pause.) Feel your heart beating and the strength in your arms as they swing gracefully to help you run. (Pause.) Just relax and enjoy the rhythm and sway of your body as you slice your way smoothly through the autumn atmosphere. (Pause.) You begin to feel slightly winded. You feel your heart beating in your chest, but it is a good feeling. You are aware of every inch of your body as an efficient and powerful machine, from the top of your head to the tips of your fingers, down to your buoyant, powerful legs. (Pause.) Even though you are feeling slightly tired, the powerful swing of your arms, the bounce in your calves and thighs and the friendly blue sky encourage you to fully enjoy and appreciate your body. (Pause.) You feel good. (Pause.) You feel strong and coordinated. (Pause.) You know you could accomplish anything you set out to do. (Pause.) Now just allow yourself to feel the joy and pleasure of running until you are tired. (Pause.) Then gradually begin to slow your run down to a brisk walk. (Pause.) Finally, savor the satisfactions of using your body. Appreciate its power and its glory. Love it for serving you so faithfully. Allow yourself to drift off to sleep feeling proud, (pause) strong, (pause) and beautiful.

Obviously, the number and types of visualizations that can be generated are limited only by one's degree of creativity. The purpose of the simple examples shown above was to illustrate some basic points concerning visualizations. First, remember to pause and to repeat anything you want to emphasize. Second, create the kind of heroine your daughter would like to be: brave, courageous, daring, and loved by one and all.

Remember, although it is only a fantasy, it is designed to increase her self-esteem; therefore, lay on the bravery and admiration thick and heavy. Concentrate on the inner feelings of your daughter as you take her on these mental journeys. It is okay for her to feel nervous or anxious in the face of danger, as long as you make certain she vanquishes it with bravery, skill, and fortitude. Always end on a positive note, with your daughter experiencing warm, nourishing feelings and a high degree of self-confidence and self-love.

It is also important to know that studies have shown individuals retain facts better and longer when they are using both sides of their brain. Therefore, try not to give your daughter any misinformation or false facts in her visualizations, since she will have a tendency to learn and remember them!

Finally, here are some suggestions for some more visualizations should you need them. They have all been suggested by the fathers in my workshops.

Activities:

Climbing a tree
Programming a computer
Lifting weights
Repairing cars, appliances, etc.
Supervising a crew
Hang gliding
Skydiving
Operating large equipment
Building a fort

Leading a hike
Mountain climbing
Accepting the Nobel peace prize
Throwing and receiving a football
White-water river rafting
Skiing
The martial arts

Occupations:

Television camera operator
Politician
Astronaut
Pilot
Movie director
Doctor, dentist, surgeon
College professor
President of the United States
Physicist
Astronomer
Chemist
Explorer
Race car driver
Rabbi, minister, priest
Jockey
Fire fighter
Athlete
Dragon slayer
Sheriff
Bank president

Judge
Trial lawyer
CEO
Architect
Scuba diver
Mathematician
Chef
Rock musician
Jazz musician
Aerospace engineer
Geologist
Sportscaster
Circus performer (lion tamer, trapeze artist, tightrope walker)
Talk-show host
Police officer
Archaeologist
Admiral
General

AFFIRMATIONS

Another tool for enhancing self-image and improving performance is the use of affirmations. Affirmations are positive self-statements designed to counteract the negative statements that some of us have learned to repeat in our heads unconsciously and incessantly. Like visualizations, affirmations have been discovered and utilized by salespeople, athletes, and anyone attempting to overcome a habit of negative thought patterns.

For those of you unfamiliar with how affirmations work, the metaphor of the computer is useful. Basically, our minds work something like computers in that whatever we "program" in, we get back; sort of like the "garbage in, garbage out" phrase programmers are fond of using. We can program our minds with garbage, or we can program them with quality.

As young children many of us were programmed with negative, energy-draining "tapes" given us by well-meaning, and some not-so-well-meaning, parents, teachers, and childhood friends. They become like tapes playing automatically in our heads. These tapes tell us we are failures or losers and that there is something wrong with us (remember "What is wrong with you?" as a reflected appraisal?). These tapes are debilitating, and they defeat us even *before* we undertake a new project or set a new goal.

By the time we are adults, this debilitating style of self-talk has become so habitual the individual no longer even hears what is being said on a conscious level. However, the individual feels the enervating and devitalizing effects of it.

Affirmations are one way to gradually silence these voices. Since the mind can only think one thought at a time, flooding the mind with positive programming slowly crowds out the negative. But first, we must become aware of what the voices are saying so that when they begin, we can vigorously assert the positive statement and reprogram the tapes to play constructive, supportive comments automatically.

Your daughter will have been programmed with all manner of garbage from the society, her relatives, and her friends. Many parents are shocked when they discover some false belief a child is carrying around and wonder where in the world the child got *that* idea.

For example, one father in my seminars told of his little four-year-old daughter, who, when invited to go outside with her dad and "run as fast as we can," replied, "No daddy, I can't. I'm a girl." When he inquired further as to what that had to do with anything, she replied, "Girls can't run fast."

Her father had not the slightest idea where she had acquired this belief because he and his wife had always taken pains to ensure that nothing of the kind was ever even insinuated in their home. As he pressed further, he discovered that the little boy who lived next door was the one who had made this startling revelation. When his daughter asserted confidently that he was wrong, he argued vehemently that it must be true because his daddy had said so. The other children playing with them at the time all agreed, so his daughter changed her mind. (Ah, our old friend, peer pressure, doing its dirty work.)

Her father went on to say, "Actually I was lucky that it happened when it did because it was the summer of the 1984 Olympic games. Everytime a female runner or hurdler was on the television, I would go get Andrea and say, 'Look, Andrea, there's a girl who can run really fast, a lot faster than me!' Finally, after a while, she was convinced.

"The next time I said, 'Come on, Andrea, let's go out and run real fast,' she said, 'OK, Daddy!' I don't know what I would have done without those Olympic games."

The point I want to make here is that even if *you* have not implanted some kind of negative belief about the abilities of females, there is a strong possibility that others have. Be on guard for clues your daughter may inadvertently drop which show some of these negative influences at work. Factual information, supportive statements to the contrary from you, visualizations, and affirmations will help to counteract these influences.

Once again, for those of you who are unfamiliar with affirmations, a few words of explanation are in order before I explain how they can be designed to help your particular daughter specifically.

First, they must be written. Not dictated, not typed, not recited aloud. The reason for this is that writing them in longhand is a slow and arduous process. The very slowness of the act can be used to advantage, for as one writes, one begins to finally "hear" the little voice that has played unconsciously for so long; one is finally able to unmask the little demon.

For example, when I wanted to learn how to downhill-ski, I began writing the affirmation, "I, Nicky, am a strong and coordinated individual; therefore, I will learn to ski with ease and grace." As I wrote, I "heard" myself reply back, "Oh yeah? What about the time you tried to learn to water-ski? Remember how often you made a fool of yourself?" I repeated my affirmation, to which the voice replied, "What if you fall down and break your leg?" I repeated the affirmation. This time the voice tried a new tactic, "You'll probably fall trying to get on the chair lift, and they will have to stop it and everyone will be mad at you because they had to stand in line longer."

Prior to writing this affirmation, I had been unaware of this voice which had done such an effective job of discouraging me from skiing that I was a first-time, beginner skier at the age of thirty-three. And I am a Colorado native! When I thought about it, it had originally come from my mother, who, concerned with my dancing career, would always say, "What if you fall down and break your leg?"

The slowness of writing affirmations, then, allows the negative voice to be brought up to consciousness, where the writer can finally hear what the voice has been saying for years. Later, when the negative voice tries its usual tricks, while you are driving down the street or walking the dog, you will hear it, be able to repeat the affirmation and abolish the voice!

Some people feel as if they are lying when they write an affirmation which is as yet unfulfilled. For example, if you create an affirmation about hating cigarettes, and each time you write it, you are dying for a cigarette, it is easy to feel as if the affirmation is a complete hoax. When this happens, the affirmer needs to remember to use the affirmation to unmask what the inner voice is saying so that it can be replaced with something more constructive and supportive.

The second rule follows from the first: never try to argue with the voice. It is endlessly creative and will win the debate every time. Simply repeat the affirmation you have designed no matter what the voice replies. Bit by bit and ever so slowly the voice will begin to relinquish its hold on your belief system and be replaced by the new statement (affirmation) you have programmed in to take its place.

Finally, many of you may be familiar with subliminal tapes using affirmations, thousands of them, playing "beneath" the sounds of ocean waves or music. These may work, but I would advise teaching your daughter to write her *own* affirmations, which she has devised herself, because by personally tailoring them to meet a particular problem, they are more effective.

Affirmations pack a powerhouse of a wallop. The reason is that *although one cannot always control one's feelings, one can control the thoughts that trigger the feelings*. Once your daughter has grasped this concept, she will be light-years ahead of any person who tries to undermine her confidence and will be able to vanquish any situation which seems to block her path. Ultimately, she will have learned how to combat learned helplessness and free herself from the debilitating influences of society, friends, and even herself.

Here are some affirmations which are particularly useful and relevant to the young female. They can be kept in a "Journal of the Positive," where she also keeps a record of her daily successes or accomplishments. Since many young girls regularly write in a diary or journal, affirmations can be incorporated with a minimum of hassle. Furthermore, the affirmations offered below can be modified to meet any situation or to whatever degree the creator wishes. Remember to tell your daughter to always use her name when she writes her affirmations.

Affirmations for ages seven to nine:

1. I, _____, like myself. I'm glad I'm me.
2. I, _____, am smart, strong, and pretty.
3. I, _____, am happy and fun to be with.
4. I, _____, can run fast and jump high.
5. I, _____, like to try new things.

Affirmations for ages ten to seventeen:

1. I, _____, am strong, capable, and pretty.
2. I, _____, take control of my destiny whenever necessary.
3. I, _____, like my body. It is strong and coordinated and pretty to look at.
4. I, _____, think independently and act forcefully.
5. I, _____, handle myself in a competent and responsible manner.
6. I, _____, feel proud, energetic, confident, and lovable.
7. I, _____, have interesting things to say and opinions that count.
8. I, _____, look forward to new and exciting adventures.
9. I, _____, am an efficient problem solver. I do not get discouraged by obstacles, because I have confidence and the ability to handle myself with wisdom and maturity.
10. I, _____, value myself as a person. I have a lot to offer.

Additional affirmations for ages twelve to seventeen:

1. I, _____, am selective about the boys I like. They must measure up to *my* standards.
2. I, _____, am lovable and attractive. Boys like me because I am intelligent and fun to be around.

3. I, _____, say what I think, even if it is in disagreement with my friends or boys around me.
4. I, _____, do not take any form of abusive language or treatment from boys.
5. I, _____, do not let boys tell me what to do, how to think or what to wear. I make my own decisions.

While these affirmations are generalized to fit nearly every adolescent girl, they can be tailor-made (as the visualizations can be) to fit specific circumstances or a particular child's needs.

For example:

1. I, _____, feel confident for tomorrow's tryouts. Nothing can disturb my poise.
2. I, _____, feel relaxed and confident about tomorrow's test.
3. In tomorrow's game, I, _____, will play with ease and grace.
4. I, _____, keep my confidence strong and bright by joyfully releasing all negative thought.
5. I, _____, deserve (to win, be happy, feel good, etc.).
6. I, _____, am perfect and lovable just as I am.
7. I, _____, accept light and happy as my natural state.

As you can see, affirmations have infinite variety, just as the visualizations do. As time goes by, your daughter will become more proficient at creating her own and will be able to meet her own needs in very specific ways.

For very young girls, who cannot yet write, these affirmations can be said before falling asleep. Have your daughter relax and close her eyes, just as she does for the visualizations. Ask her to repeat after you any phrases that you think she would understand and benefit from. Here are some suggestions:

Affirmations for ages three to five:

1. I am smart.
2. I am strong.
3. I am pretty.
4. I feel happy.
5. I feel safe.

All of the above, not just one or two, should be repeated by your daughter. Obviously these can be altered, embellished, rearranged to suit your daughter's needs. Finally, they can be quite effective when used following a visualization just before falling asleep.

TEACHING A LOVE OF PERSONAL FREEDOM

A discussion of freedom is nearly as tricky as a discussion of risk taking. Most fathers want to maintain a certain degree of control over their daughters; they just differ on the degree of control.

If you want your daughter to value her freedom and independence, if you want to increase the likelihood that she would reject a potential boyfriend who was possessive, rigid, or controlling, then she must be given the *experience* of freedom. In other words, she will never miss what she hasn't had.

If she has been kept under rigid control by her parents, then it will not feel any different when a boy enters her life and begins setting up restraints or insisting she follow his lead. Since she will have already learned how to adapt to limitations set by others, it will not feel uncomfortable, and she will not put up a fight when her rights are threatened. She will not even *know* her rights are being threatened.

It happened to me. When I was in college I dated a boy my parents disliked intensely. One of the reasons was because he was extremely domineering and insisted on directing the course of my life.

At first, I kind of liked his controlling attitude. It was flattering, and I was touched by his "concern" over my affairs. Being twenty-one and in love, I made excuses for his behavior and interpreted his possessiveness as protectiveness. It made me feel safe.

After a while, however, his incessant questioning, his demanding attitude, and his insistence that I follow his lead became a thorn in the relationship. I began to feel trapped. One day I remember thinking, "God, he's worse than my parents! I had more freedom at home than I have with this guy." It was the beginning of the end.

Had I become accustomed to a tight rein during my years at home, I probably would not have chafed against his constraints as I did. Luckily, my parents had (accidentally) instilled a love for freedom and independence by having allowed a great deal of it while I was growing up.

I know this is difficult for many fathers to accept. Their fears for a daughter's safety are a major concern. I also realize that granting a daughter freedom depends, to a large extent, on the particular girl. Some daughters can be trusted with freedom because they have shown they make wise decisions, while others have made bad choices and must earn the right to freedom, as well as the trust of their parents.

However, consider this as food for thought. If you have a daughter whom you trust and who has learned to be responsible for her own safety, give her as much freedom and independence as *you* can tolerate. It will teach her to value her freedom as a cherished but fragile prize and to fight for it when it is threatened. Since females typically give up "everything" to become "slaves of love," whatever emphasizes the urgent need to zealously guard the precious right to personal freedom should be practiced and reinforced.

Checklist I

The following checklist represents an overview of the ideas presented thus far. At the end of the book will be another checklist summarizing the suggestions made from Chapters 9 through 11. Let me stress that simply reading the suggestions, without reading the explanatory material in the chapters themselves, will leave you with only a partial and inadequate understanding of the suggestions.

1. Never assume she may not be interested in a particular field.

2. Teach her repair skills, woodworking, electrical wiring, car maintenance, etc.

3. Give her a subscription to a magazine not traditionally chosen for girls, like *Omni*, *Popular Science*, *National Geographic*.

4. Encourage her to browse through your library, both professional and recreational.

5. Show her scientific diagrams, charts, graphs, etc., and explain them, even before she is actually ready for them. Do not make it an ordeal or a test, just some time spent together.

6. Counter negative input she has received like, "Girls are not supposed to be good in math." Maybe your daughter is the one who is.

7. Teach her to play poker, chess, backgammon, "Go," or any other game of strategy.

8. Teach her how to make paper airplanes and how to alter them to improve their aerodynamic properties. Experiment together.

9. Consider sending her to an all-girl school.

10. Teach her how to handle money. Begin on a simple level and progress to more sophisticated concepts. If you are not good with money, have your wife do it. If neither of you are, at least make her aware of what a handicap this can be and help her get some instruction from *someone*—friend, relative, or professional.

11. Pass on what you know about the business and professional worlds. Teach her what is expected of the participants in these worlds.

12. Think about what female role models (other than your wife) you would like your daughter to emulate and discuss them with her, giving your reasons for your choices.

13. Do not rescue prematurely!

14. Have high expectations.

15. Teach her that both feminine behavior and masculine behavior are available to her depending on the circumstance in which she finds herself. Teach her to modulate her behavior according to the circumstance rather than according to her gender. Teach her to be adaptive.

16. Help her overcome the stigma against girls and computers by doing the following:
    a. play video games together.
    b. let her "play" with your personal computer.
    c. verbally counter any negative input she may have received at school or elsewhere.
    d. encourage her to read computer magazines, but teach her to spot the high degree of sexism in these magazines that we discussed earlier.

    e. send her to computer camp if she has the interest.

    f. if she gets hooked into the "boys program; girls 'word process' " myth, debunk it immediately as per the suggestions in Chapter 3.

17. Teach her how to take risks and overcome fear.

18. Make sure your actions do not belie your words. Remember, real support goes far beyond mere lip service. (More about this in the following chapter.)

19. Be your daughter's friend. Avoid playing the role of authoritarian, softie or protector.

20. Take your daughter on Saturday errands with you.

21. Encourage participation in activities that contribute to a broad self-concept, which means encouraging participation in some traditionally masculine endeavors.

22. Pay attention to what kind of messages you are giving her brothers as well.

23. Pay attention to the unspoken messages of your behavior.

24. Provide behavioral evidence that indicates your belief in her abilities.

25. When teaching your daughter to take risks and master situations, do not incorporate war and sports models, ones that require you to act militaristically, rigidly, or without feeling. Be loving, kind, and humane in your approach to risk taking and assertive behavior. Do not shout and become impatient.

26. Reread the chapter entitled, "Self-Concept and the Importance of Daddy."

27. Read your daughter the brief biographies of the successful women offered in Appendix B. Take a trip to the library together to check out some books on her (or your) favorites.

28. Remember it is never too late to alter the direction or tone of your relationship with your daughter. If you have already made some mistakes you would like to correct, reread "Delivering Difficult Communications" in this chapter.

29. The hardest thing of all: remember that your daughter's life is her own and regardless of how much you may want her to pursue a particular profession or field, the final decision is still hers. (Remember this for your sons as well.)

CHAPTER 9

❧

Male Advocacy

The need for male advocacy in recognition and support of female talent is absolute. Although it is inevitable that females will continue to progress, it is just as certain to be an arduous uphill climb if they lack the support of those in a position to help.

Generally speaking, men are the primary people in positions of rank and authority. Therefore, they play a key role in the development of female potential, on the job and off. With a strong male support system behind her, a woman can progress rapidly and smoothly, just like a man with the same mentorship and network behind him. Without this support, her climb can be a struggle bogged down with emotional baggage men do not experience in their rise to the top. Sometimes, this conflict can drain her of her will and energy to succeed. (It is true that other women who have made it can be mentors as well, but unfortunately, women in key positions remain enough of a minority that to rely on their support is risky indeed.) But what has all this to do with your role in the development of potential in your daughter?

If your desire to help your daughter is sincere, then ideally your commitment to this goal must go beyond your role as a father to that of your broader role as a male participant in society. Why? Because change does not take place in a vacuum. Your protected little home environment does not exist as an island unto itself; it exists against the larger backdrop of the society. If that society remains resistant to accepting the achievements of females, then ultimately your daughter's struggle intensifies.

The reality is that there are still countless numbers of men who do not want to see females achieve and progress. Some believe their position of power is their right and privilege. Others guiltily perceive that it serves their needs to keep women in their place. A few actually believe that females are inferior. Still others perpetuate the concept of the natural subservience of women. Some simply fear change. Whatever the reason, the result is the same— a world against which your daughter must fortify herself if she is to overcome the narrow, ignorant prejudices of those who would use their power and authority to obstruct her path. Consequently, it must be the job of those who believe in the development of female talent to create a world willing and able to accept feminine contributions. The sooner this happens, the less your daughter must struggle.

You can be in the vanguard of this change. It won't be easy. Being among the first is always a challenge. The world will someday recall the men who had the courage to promote female potential before it was fashionable and regard them with respect, but until then, you may be required to endure the taunts of those less enlightened than yourselves. I am not being melodramatic. As you will see in the rest of this chapter, the kind of behavior I am referring to goes beyond the safe confines of home to the public arenas of work, politics, and community involvement. It will require courage, commitment, and clear vision.

We will be discussing a variety of options through which you can demonstrate your solid support of talented females and thereby remain faithful to rule number 1 of fathering: actions speak louder than words; behavior is a more accurate gauge of support than verbal encouragement alone. The first set of options involves your personal interactions with others—your wife, your daughter, other family members, and male friends of yours. The second set examines your social interactions with other men in groups and how these interactions contribute to your public image, which, in turn, will influence your degree of motivation and commitment to the issue of female achievement.

A word of warning. From the fathers in my seminars I have learned that the actions required of male advocates can be threatening for a variety of reasons. We will go into these reasons in greater depth later. However, for now, suffice it to say that because these actions can be personally threatening, many fathers choose to diminish their importance by labeling them as ''frills,'' not very important in the overall scheme of things. However, like the other suggestions in this book, they carry a potent message to your daughter as she observes you interacting in the world. If you find yourself thinking, "Oh, I don't really need to do that," stop and ask yourself, "Am I afraid of what other men will think?" If the answer is yes, it is time to reevaluate your motivations and degree of commitment to your daughter and her potential.

To understand how the other roles you play (besides Daddy) influence your daughter's chances of success, we will take what seems to be a circuitous route. Eventually, our detour will lead us back to the topic of your participation as a male advocate and what it means to your daughter, so try to be patient during the detour. It is a necessary part of the journey.

The question is, quite simply, why is there a lack of female representation among the recognized geniuses of the western world? If indeed women are as intelligent and creative as men, then where are the female Shakespeares, Beethovens, Einsteins, and Edisons? It is a genuinely provocative question and a significant one for our purposes.

A book entitled *A Room of One's Own*, by Virginia Woolf, presents an insightful analysis of this intriguing question, and we will look at it in greater depth. But first, it is pertinent to look at Virginia herself, a brilliantly gifted writer and thinker who enjoyed strong male mentorship throughout her troubled life.

Her father, though definitely not a good role model due to his dictatorial and demanding behavior, nevertheless did provide little Virginia with unparalleled intellectual stimulation. He was to instill in her a love of books and the "examined" life. He developed her critical thinking skills at an early age by expecting her to read books, form opinions, and be able to discuss and defend them. He encouraged her to be intellectually adventurous, and when she was fifteen, he expanded her horizons tenfold by giving her carte blanche to his famous library, saying to her, "Read what you like."[1]

Later, Virginia married Leonard Woolf, an equally great mind and an extraordinarily sensitive man who respected, loved, and cared for Virginia even during her periods of madness. He recognized in her the imagination and perceptions of a great artist and was enthralled by the depth and breadth of her intellect. But Virginia was vulnerable (she suffered from what today would probably be diagnosed as a manic-depressive condition) and required a very structured and protected environment. She was sexually unresponsive as well. Leonard adjusted his life to meet the stringent needs of Virginia's illness as well as her genius and provided the emotional support she required to cling tenuously to her sanity and develop her great talent. Today, we can thank Leonard as much as Virginia for the great works of this gifted artist, for without his sacrifice, she may have never had the opportunity to create.

Virginia Woolf was concerned with the lot in life that most females in her society endured, and as was stated previously, examined the problem of female geniuses in her book *A Room of One's Own*. According to Woolf, a "great contribution," that culmination of an innate gift and sheer grit, requires two essentials beyond the raw talent and perseverance of the individual. These two essentials at first seem deceptively simple, but upon further reflection reveal profound implications for the development of talent in females. These two essentials are, quite simply: time and space.

An artist with a great gift or with genius (or any calibration thereof, for what we are discussing is a matter of degree, not substance) can produce nothing of value if subjected to a constant stream of interruptions. Creativity thrives best in an environment where unbroken time is available, during which the intense demands of critical thinking and problem solving can be met. To withhold these essentials (of uninterrupted time and the space which permits it) is to hinder the process to whatever degree they are withheld. Constant intrusions and lack of privacy are anathema to the processes of critical thinking and problem solving.

And what is the reality of the lives of most women who also happen to be mothers? Even in today's so-called liberated society? The truth of the matter is that child care requires an almost total sacrifice of the right of privacy—in terms of both time and space. The infinite needs of a growing child demand that the adult caretaker forfeit his or her privacy. Since in most cases the primary caretakers are still women, it is their time which is interrupted, their space which is intruded upon, their contributions which never see the light of day. By the time children are raised, it is often too late to make the kind of major contributions that require years of dedicated study and commitment.

While it is always possible to cite exceptions to the rule, for the most part, these realities will weigh heavily on your daughter. She must be made aware of them in order to make realistic choices for her future. She cannot escape the expectations placed on her by society or the decisions she will face concerning her own reproductive destiny. This is inevitable. What can be done, however, is to provide her with the facts of motherhood, its sacrifices as well as its rewards, in order to facilitate enlightened decision making on her part.

It is important to bear in mind that we are not discussing holding down a job and being a mother. Many women accomplish this difficult task with competence and grace (and often, a good deal of exhaustion). What we are discussing is achievement, the chance to make a lasting contribution. Since the demands of motherhood will intrude upon your daughter's time and space and will diminish proportionally your daughter's opportunity to achieve, it is imperative that she be made aware of these realities. In so doing, you provide the tools of choice to make enlightened decisions, rather than the romantic visions of "gootchy" little babies which most young females currently use to make their choices.

Lest I alienate every mother (or would-be mother) by implying that motherhood is a bad choice, or every father by implying that fathers lack a sense of responsibility for child care, let me reiterate two points.

First, to women: motherhood is a viable, fulfilling, and natural option *for some women*. Let's face it, though, most of us never heard the truth about the role—its sacrifices, its loneliness. We held rolypoly, adorable little babies in our arms and felt the maternal blood rise in our veins. We were total innocents concerning the realities. Since most girls still see only this lopsided version, it is essential to present both sides of the story. Second, to men: of course fatherhood carries responsibilities. No rational person would suggest otherwise. But the actual minute-by-minute daily interaction with a child still remains a female obligation in most households. These facts must be clearly understood by your daughter. To allow her to make her life choices based on rose-colored illusions is not only unfair but counterproductive to her achievement.

Males do not have to contend with a choice in this area. They just accept that they will have both because the woman will assume the role of primary caretaker. Even though it *is* often the case that a family interferes with a man's goals and aspirations, it is certainly not something he confronts as an adolescent or young adult. (It could be argued that he should.) At any rate, the point is: it does not even occur to him that this is a possibility.

Females recognize at an extraordinarily tender age, however, that it is different for them. Remember the pregnant doctors? This was an attempt through play to fuse divergent roles and resolve the future conflict of their adult lives. When we encourage a young girl to go out and achieve, we must remember that a high level of skill and sophistication is required to sort out the choices and priorities. As was previously mentioned, this can be a colossal task for a mature woman, much less an adolescent.

At this point, you may be wondering what your daughter's reproductive destiny has to do with your role as her father, not to mention what the other roles you play have to do with her achievement. They are all interrelated and interdependent. We will use both the insights and life of Virginia Woolf as a central point around which to discuss the interrelatedness of your roles as father, husband, and male participant in society. We will then discuss what these roles have to do with your role as a male advocate for females in general.

First, if you accept Woolf's contention that motherhood severely curtails a woman's opportunity to achieve other goals, then your feelings toward motherhood for your daughter may need some sorting out as well, because whatever you feel and/or believe will be communicated to her. For example, do you encourage her sense of adventure, but secretly see her as a traditional homemaker and mother? Perhaps you have dual expectations—the old "you can have it all" syndrome. While there is certainly nothing wrong with this approach, it is best to keep in mind that the degree of developmental maturity required to cope effectively with the rigors of achievement *and* the responsibilities of motherhood is beyond the scope of most young women. As Woolf correctly observes, it becomes impossible to ignore the duties of child care, so it is the area of achievement that takes secondary position.

Consequently, then, a father should examine his own expectations of role fulfillment by his daughter. If he sends double messages, he will be contributing to the conflict she will face. If he has his own feelings and beliefs sorted out, he will naturally behave in a more consistent fashion.

Remember Deana Bennett and her two sisters? Listen to how thoroughly her father had internalized the undifferentiated expectations he had for his daughters and his son.

"I really don't believe my father ever thought about any of his daughters having children. Isn't that something?

"I remember one time saying to him that I had made the decision to go into business. It was truly a life choice because of the motherhood issue. I reminded him that my decision sort of ruled out children because I really couldn't manage the two. He paused and gave me a blank look. It was obvious that it had never occurred to him it might be a problem. It was his first realization.

"I think my father would have been disappointed if we had chosen traditional roles for ourselves, because he had trained us for other things. He would have considered it a big mistake.

"When my two sisters did have babies, it was kind of a surprise to him. It didn't cross his mind that there was anything unusual that each of my sisters got up just three weeks after birth to go back to work.

"Actually, now that I think about it," she adds with a chuckle, "it never crossed his mind they might stay home and raise them!"

Many women today are trying to have careers and raise children, but they pay a heavy price. The conflict spawned by the feminine desire to nurture in conjunction with the desire to achieve causes many women to exhaust themselves trying to do it all. They begin to feel like anything less is some kind of moral reflection on them. Women who are "just" homemakers are made to feel lazy and unproductive and must fight to maintain their feelings of self-worth. Women who are career-oriented professionals are made to feel unnatural and masculine and must fight to maintain their femininity.

Again, let me stress that it can be done. There are women who raise children and make lasting contributions to society. But it takes an extraordinary kind of woman to do this. Furthermore, it requires the help of the husband/father as well, and there is no guarantee that your daughter will marry the type of man who will do this. Therefore, it is crucial that you make her aware of three things: (1) childcare responsibilities will likely fall primarily to her, (2) the demands of motherhood will impose on her time and privacy, and (3) the consequences of these demands will affect her ability to create and achieve.

Some fathers have said this is a mother's job, but suppose a mother, for whatever reasons, is unwilling or unable to model a different kind of choice for your daughter? If this is the case, you, as her advocate, must take the responsibility for making your daughter aware of the responsibilities and sacrifices she will be making if she chooses motherhood over achievement. Furthermore, since this is yet another issue where male approval enters in, your stand on the issue can be a major influence. Perhaps for your daughter motherhood is a better choice, but the decision should be based on facts, not on wistful illusions.

Finally, in households where the mother stays home, the father usually represents the world of adventure, wheeling and dealing, smoke-filled boardrooms, and major mergers. Therefore, a daughter is more likely to pay heed to a father's advice in the world of business, academics, or finance. This is unfortunate but often true.

One successful businesswoman put it like this: "My mother is a very intelligent woman. She was married late in life compared to her peers, at twenty-five, and took care of herself for years. She put herself through college. But whenever it came to advice about the world, she just sort of left everything to my father. He was the one who taught us how businesses work and how to deal with people in a businesslike manner. She let him form us in that area.

"She was just tickled pink that there was food on the table, and her bills were paid, and this man was kind to her. In spite of her intelligence and experience, it never seemed to us kids that she was anything other than a person who was at our beck and call. Our father was the worldly authority."

Let us return for a moment to the issue of time and space as mandatory to the creative process. We are all somewhat familiar with the following scene, whether as a moment from our own lives, or a moment from those of friends and relatives: a young mother anxiously keeps her children away from a certain room in the house, a room with a door closed, fortified against the incessant interruptions of a household. This same young mother not only keeps the children from knocking on this door, she ensures that they are quiet so as not to disturb the peace that must also surround this room. What is in this mysterious room? Why is the door locked against the world? Is it a gravely ill human being? Is it a feebleminded family member? No, it is Daddy writing his dissertation for his Ph.D. or studying for his law exams.

I do not blame the father of these children, who must indeed have the quiet and space in which to create and study. I do not begrudge him this luxury, because it is a requirement if he is to achieve his goals. But, gentle reader, I ask you to visualize the same scene with your daughter being the individual behind the closed door, the one who must be granted the time and space in order to achieve intellectual goals. Picture a young father keeping the children away from Mom, entertaining them and keeping them quiet, not for just a day or a weekend but for protracted periods of time. Seem unlikely? I would venture to guess that it is so unlikely as to be nearly nonexistent.

To be fair, most young fathers will gladly pitch in with child care. Unfortunately, the term "pitch in" is the giveaway. It does not imply full-time care. When a woman seeks a Ph.D. or a law or medical degree, a Saturday afternoon here or a Thursday night there will not be sufficient to relieve her of the burden of child care necessary to realize the dream. It is essential your daughter be made aware of these realities, *before* she chooses a husband or decides to have children. If her mother is not making her aware of these issues, then you must.

I have several reasons for bringing this up. One is candid and straightforward. The other is ulterior and subversive.

First, the candid, straightforward reasons. In terms of your daughter's achievement, her choice of a mate will have obvious implications. Obvious to you and me, that is. Probably not so obvious to the young female who has no idea of the commitment and dedication that lofty goals require. Without information to raise her awareness, most of this will not even enter her mind. Waiting to inform her of these exigencies when she is madly in love with a boy is hardly good timing. Love will make her anything but receptive to the practical matters of success. Planting the seeds when she is a child, then carefully watering them with frank discussions as she grows older, is a more fruitful approach. Your advice is more likely to become a part of her own thinking if it has that gentle but repetitive quality.

Now for the good stuff—the subversive motives I mentioned earlier. Now, hold on. The next few paragraphs may challenge and threaten you but they must be said. To leave them unsaid perpetuates the kind of empty support and lip service that routinely undermines the development of potential in your daughter.

What if your wife were to walk in the door this very minute and state boldly that she had reached a turning point in her life and intended to pursue a law degree, finish medical school, write a novel, compose a symphony, or finish her dissertation? Many women have been faced with just such a statement from their husbands and have supported him in the change. Some go back to work *and* take care of the kids so that he can pursue the dream. This is because both of them are committed to his success. Why? Because both partners see *his* success as *their* success. Unfortunately, and too often, a woman's pursuit of a dream is not perceived by the husband (or the larger society) as a mutual success, but a dangerous threat to the traditional family structure. Leonard

Woolf sacrificed himself to a certain extent in order that Virginia might write and give the world her gift. He cherished her pursuit of art as much as his own. And while you may not be living with a genius the scope of Virginia Woolf, again we are simply talking about a matter of degree not substance.

Where do you stand on this issue? Would you be willing to make these sacrifices for your wife? Would you take over full-time childcare duties? (Ted Koppel did it!) Would you be willing to spend your time every day listening to the tedious descriptions of a first-grader's adventures, bandaging hurts and cleaning up spilled milk and dirty little fingerprints? Perhaps your children are school-age and the daytime hours are not a problem. Would you be willing to take on most of the responsibilities of cooking, cleaning, laundering, and shopping? Suppose you and your wife are perfectly comfortable in an unkempt house. The problem is not resolved, because the obligation to nurture little human beings goes far beyond washing stains out of rompers and making beds.

Usually, at this point in my seminars, the room grows deathly quiet. This is because we are now discussing major sacrifices as well as all the risks that go with role-reversal experimentation. Some fathers ask what this has to do with fostering achievement in their daughter or how it is pertinent in their role as a father. The answer is: children learn what they observe. It is usually the unspoken messages—the things that parents *do* rather than say—which have the most impact.

If a daughter observes that it is Daddy's career, Daddy's education, Daddy's goals which come before Mommy's, a powerful message is communicated. If this is coupled with verbal encouragement saying, "Go for it, kid. Girls can do anything!" you create a chaotic, discrepant message.

Imagine a daughter's confusion if her father tells her that she can achieve and be strong, competent, and adventurous and then shows disapproval of and noncooperation with this type of independent behavior in his wife! Imagine her distrust when she learns that this type of female behavior is not valued, even by her "supportive" father. Imagine her anger when she discovers that it is okay for females to *believe* they can achieve their dreams, but not okay to *act* on them. Imagine her disapproval when she discovers the hypocrisy of your words. It will become obvious to her that the consequences of direct action will be male disapproval and perhaps even a lack of male companionship. It will aggravate the conflict your daughter will face regarding her role when it comes time to make a decision.

* * *

The final issue of advocacy revolves around an even touchier subject than those discussed above. Perhaps the best way to approach it is to create another "scene from reality." See if this one is familiar to you.

A group of men are in a bar having a business luncheon. The waitress, a well-built, attractive young woman, comes to take their order. When she leaves, one of the men says, "Nice tits." Another responds, "I'd like to hold that cute little ass in my hands, right about waist level." The rest laugh in camaraderie and good-natured understanding.

We all know these scenes take place, hundreds and thousands of times per day. I overheard the one related above just last week. Most men take this rather lightly, and some even get irritated if a woman is not flattered by the attention. They think she has sex and sexism confused. In reality, *they* are the ones who have it confused.

At any rate, this may all seem innocent and harmless; after all, the waitress will never hear the conversation. Perhaps I am beating a dead horse. But let me add a slight variation to the scenario while you carefully monitor your own reaction.

This time, visualize the cute little waitress as your daughter. When she comes up to the table, she gives no signs of sexual enticement. She simply walks up and cheerfully takes their order. (I can vouch for this behavior, since I was there and witnessed it.) How do you feel knowing that these remarks are directed at your baby?

You have probably already confronted this to some degree if your daughter is over the age of twelve. It usually accounts for at least part of the reason why men are so protective of their daughters. They are all too painfully aware of her status as "prey." Instead of overprotecting your daughter, I have another suggestion.

Suppose the next time you hear a comment like the one mentioned above, you indicate your disapproval. Something along the lines of, "You know, I think we should stop talking about women that way. It is demeaning to them and to us. Besides, I have a daughter, and it bothers me that that might be her one day. I hate to think the world is never going to change. I would like to believe the change can start with us."

Now, I know what you are thinking because fathers in my class have made the following comments:

"What if this were a client? I couldn't risk losing his (her?) goodwill for the sake of a little sexist remark."

"What if they think I'm a wimp?"

"I just can't insult my friends or business associates like that. I would be ostracized."

"Suppose they they think I'm 'pussy-whipped'?"

"It is rude to make a scene at a business or social function. It spoils everyone's fun."

"The waitress will never know the difference, so why make a big thing?"

"That's not the way to change other people's attitudes."

Etc., etc., etc.

I'll bet you also think I'm going to rant and rave at you to take a stand, right there in front of God and everybody. You're wrong. Every one of those doubts (excuses?) is a realistic fear. I can understand your reluctance to take a public stand as an advocate for females. It is not particularly popular or considered "masculine." Therefore, I, and many other females, forgive you for not coming to our defense. I would however, like to give you a little food for thought. For some of you it may make the difference between your silence (which can be interpreted by others as approval) and vocal opposition.

Suppose the lecherous boss who pinches females in the elevator (yes, they really do) or makes public comments about his female employee's legs is the person to interview your little girl for her first job?[2] Do you want her to be hired by him? He may reject her if she is not pretty enough, slim enough, or sexy enough. On the other hand he may hire for the same reasons. It's hard to know which is worse.

Suppose this guy's *son* arrives on your doorstep one night to take your daughter on a date. Being raised by a father like this, what do you suppose his attitude toward your daughter will be? Do you think he will graciously take no for an answer in the backseat of a car?

Now you're probably thinking, "Yes, but my remarks are not going to change this guy or his son." True. Perhaps. But where will it start? It is a foregone conclusion that the sexists of the world are not going to pay attention to the pleas of women to be taken seriously. To them, the complaints and demands of women are amusing. That leaves only one alternative to try to make the point to these Neanderthals—other men have to do it. And although the sexists are likely to reject the point from you as well, you stand a better chance than any female. For the most part, these guys are not going to be swayed by your principled stand. On the other hand, they are more likely to listen to you than they are to the other 50 percent of the population.

There is also something to be said for witnessing. As one of the fathers in my class remarked after we discussed this issue, "Well, I wouldn't stand by and let someone call a black person a nigger without saying something. I guess this is sort of the same thing." Simply voicing your opposition to a traditional but discriminatory practice is good for *your* soul. And who knows? Maybe, just once, you'll say it with particular depth of feeling, to a male ready to hear it, and one life may be changed. A slight shift in perspective. A feeble but registered click in the brain. These are all it takes to plant the seeds of change in a person's mind. Hasn't it ever happened to you that someone else's passing and forgotten remark struck you with peculiar intensity and caused you to look at an old situation in a new way? It's what being a change agent is all about—Johnny Appleseed. Imagine what would happen if all fathers who believe as you do were to take a public stand. Alan Alda has done it, and it hasn't hurt his image any. It's something to think about.

PART 3

Your Daughter at the Crossroads

C H A P T E R 10

❧

How to Act as Your Little Girl Becomes a Woman

One day in your life as a father there will come the first vague and disquieting signals of a change. At first, they won't amount to much. A voice, struggling toward a baritone, may crack on the other end of the phone requesting to speak to your daughter. No big deal. You can handle it. Besides, you think to yourself, the telephone is safe.

Next, she may begin spending hours poised in front of the mirror preparing to go to the shopping mall with her friends. She will scream and cry if the "right" pair of jeans is in the laundry. You may calmly suggest another pair, but she will only wail contemptuously, "I'm *sure*. I can't wear *those*." If she thinks her hair looks stupid, she may not even go.

One balmy summer night a "muscle car" may roll casually into your driveway—or worse, a motorcycle. If the boy has been raised with some manners, he may come to the door. If not, he may just honk the horn. It probably won't make any difference to your daughter, who will act as if her knight has just arrived on his snow-white, trusty steed. Indeed, he has. Your baby will dash off in a thundercloud of flying gravel and blaring stereo speakers, eagerly seeking the adventures that await her in the land of The Great American Teenage Experience. Remember how much fun it was? But instead of feeling happy for her, you stand there feeling frightened, alone, and old.

The arrival of *BOYS* in a daughter's life may seriously unsettle a father. It signals a metamorphosis that he almost always feels has come too soon, primarily because, regardless of what age the boys arrive, a father is not ready to lose his little girl. He is not ready to relinquish her to these strangers who do not love her as he does. He knows it is inevitable but resists acceptance.

His feeling of loss is acute. He may feel helpless. He may feel jealous. It is almost certain he will feel protective. Having once been a teenage boy himself, he has little room for tolerance, feeling he understands them only too well. His daughter may look more vulnerable and naive to him than ever.

If he has authoritarian tendencies, they may be aroused at this point in an attempt to control his daughter and prevent her from exercising the very independence she needs in order to break from him. If he has trained her in the past to be an independent person, or if he secretly views his children as his "property," the situation can get very hostile indeed. It becomes obvious to all concerned, particularly his daughter, that he has had a hidden agenda; that is, her independence is limited to his rules. Although this seems perfectly reasonable to the father who knows he has her best interests at heart, it does not appear that way to the adolescent female. A rift may be established that takes years to mend.

A less aggressive father can simply withdraw, feeling hurt and betrayed when his daughter begins to show interest in boys and exercise her independence. He may emotionally retreat (due to fear and confusion about his new role in her life as a woman) just at the time when she needs him the most. His daughter is left with a strange sense of abandonment, baffled by her father's withdrawal and feeling vaguely guilty that she is somehow responsible.

To successfully negotiate the hairpin turns in the road ahead, a father must allow himself to grieve the loss of his little girl in order to celebrate the arrival of the woman. It is a bittersweet time, full of the most profound human emotions.

One father remarked, "Before, when she got a new dress or a new pair of shoes, she would come in to show me and ask my opinion. Now, she shows her boyfriend. It doesn't matter any more what I think. It hurts."

Another father remarked, "All of a sudden she started closing the bedroom door. I felt so shut out. I know she needs her privacy, and I'm trying to understand, but it's hard. It's not just privacy to dress that I'm talking about. Her door is shut all the time. It's like she wants to shut *me* out."

More than at any other time in their relationship, this time in a daughter's life (and her father's) will test his sensitivity and strain his understanding. The teenage years are always difficult between parents and children, but the father-daughter relationship has a separate, unique issue with which to deal. The conflicts created by a daughter's budding sexuality and her father's fear of it require very mature behavior on a father's part, as well as a great deal of love and understanding. The more sensibly he handles himself and their relationship, the more profound the support he can give his daughter at this very precarious time in her life.

Unfortunately, on top of everything else, his once adoring little girl has become an alien creature. Her mysterious emotional outbursts; door-slamming temper tantrums; critical attitude; and super-, ultra-, extra-sensitivity leave him seemingly at the mercy of her hormones.

Up until now, he has been the most important male in her life. When he realizes that other males are becoming more important to her than he is, he can feel powerless and jealous. He may become concerned with what type of behavior the new hormones coursing through her body will activate. And finally, the most difficult thing to admit is his own masculine response to her new body and womanly ways.

What Became of Daddy?

The first and most important thing for a father to remember is that now more than ever, she *needs* his love and approval. His support during these teen years, when she is first discovering what it means to be a woman, is critical. When fathers do an emotional disappearing act, as so many of them do during these years, many young girls simply do not understand "what became of Daddy." Just a short time ago he was there, her companion and devoted escort to the world. Suddenly one day he disappears. He is physically present, but for reasons she does not understand, he has stopped hugging, kissing, tickling, and horsing around.

His daughter is left to create her own reasons as to why she has been "abandoned." It can be a sorrowful experience for both of them. Both of them feel the loss, both of them miss each other, yet neither knows how to proceed with their relationship.

A close friend of mine expressed these difficulties quite succinctly, "She'll close her door for hours on end. Then, all of a sudden, she wants to sit on my lap. She has a fairly well developed body, and I'm just not comfortable with that kind of close contact.

I don't want to turn her away when she needs attention, but I just don't know what's appropriate any more.''

A father walks a fine line with a teenage daughter who has just acquired breasts and all the rest that goes with it. It is imperative that he learn to give and receive affection in new ways. If he withdraws, as my father did, he creates a lasting impression of abandonment. With his daughter's limited experience of the world and lack of understanding of her father's dilemma, she often comes to all the wrong conclusions. She can feel that if her own father does not find her attractive or lovable, how could anyone else? My story is a perfect case in point.

It was prom weekend. Like every other girl in high school who had a date for the prom, I spent the entire day getting ready for this blessed event. I worked on my tan. I soaked luxuriously in a tub filled with fragrant body oils. I had my hair done in a chic new style. I manicured my nails and pedicured my toes. I pressed and repressed my dress. I applied my makeup with the skill of a trained professional, complete with false eyelashes and three shades of eyeshadow. I ''highlighted'' my cheekbones. In short, I did everything humanly possible to make myself beautiful.

While performing this sacred ritual, I thought the purpose was to impress my boyfriend, of course. It wasn't until I made my appearance in full regalia in our living room for my father that I realized that the person I was really getting ready for, the one I really wanted to impress with my breathtaking beauty was my dear ol' dad.

I stepped ceremoniously out of my bedroom. My mother was standing there smiling proudly. She was as expectant as I was to see my father's reaction. He was reading. A few seconds went by. I stood there patiently. A few more seconds ticked by. Finally, I said, ''Well?'' He never even looked out from behind his newspaper. I might as well have been standing there in my jeans and a T-shirt. He said nothing. Not one word. I felt humiliated and stupid in my prom dress. I was crushed and brokenhearted.

My boyfriend arrived. He gave all the right responses. He appropriately ooohed and ahhhed and acted proud to take me to the dance. My mother tried desperately to compensate for my father's lack of response. She pulled me aside privately to say, ''You know how your father is. He thinks you look great, but he's just too embarrassed to say it.'' (I wonder how many times children have heard that line, ''You know how your father is. . . .'') Anyway, none of it mattered. The one person I cared about the most had not even noticed. I went to the dance convinced I was fat and ugly. I spent the next ten years convinced I was fat and ugly.

My father's behavior had confirmed my darkest teenage fears; that I could not pass my first test of womanly beauty, even after a day's work and preparation! Obviously, my father had been too embarrassed to tell me the truth, and because he loved me, he chose to say nothing at all rather than hurt my feelings. If my own father did not find me attractive, things must be worse than I thought.

I must say that looking back on it, this still seems like a plausible explanation, but age and objectivity have mellowed me, and I now believe that my analysis is incorrect. The more likely possibility is that he was embarrassed to respond to me as a woman. Little girls don't put on makeup and do their nails. Big girls do. Little girls don't spend hours cultivating a golden tan to be sexually alluring. Big girls do. I think it was my father's first conscious realization that his little baby wanted to be sexy and attractive for her date, and he disapproved and was even embarrassed in a puritanical sort of way and didn't know how to respond.

From my point of view, it was so much more innocent than that. I just wanted my dad to tell me I looked pretty. I wanted him to notice that I was growing up and to reassure me that the person I was to become would be attractively feminine and charming to men.

I am embarrassed to admit it, but to this day I have not really forgiven him for that night. It was not until after his death, when I really began to analyze my relationship with him through the help of a therapist, that I acquired even the slightest objectivity about the events of that night. Sometimes, though, even now when I'm getting ready to go out, I get an empty, scared feeling in the pit of my stomach that I won't pass muster, that all the preparation in the world won't make any difference. I fight the feeling with the force of my intellectual understanding, but the emotional reality is as indelible as ever.

The purpose of telling this story was not to lay a burden of guilt on my father. We are all human, and we all make mistakes, especially with the daily demands and intimacy of parenting. The story was told to emphasize the power a father has to shape his daughter's self-image.

The truth is: your power lies in the ability to give male approval to your daughter at a time when it is her greatest need. This gift, which is in your power to grant or withhold, is profound and far-reaching. Your influence is felt at the very core of your daughter's psychological self, where mental health is formed through self-acceptance.

Once this is accepted, many questions may enter a father's mind. How does he walk this fine line without crossing over into inappropriate behavior? Will he be able to control his own feelings? What if his gestures of love and affection, albeit innocent, are misinterpreted? How does he appropriately express love and approval for a daughter who is now a full-grown woman?

A New Style of Affection

I am not suggesting a father should hide his loving feelings for his daughter. That is what my father did. What I am suggesting is that he must learn to discriminate between loving feelings and sexual feelings, as well as between feelings and actions. Furthermore, he must act on only the appropriate, constructive, safe emotions.

Feelings are the internal emotional states we experience in response to life situations. Actions are the outward, observable behavior we manifest in the world. Feelings do not have to be acted upon. They are an internal experience only. In a way, a father has already had practice at this, for society trains its males to hide their emotions.

A man who begins to notice his daughter is becoming a woman most often experiences apprehension mingled with anything from fear and confusion to guilt and disgust. In some cases, he may even feel self-loathing. This feeling is so unpleasant that it may be easier for him simply to sever his interaction with her than face what seems like a sick and repellent emotion.

One brave father expressed his feelings to his wife. She told it to me in the following way.

"One night David came to me very upset. He said that Angela had come to sit on his lap. She is twelve years old and beginning to develop. She had been squirming around, and suddenly, David found himself with an erection. He asked me if I thought he was sick.

"I asked him if he had ever had these feelings before. He said no, he wasn't sexually aroused but thought it was because she had been squirming around in his lap. He was so worried. I told him that if he thought he needed help, he should go and get it, but that he may have just been reacting to physical stimulation.

"We talked some more about what he should do. He came up with the answer. He said 'Obviously, I'm going to have to make some changes in the way I relate to her. I can make up some excuse for why she can't sit in my lap anymore.'

"At that point, I watched their relationship carefully, aware of my responsibility to my daughter. He made the changes he had talked about. He was very careful. I don't think Angela knew the difference because he still hugged her and paid attention to her. Also, she seemed just as happy and carefree as ever, so I relaxed." She paused for a moment before continuing. "By the way, he thanked me for not making him feel like a sicko."[1]

This real-life experience illustrates the double-edged sword a father must deal with. He must restructure his relationship with his daughter in order to be comfortable with the difficult feelings that may surface at this time *and* he must do it without creating the impression of abandonment.

A father must learn to express his physical affection in new ways which are nonthreatening to both of them. He must examine his interactions with his daughter in order to avoid situations which produce anxiety in him, but he must continue to let her know he loves her. For example, he will discover that certain types of play, in which they used to engage when she was a child, are no longer appropriate. Any type of full body contact horseplay is out. Tickling, wrestling, and the like belong strictly to the past. Respecting her privacy by never entering her room without knocking is a new and emphatic requirement. Lap sitting is potentially risky. Frontal hugging may present some problems. But, basically, common sense will give fathers guidelines they can trust.

On the other hand, many forms of physical affection are still appropriate and necessary if a daughter is to feel loved. A warm kiss on the cheek or a pat on the back will go a long way in making her feel your approval. A hug (from the side, if a frontal hug is difficult for you) will make her feel wanted. Holding her hand or putting your arm around her if she is upset is a harmless way of making emotional contact. Even something as simple as direct eye contact sends the message that you are giving your full attention and concern. In other words, it is not necessary to completely forgo all physical contact with your daughter out of fear and confusion. Let her know you still love her, but be aware of appropriate and inappropriate activities.

One last issue needs to be addressed before continuing. A teenage girl will often practice flirtatious behavior on her father. As was mentioned previously, she is learning for the first time how to act like a woman. You will be the handiest man available, so she may practice on you. It is imperative to remember that her conduct is not what it seems. (See "Special Note to the Sexually Abusive or Potentially Abusive Father" that appears later in this chapter.) She is still innocent, regardless of how skilled she may be at her new technique. This is something adult men forget. They assume that a certain worldly knowledge accompanies this flirtatious, even sultry, behavior. Nothing could be further from the truth. So when she gives what appears to be a come-hither look or acts cutesy and flirtatious, don't be shocked. Remember she is just trying out her wings on the man she knows she can trust. It is your responsibility as a loving father not to betray that trust or inappropriately punish her behavior.

Body Changes

Now that we have established that your daughter needs to feel your affection and support, it is time to address the uncomfortable subject of her budding sexuality and what you can do to help her like her new body and accept her identity as a woman. Remember, this must be accomplished without sexual overtones on your part.

This process should begin at birth as has been reiterated periodically throughout this book. But puberty is an especially precarious time with regard to self-esteem, particularly for females. It is during this time when many girls lose their confidence and "disappear." Some do resurface, but the amount of lost time varies from child to child (or should I say woman to woman?), and any time lost represents a waste of human potential.

Most of the turmoil of the teenage years is due to the momentous changes occurring hormonally. Your adolescent daughter will be coping with the arrival of a new body, as well as menarche (the occurrence of her first period). Girls become much more intensely private at this time than do boys. As her father, there are several important things for you to keep in mind and to act on accordingly.

First, she may be embarrassed or even annoyed by the process. The physical effects of puberty are more sexually obvious for a girl than for a boy. A boy just sort of gets bigger and stronger. A girl actually changes shape. Second, a girl is forced to deal with a whole new set of secrets, from bras and tampons to monthly mood swings, cramps, and the possibility of embarrassment if she is unprepared. Until she adjusts, this new world may seem like little more than a disconcerting hassle.

From my observations as a teacher, I would say that today's teenage girls are much better equipped emotionally to deal with menstruation than previous generations. They are better informed and more sophisticated. With the arrival of sanitary-napkin ads on television, which most females detest by the way, the menstrual taboo has lost some of its mystery and power. Keeping this in mind, it is still important to recognize that for most females the onset of menstruation remains an awesome and potentially embarrassing event.

We will look at the two major events of female puberty, how they are likely to affect your daughter and the best responses for you to make. Those events are: the development of breasts and the onset of menstruation.

BREASTS:
THE MOMENTOUS DEBUT

As your daughter approaches puberty and her need for male approval intensifies, she will eagerly look forward to breasts, believing that they are proof of her physical desirability. They may or may not arrive. Either way can be a traumatic experience.

The female adolescent who matures more quickly than her peers, or who develops large breasts, must endure the taunts and false assumptions of her classmates that reflect those of the larger society. The boys will assume that she is "available" and perhaps even promiscuous because her breasts are large. Both boys and girls may assume she is stupid due to the "dumb broad with big tits" stereotype left over from the fifties.

This may come as quite a shock to your daughter. Remember, this may be her first *personal* confrontation with a negative female stereotype. Suddenly, it is being applied to her, and she may react in several different ways.

If she is in need of male approval because she hasn't received it at home, she may begin to use her body to get the attention and validation of her femininity (desirability) that she needs. Unfortunately, she may come to feel that she *is* her body, that nothing else about her is worthy, valuable, or lovable. She may see her body as a ticket to love and acceptance. As adults, we know this is a false and empty kind of approval, one which has nothing whatsoever to do with love. But the needy adolescent has no worldly experience to help her differentiate between exploitation and love. To her, attention may feel the same as love, or at least an acceptable substitute.

Getting angry at her and assuming that she has the carnal motives of an adult is generally dead wrong. For the most part, the average teenage female has no idea of the power of the male response and is often frightened when she discovers it. Also, falsely assuming that her motives are sexual can make her feel dirty or guilty—one more tool to destroy her self-confidence. Instead, the best thing to do is to look at your relationship with your daughter and try to determine what is missing.

This may be a time to give her more attention and approval than ever before. Let her know you love her, being careful of the physical expression of your love that we discussed earlier. But do not emotionally abandon her. If you do, you are leaving her exposed and undefended for the predatory types who prey on emotionally insecure females. She will be left with no choice but to seek the males "out there" who are only too willing to give her the attention and approval she craves.

If she receives enough love and attention from her father at home, her reaction to large breasts may be quite different. In this case, she may just be embarrassed by them. She may wear loose and baggy clothing in order to hide them. She may slouch over when she walks.

It is quite possible that she will not welcome the kind of male attention she is receiving. It will probably be her first encounter with whistles, catcalls, and shouted obscenities aimed at her. Since boys are usually en masse when they indulge in this kind of behavior, it can make a female feel quite vulnerable and even resentful, particularly if she is alone.

Again, as her father, you can play an important role. Show her you love her for who she is, not what she looks like. Be sure to express your love and approval of all areas of her personality with special emphasis on athletic or academic achievements. If you have a close and open relationship, you may even be able to discuss the boys' behavior and help her handle it, explaining that all boys do not act this way.

Breasts that don't arrive are as traumatic as those that do. For a female, the trouble with breasts is that they have to be just right. They can't be too big and they can't be too small. Because they are an American fetish, symbols of femininity and sex appeal, their size and shape will be carefully monitored by the female adolescent anticipating their arrival.

When breasts don't arrive, or are considered too small, the

teenage girl may feel inadequate as a woman. Again, she may have several different responses, but they follow the same paths as the responses of a girl with breasts that are too large.

Once again, if she needs to feel male approval, she may begin to use sex appeal to get it (with or without breasts). Again, your best response is not to blame your daughter, or treat her as if she were a streetwalker, but to look carefully at your relationship with her and fill in the void of love that is causing her behavior.

On the other hand, her feelings of feminine inadequacy can cause her to become timid and shy, lacking in self-confidence and self-esteem. This is the time for lavish praise of her physical (not sexual) appearance. This is the time to tell her she is pretty, that you are going to have to keep the boys away with a baseball bat, that she is feminine and attractive. Your demonstrated approval at this time will go a long way to help her through this precarious period in her life. Your efforts may not produce any immediate results, but will pay off in the long run.

"When I was fourteen, I was skinny with knobby knees and absolutely no boobs," says one woman. "I thought I was the ugliest thing around. But my father didn't. He was always telling me how pretty I was and how proud he was of me. I loved him so much for that. I didn't believe him, but I loved him for it anyway.

"Later, looking back on it as an adult, I realized that his love for me, regardless of my figure, was what helped me to like myself while I waited for some curves to emerge. Actually, they never did. Not the way I wanted. But his love and support got me through it until I realized that there were other things I had to offer besides boobs."

Therefore, never, never tease her about her body. Many men do this and say they mean no harm. I believe them, but not meaning to do harm and not doing harm are two different things.

A lot of men excuse teasing as an expression of love, but teasing requires walking a very thin line. It can easily become sadistic, much like tickling. Unfortunately, it is rarely interpreted as love by the person being teased. It requires a healthy, solid relationship in order to tease without hurting. This is particularly true in a parent-child relationship where ancient power struggles have polluted the waters to such a degree that teasing is not humorous but humiliating.

Remember, your daughter will be having enough trouble coping with her new shape, wondering how it will look when it reaches maturity, without having to discriminate between playful remarks and hurtful ones. Because she is so sensitive at this time, she will be likely to take even playful remarks seriously and be hurt by them.

A story told by a father in one of my classes illustrates this point.

"A friend of mine" (hmmm . . .) "told me about the day his daughter got her first bra. When he arrived home from work, either his wife or his daughter, I don't remember which, told him about it. He said he could tell his daughter was embarrassed but proud. Then he said he would never forgive himself for his reply, which was, 'Why don't you just use a couple of Band-Aids?'

"The minute it was out of his mouth, he said he regretted it. He saw the expression on his daughter's face and realized he had humiliated her. Now the last thing you want to do is humiliate someone you love. She burst into tears and ran to her bedroom.

"He tried to apologize, but the damage was done. He tried to tell her he thought she looked good, but she didn't believe him. All she would say was, 'You're just trying to make me feel better. Go away and leave me alone.'

"I guess the moral of the story is to think before you talk. He was just trying to be funny, but it backfired. Maybe he was embarrassed himself. After all, it's kind of a shock to realize your little girl is into a bra.

"Anyway, to this day he tells that story. It will always be one of those things he feels he can never correct."[2]

Since your daughter's sensitivities will be so close to the surface, it is best to play it safe and not tease her about her body or her appearance in any way. Period. As you will see in the next chapter, many girls who suffer from eating disorders have fathers who tease them about their bodies.

If you must tease, find something else to tease about. Something innocuous. Something harmless. But remember, do not make it related to her appearance. Don't tease her about her hair, or her clothes or her makeup, even if it seems harmless enough to you. In this way, you will accomplish two goals. First, you will be demonstrating your love by showing sensitivity to her feelings, which at this time are raw, close to the surface, and "hair-triggered." Second, you will be contributing to a more peaceful household atmosphere by eliminating a few of the door-slamming screaming matches that seem to erupt so easily when sharing life with a teenage girl.

''DON'T TELL DADDY!'' (THE ARRIVAL OF MENSTRUATION)

''It's not that menstruation itself is so difficult, although it certainly can be painful, it's that it marks so graphically the change from girl to woman. You know there's no turning back.''

''Then, there's the embarrassment of having to tell your mom.''

''And let's not forget the hassle of learning how to take care of yourself.''

''I can remember thinking, 'Oh, yuck! I'm going to have to do this for the next forty years.' ''

''I thought I wouldn't be able to do anything fun anymore like ride bikes or play basketball with my brother. Nobody ever actually told me that, I just thought it up myself. But that didn't make it seem any less real.''

''All I can remember is the cramps!''

''I remember saying to my mother, 'Promise me you won't tell Daddy.' She said he would be proud, but I was so embarrassed, I just wanted to hide.''

You have just been given the rare opportunity of being privy to a conversation of women recalling their first periods. If you will notice, there isn't a lot of flowery, inspirational language about ''the beauty of becoming a woman.'' Mainly, when women look back on this unforgettable event, they do so either with humor, embarrassment, or a sort of bittersweet nostalgia. It takes a while for them to fully appreciate the awesome mechanisms of their complicated reproductive systems.

The changes that your daughter will be experiencing in her body will require you to make some delicate adjustments and to learn to perceive some of the finer nuances of behavior and body language. Your careful handling of your daughter's feelings can help make the difference between a female who matures into an appreciation of her body, one who is embarrassed by her body, or worst of all, one who hates her body.

First and foremost, recognize her need for privacy. This is a requirement that may include not only bathroom and bedroom privacy, but the right not to be touched as well. You may notice your daughter sort of ''hiding'' her body at first. She may visibly withdraw if you touch her. Don't be hurt. Try to understand that her modesty is born out of insecurity and anticipation of the unknown. After all, she is forging a new identity. Once her woman's body has fully emerged, she will probably be her old self again.

To reiterate then, try to be aware of certain kinds of body language that indicate her confrontation with a new identity. Lots of time spent in the bathroom, hiding behind clothes, skulking around looking guilty, and locking her bedroom door are all indications that she is handling this new situation. It will require time, love, and patience on your part, but rest assured, she will eventually "recover."

Incidentally, it is important for you to have the right attitude about your little girl becoming a woman. Some daughters are made to feel guilty or even "dirty" about physically maturing. There are fathers who become intensely suspicious, protective, or even angry when their daughters mature. Some begin to mistrust their daughters, viewing them with accusing eyes. Others do not necessarily mistrust, but feel cheated that the childhood years are over. All are reminded of the passage of time and their own relentless aging process.

Remember, it is natural for your daughter to mature. For some girls puberty arrives earlier than for others. Your daughter's body will have its own timetable, which will bear little, though research shows it may bear some, relationship to her mental maturity.

It is a process that you should look forward to in order to develop her self-esteem, which is usually on very shaky ground at this point in her life. Remember what the research shows about females losing their confidence and feelings of being OK right about this time. Any disapproval on your part will be keenly felt by your daughter, and she may conjure up all kinds of incorrect assumptions to explain your behavior. She is most likely to think there is something wrong with *her*, since children tend to blame themselves for any inadequacies or problems they feel.

Remember that the emotionality of puberty is a temporary state. As your daughter relaxes into her new body, you can reduce your vigilance a little and tease her with the affection she once understood.

Enjoy the metamorphosis from child to woman, and see it as the fascinating and exquisite transformation it is. Don't be frightened by it. It will be an exciting and moving experience to watch a new person emerge from the cocoon of childhood. To behold it is no less inspiring than watching a flower bloom or the seasons change. It is deserving of our greatest admiration for nature's cycles. You will see it only once per child. Cherish it.

To the Weekend or Single Father

Weekend and single fathers may face unique problems as their daughters begin to mature. Not only must they deal with the developing daughter, but they often worry about what she might say that could be misinterpreted by ex-wives or other family members. (To all the ex-wives who may be reading this, let me stress: I am referring to the father who does not have a problem and is just attempting to handle, as smoothly as possible, his daughter's rite of passage to womanhood. I am not in any way excusing the behavior of an abusive father.)

One father related the following story.

"My daughter comes to visit me on the weekends. She is ten years old with a very prepubescent body. My shower doesn't work right, and she is not strong enough to turn it on. She comes traipsing out, stark naked from the shower, to get my help. I just ignore it. I know she's too young to think anything of it.

"What bothers me, though, is I sometimes think to myself, what if she were to tell this to her mother or grandparents? How would it sound? What would they think? Even if they didn't say anything, what might they be thinking about me? I suppose I'm being paranoid, but in the future as she develops, I can see where it might become more of a problem."

I sympathize with fathers who worry about this touchy issue. After all, there are some pretty bitter divorces out there, and the leftover rancor, in an unstable ex-wife, might make her more protective and suspicious than is warranted. Furthermore, some men may feel a deep sense of guilt surrounding the circumstances of their divorces, and if they have been delinquent in some way, their fear is exacerbated by their guilt.

It is only fair to point out that many newly divorced men feel their ex-wives are unstable. Most often, this is just the product of the emotional process of separation that must occur in a divorce. It is difficult for many men to believe, after the wildly emotional scenes that accompany some divorces, that their ex-wives wouldn't do everything conceivable to ruin their lives. However, if you talk to men who have been divorced for a longer period of time, most will say that these rampant and tumultuous emotions gradually subside. Some divorced couples even manage to achieve a degree of civility, even friendliness, in their new relationship.

For the man who truly believes his ex-wife may be vindictive enough to purposefully cause him harm with his daughter, there is one consoling thought. Your little girl knows the truth. If your ex-wife attempts to falsely charge you with abusive behavior, she risks losing the love and trust of her daughter, who will hold her responsible for your severed relationship. This "blame" that will fall on your ex-wife will only worsen as your daughter matures. Your ex-wife knows this, and probably will not want to risk alienating *her* relationship with your daughter. In their hearts, many mothers realize that daughters need and love their daddies and would not want to ruin that relationship, no matter how much they may personally hate the men who fathered their daughters. I know this is a slim consolation.

While all this may seem slightly tangential to the topic of the father-daughter relationship, it has a closer bearing than may be readily evident. If you are a divorced father with these problems, it may adversely affect the way you relate to your daughter, making you hesitant, fearful, and distant. Your daughter will not understand this coolness in your relationship and may interpret it as being caused by something "unlovable" about her. Keep this in mind, and try to give as much love and affection as possible in your situation.

SINGLE FATHERS: TALKING ABOUT MENSTRUATION

If your daughter is premenarcheal (has not yet had her first period) and you are a single-parent father, you may need a little advice.

First, if you are comfortable talking to your daughter about menstruation, I don't see anything wrong with it. It is important to remember that, as adults, we see it differently than children, particularly because we have been raised with a strong cultural taboo (which seems to be weakening, I'm glad to note). Therefore, if you present it very matter-of-factly, without a lot of red-faced stuttering and stammering, or worse, disapproval or distaste, your daughter will simply view it as a bodily function; that is, if you present it early enough. Don't wait until she is thirteen and already feeling embarrassed about her body.

Furthermore, if you are contemplating when to discuss this physiological change with your daughter, remember that some girls experience it quite early. Therefore, it is important to tell her prior to age ten.

The only problem that I can foresee with a single father may be that he cannot give her the benefit of his experience, since only a woman could do that. He can give her the necessary biological information she needs in order to understand what is happening to her body, but matters related to hygiene, bodily sensations, cramps, mood swings, etc. are out of his realm. For this reason, I recommend that he find an understanding woman, preferably one who already has a relationship with his daughter, to answer questions, discuss these matters, and show her how to manage sanitary napkins and tampons.

If her own mother is unavailable, the most obvious choice is a grandmother. If she is unavailable, then try aunts, family friends, teachers, a female doctor, or an older sister. Let me stress that it will be easier on your daughter if she already has a relationship with this person.

If the only person available is a teacher, I have a few suggestions. Pick a female teacher whom your daughter likes. Write the teacher a note. Do *not* send it to school with your daughter, who will be mortified to be the messenger of this request. Instead, send it in the mail.

It isn't necessary to be explicit. You can use euphemisms and vague statements to allude to what you mean. You may say things like, "There are certain things she needs to know about becoming a woman, and I can't teach them to her," etc. The teacher will understand.

It is important to allow the teacher (or any other female you may be writing this to) an escape hatch in case she does not want to do it. Simply state that you will understand if she is uncomfortable, but since your daughter is so fond of her (I know, it's a little manipulative but some manipulation can have a positive intent), you thought she was a good choice. If she refuses, leave it at that and search out a new person.

Finally, be aware of how difficult it is for a young girl to walk into a store and casually buy her first box of sanitary napkins or tampons. (It's kind of like when boys buy their first box of condoms. I'm sure they feel as though the whole store is watching and stifling their laughter.) Anyway, you might be able to take some tips from the way my mother handled the situation.

Long before my first period my mother came into my room with all the necessary "equipment." She showed me what to do and how to do it. She made sure I understood, then she said, "I will leave this stuff right up here on this shelf in your closet and when you need it, it's there for you. That way, if I'm not here when the time comes, you'll have what you need."

Sure enough, she wasn't home at the time. I followed her directions, absolutely sure that my father somehow just "knew." I wouldn't go into the den and watch television with him that night because I was too embarrassed!

If possible, use this technique. If a grandmother, aunt, or older sister is available, she can be the one to purchase the supplies and give them to your daughter. By allowing her this freedom and responsibility to take care of herself when the time comes, you eliminate her embarrassment and dependence. Finally, be sure to remember that when your daughter reaches this monumental point in her life, she will need money to buy what she needs. Give her an allowance to cover her expenses if she is too young to hold a job.

Sexuality: A Father's Fear

This is a topic with which most fathers are uncomfortable, feeling it is not proper for a father to advise his daughter about this. They feel the mother should handle the delicate and private issues of a daughter's budding sexuality. This is accurate to a certain extent, but even here a father's behavior can have important consequences.

Remember the woman who returned home after a bad experience at college, only to be put on the next bus back by her father? Let us turn to another example set by this same father to provide a positive model. Later, for an example of what *not* to do, we will turn to the example of another father-daughter relationship.

According to Marie (not her real name), her father was embarrassed by any references to sex around his daughters and avoided the topic. Nevertheless, he managed to relay some important and relevant information with regard to their futures. Listen to his approach.

"His idea of sex education had nothing to do with morality. It was strictly practical. He drilled into us that you had to be careful or you could get stuck in a situation where you wouldn't be able to finish college or pursue other goals. You would be stuck in a dependent situation. His sex education had more to do with the hard, cold "facts of life" than with anything overtly sexual. He made us very aware of reality.

"He used to say, 'It may be fun at night, but you have to know where the bacon is coming from in the morning.' This kind of advice can kill a lot of romantic interludes because you can't argue with that kind of realism. It would have been much easier to reject if he had said 'Good girls don't do that,' or 'It's immoral or evil,' and I probably would have rejected it. But it's much harder to reject reality.''

What Marie's father did was to allow his daughters to make their own moral judgments concerning their personal lives. At the same time, however, he armed them with the facts in order to help them make informed decisions. This demonstrated his trust in their ability to discern the right course of action and to act in their own best interest.

It is worth emphasizing the point about the power of reality as advice. As she states, it is quite easy for children to pooh-pooh the moral castigations of parents. Many young people actually believe that parental warnings about sex are based on ignorance, disapproval, or even a downright nastiness designed to spoil their fun. Very few realize that the admonitions are based on loving concern and knowledge of the pitfalls. What Marie's father did was to make his children feel that he was not passing judgment on them morally, but educating them about the world. To a teenager, this method of giving advice is more palatable.

Like everything else in the complicated task of parenting, there is a right way and a wrong way to make your daughter aware of the pitfalls of unprotected sex. A conversation with one of my gifted female students several years ago revealed the *wrong* approach with vivid clarity.

Kelli (not her real name) came to talk to me after school one night following parent-teacher conferences. She wanted to know what her father had said to me. Since he and I had had a rather uneventful conversation, I was unsure what she was driving at. There was little to discuss about her grades, which were good, but I did remember her father asking how much time she spent with her boyfriend.

''I knew it,'' she said bitterly, ''he's always embarrassing me with this pregnancy bit. It's driving me crazy. He says it in front of everybody. 'You're gonna get pregnant. You're gonna get pregnant.' Can't he see how it makes me feel?''

I tried to explain to her that what appeared to be an accusation was really concern for her welfare, but my explanation fell on deaf ears. Frankly, I knew she was right. He was accomplishing nothing but making her feel dirty and guilty. He was humiliating her, undermining her self-confidence, and damaging their relationship, all in the name of paternal concern.

There was little I could do in the way of counseling this father, since he was not the type of man open to an outsider's advice. He clearly felt he knew what was best for his daughter and would have resented any interference with his methods. But knowing about Kelli's humiliation should help you think about this issue further.

First, waiting until your daughter is involved with a boy to begin discussing the pitfalls of sex and pregnancy gives the appearance of a lack of trust. It will make your daughter feel guilty and embarrassed. If you have waited this long, you should present the unvarnished truth about motherhood, its sacrifices as well as its rewards. Don't concentrate on her possibly immoral behavior. This is a good way to alienate your daughter and lose her trust.

It would be ideal to begin discussions about sexuality at an early age, in small, palatable doses your daughter can understand. Obviously, you can begin this too young, but waiting until she is in love with a boy is risky indeed. Use the example of Marie's father, and you will convey the message that you believe in your daughter's ability to make wise decisions regarding her life. Giving her the experience of baby-sitting and then discussing the responsibilities, the lack of freedom, etc. is a good way of initiating the subject.

When I was a teenager, my own parents gave me honest feedback about the sacrifices of child rearing. My mother used to say, "You don't have to have children just because everyone else does. People don't stop to think about what they're doing. Especially women. Kids are adorable, but they tie you down."

My father would add, "You got little kids, you got little problems. You got big kids, you got big problems."

Even at the age of thirty-three, as the biological clock ticked relentlessly away, I began to feel that maybe I should have a child. It wasn't that I had an overwhelming desire to be a mother, but my social conditioning had trained me to believe I would be missing out on fulfillment as a woman. My mother gently pointed out that I didn't even want a dog because it would interfere with some of the plans I had made for the future. I was grateful for the reminder.

Finally, if all your counseling should go awry, and your daughter finds herself pregnant and unmarried, give her all the support, encouragement, and loving care you can possibly summon. Regardless of how angry, hurt, or betrayed you may feel, rest assured it is nothing compared to the hell she has been going through.

Paternal rage is often the greatest fear a girl has—*even greater than the anticipation of responsibility for a new life*. A counselor in a girls' dormitory at a state university says, "Very few girls are frightened over their mothers' reaction. They feel that somehow, although they may cry a lot, mothers will always try to help. But they fear their fathers. The most standard comment is, 'My father will kill me.'

"To us, this may sound like an exaggeration, but they really believe it. It can cause girls to act out some pretty desperate behavior, from self-induced abortions to abandonment and homicidal neglect of a newborn.

"At the very least, a girl feels as if she has failed him. In fact, that's another difference. She doesn't worry that she will lose her mother's love. She knows her love is unconditional. It's her father she doubts."

Marie's family was forced to deal with just such a crisis, and her father demonstrated that concern for his daughter's welfare was his primary consideration.

"One of my sisters thought she was pregnant, and she did not want to come home and tell Daddy," Marie says with a furrowed forehead. "I finally told her she had to. We came home from college and sat down with Mom and Dad. She just looked at him and said, 'I think I'm pregnant.'

"He looked at her without flinching and said, 'What do you want to do?' No shock, no yelling, no moral outrage. He asked her if she wanted to get married. She said no. He asked her if she wanted an abortion. Mainly I remember him saying, 'What do you want us to do?' Instead of telling her, he was asking her. Then he got up from the table, walked over to her, hugged her, and said, 'We love you.'

"I loved him so much for that because his first concern was her well-being, emotional as well as physical, and not his idea of morality, which she didn't need to hear at that point. He didn't worry about how it would reflect on *him*.

"Well, it turned out she wasn't pregnant after all. But he never brought it up again. Obviously he knew she had been screwing around, but he never rubbed it in or made her feel guilty. He didn't question her when she went out on dates and never, never made a derogatory comment. It was then that I realized fully how much he loved us."

Marie's father is an inspiration. His unwavering support, even in the face of what must have been a horrible blow to his hopes for the future, demonstrates the kind of unconditional love that may be necessary. Hopefully, you will never have to face this crisis, but if you should, do not withdraw your love. Your daughter will need you more than ever.

SPECIAL NOTE TO THE SEXUALLY ABUSIVE OR POTENTIALLY ABUSIVE FATHER

I would be remiss if I did not address the issue of the father with a problem who is not in control of himself and therefore represents either a potential or actualized threat to his daughter. *Get help immediately. Do not make excuses. Do not wait.* For every day you put off getting the help you need, you increase the danger and the damage, not only to your daughter (who should be your first priority), but to yourself and your entire family.

Do not try to find loopholes in the information given earlier in this text in order to exonerate yourself. Do not delude yourself that what you are doing is an expression of your ''love'' and ''support.'' Do not attempt to console yourself with false but comforting notions that it is somehow ''natural.'' Most importantly, do not blame your daughter in any way by inferring that her behavior leads you on. Regardless of your daughter's behavior, you have no right to her body. In any way. For any reason. Period.

You know in your heart if you are this type of man. If you are, you pose a threat to your daughter, your family, and your society. You are doing serious damage. You must get professional help. *Trying to cope with it alone is not the answer.* I realize that it will take every bit of courage you can muster to walk into a health professional's office and admit your problem, but remember, these people are trained to understand and help.

The actions that will be taken will vary depending on what has already occurred. If your problem is still just potential and not realized, they *may* not remove your daughter from the home. If actual physical abuse has taken place, they *may* not allow your daughter to remain in the same house with you. The action taken is difficult to predict. It will vary with your individual situation, environment, and family members.

I know your greatest fear is disclosure, to your wife, to your family. But keep this in mind: many abusive fathers live with their guilt for years, only to have it eventually revealed anyway. More and more children are becoming aware that there is help available to them. More teachers are being trained to look for the signs. More mothers are taking action. So do not rely on good luck to keep your secret, and do not threaten your daughter. This will only fuel the hatred she will one day feel for you. Get the help you desperately need, and end your mutual misery before it destroys you, your daughter, and your entire family.

FOR ALL FATHERS: A FINAL COMMENT ON INCEST

A man's beliefs about what a woman is affect the way he treats his daughter. If a man believes that a woman is a "thing" to be used to meet his needs for comfort and pleasure, then when that man's daughter becomes a woman, that is what he believes *her* to be. This then makes it easier for that man to indulge in sexual behavior with his daughter. His belief about women carries a built-in escape hatch for him to excuse his behavior.

This is why it is imperative for a father to examine, in a brutally honest fashion, what his beliefs about women really are. When his daughter becomes a woman, this is what he will believe about her.

It has been said before by others, but bears repeating: our society fosters incest between fathers and daughters. The titillating pornography of men's magazines which features naked females only a few years older than your own daughter (and perhaps even younger) may exacerbate the problem. In reality, these magazines give you permission to look at other men's daughters. Think about it.

Staying Sane

Regardless of all the advice, puberty is a frightening time for parents. It all seems so out of control. That's precisely the point. It is. It is this very aspect that may drive some fathers to distraction, for it is men who have been taught to feel most uncomfortable when they are out of control.

Being out of control implies unpredictability. It implies vulnerability. It implies the dangerous intrusion of the irrational. Like it or not, your ability to "go with the flow" and experience the spontaneity of life will be tested and exposed throughout your daughter's teenage years. In this way, her journey to adulthood will be your journey as well. As you help her establish her identity, you will be learning more about your own. What a glorious opportunity. It's heady stuff.

CHAPTER 11

❧

Eating Disorders: What a Father Can Do

Years ago people lived in fear of tuberculosis or polio. Now they live in fear of fat. I am not being humorous. The fear of fat can generate a panic so severe it demolishes self-esteem and destroys an otherwise happy life. This fear must not be taken lightly, since it is a contributing factor in two devastating mental disorders—anorexia nervosa and bulimia—both of which most frequently strike females in their adolescent years.

You may be wondering what a chapter on fat and eating disorders is doing in a book concerned with fathering successful daughters. The following statistics speak eloquently enough.

Estimates say that 90 to 95 percent of all anorexics are female while 95 to 99 percent of bulimics are female. As high as 20 percent of all college females engage in bulimic behavior at least occasionally, while 10 percent do so habitually. A third group suffers from both, ricocheting crazily between starvation and gluttony in a desperate attempt to get control of their lives.

A recent study of thirty-nine anorexic girls revealed that *thirty-six* of them experienced withdrawal of affection from their fathers (which they perceived as the withdrawal of love) upon reaching puberty.[1] This is a sobering finding. The researcher, Dr. Margo Maine, theorizes that anorexia may be an attempt on the part of an adolescent girl to stave off maturity by remaining ''daddy's little girl,'' that is, undeveloped and childlike. In other words, anorexics may be trying to win daddy back.

The research also shows that bright, high-achieving young women from middle-class and upper-middle-class families are at greater risk than the rest of the population. Furthermore, for every girl who actually develops the disorder, hundreds (perhaps thousands) do not, but will exhibit the symptoms to varying degrees, wasting precious energy obsessed with food and dieting, hating their bodies and themselves.

It is also significant that the problem will not necessarily be grounded in reality. Your daughter may or may not be overweight. It is her *perception* of herself and her beliefs about food that will cause the difficulties.

Trust me. I do not wish to alarm you, nor do I wish to set off your panic buttons and cause you to look for trouble where it doesn't exist. *But*, the statistics illustrate the need for fathers of bright, high-achieving females to be aware of what the research is saying, and that is, eating disorders strike females—who are high-achievers—and fathers play a major role.

Because the experts say that fathers typically have a more difficult time than mothers in coping with an anorexic or bulimic daughter (often expressing anger and rage), it is crucial that you understand the dynamics of these disorders. Only in this way can you avoid the paternal behaviors that contribute to their appearance.

We will begin with a general description, and progress to a more in-depth discussion of each disorder.

Anorexia

Anorexia causes a person to see a fat body in the mirror regardless of the actual size. Anorexics literally starve themselves to death, becoming so thin they resemble concentration camp victims of the Holocaust. In many cases, the skeleton actually becomes visible, with knees protruding below skin-covered bones which cannot really be called thighs. Faces become skull-like, with deeply sunken eye sockets and bulging eyes. Yet, as unbelievable as it may seem, the anorexic continues to perceive only fat.

An anorexic's perception becomes so distorted by her irrational fear of fat (or even normal feminine curves) that a fully grown, adult woman weighing only 75 pounds will continue to "diet," convinced that she is still overweight. She will discount the frantic pleas of her friends and relatives by believing that they are jealous of her thinness. She is resistant to treatment because she doesn't believe she has a problem.

One emaciated woman called a friend who was 5 feet, 5 inches tall and weighed 115 pounds a "fat slob." The anorexic, a home economics teacher, by the way, literally ate nothing. She survived on diet soft drinks and cigarettes. She further tortured her already devastated body by jogging every day. The fact that she was a home-ec teacher, and constantly preparing food, is not unusual. It illustrates one of the many ironies of the disease. Many anorexics are understandably preoccupied with food and will prepare elaborate meals and give them away to friends, smugly refusing to eat any of their concoctions.

Obviously, anorexia is a life-threatening disorder. Professionals estimate that somewhere between 10 and 15 percent of anorexics die of starvation or complications arising therefrom. They often stop menstruating and ovulating, as did the females in Nazi concentration camps. If the disorder persists untreated, the anorexic will begin to show signs of malnutrition: fatigue, mental disorientation, chills, hair loss, dizziness, and skin problems. If she continues to refuse to eat, she may require hospitalization. Later in life, if she survives, she will be more susceptible to crippling osteoporosis.

If the disorder is diagnosed and treated early (within the first few months), the cure rate is quite high. On the other hand, if the disorder is not treated early, it becomes progressively more difficult to cure the anorexic, who perpetually returns to the behavior in times of stress or low self-esteem.

Bulimia

Bulimia is an eating disorder in which the victim consumes incredibly large amounts of food, usually in secret and sometimes in excess of 10,000 calories, and then induces vomiting. This is called "purging." This may occur numerous times throughout the day. Also, purging is not limited to vomiting alone. Many bulimics purge through the abuse of laxatives, diuretics, cocaine, and amphetamines. Others will fast for long periods of time or engage in bouts of excessive and compulsive exercise. Many sufferers use various combinations of the above to rid their bodies of the unwanted food.

Bulimics can be hard to spot because so many of them are at a normal weight or only slightly below. Also, their behavior almost always occurs in secret. They become so adept at keeping their secret that parents and families can be unaware of the problem.

As was mentioned previously, the bulimic deprives herself of the nutrition her body needs due to her extreme and distorted version of ''dieting.'' When the hunger and deprivation become too much to handle, she gorges and then feels morbidly guilty. She can purge herself of her ''sin'' and punish herself by vomiting. The important thing to be aware of here is her perverted sense of what constitutes failure and discipline.

To illustrate this point, allow me to contrast the information provided by health care professionals with the testimony of an ''average'' bulimic.

Doctors and nutritionists recommend a caloric intake of *not less than* 1,200 per day, since this is the minimum required by the average woman to maintain healthy bodily functions. Caloric intake under this amount is considered a starvation diet. Even the doctor willing to recommend fewer calories only goes as low as 1,000—the bare minimum to maintain health.

One bulimic I interviewed became convinced that any intake over 350 calories per day was proof of her failure and lack of discipline.

''It started after I went on one of those commercially available liquid diets which allows only 330 calories per day. When I first started to eat real food again, I felt that even 350 calories was too many because it was 20 calories over the liquid diet I had been on.

''Can you believe that? I would become frantic, completely berserk, over 20 calories! It was because I felt that if I couldn't succeed on this diet, my whole life was at stake. I would be fat, lonely, and unloved for the rest of my life.

''The only way I could maintain that kind of deprivation was to have absolutely no food in the house. And I really do mean *no food*. Not even skim milk or celery.

''Of course the inevitable would always happen. I would become so ravenous and weak from hunger that if I were accidentally placed in a situation where there was food, I would eat everything in sight. Then I would *really* hate myself because I had just ruined a week of suffering and deprivation in the space of an hour.

''I decided to solve the problem by never again accepting another invitation to go out because there might be food present and I was too afraid of my 'lack of self-control' to go out.

''At the time, I actually thought this was a sane and rational way to approach my problem. You can see how crazy I was. I thought I had to keep cracking down on myself harder and harder because I couldn't be trusted around food. In reality, I was starving to death. It's no wonder I would consume everything in sight when I had the opportunity."

During the binge, the bulimic is temporarily freed from her self-imposed prison. There is a momentary release from the rigid controls by which she leads her life. She begins to use this release to console and nurture herself whenever *any* strong negative feelings surface. What begins as a way to eat forbidden food, or in some cases any food at all, eventually becomes a way to cope with conflict. Once the need has been fulfilled, the self-loathing and panic set in, and she must purge herself of her terrible guilt and sin.

Victims loathe and despise themselves for their behavior. In the Judeo-Christian ethic, gluttony is one of the seven deadly sins. The lack of control around food is regarded by our culture with disgust and revulsion, and our collective view of this behavior lacks any semblance of compassion.

Bulimics come to see themselves exactly as society sees them—as gluttons and "pigs"—not as severely disturbed victims in need of professional help. Despite their self-hatred, they are unable to stop. Since food becomes the way to cope with powerful negative feelings, and self-loathing is among the most powerful of negative feelings, it is easy to see the cruel cycle they fall prey to.

While bulimia is less immediately life-threatening than anorexia, it *is* insidious and sinister. It is just a slower process of life destruction. Tooth and gum decay are common problems from frequent vomiting as are an irritated throat and swollen salivary glands. In more severe cases, a torn esophagus can lead to internal bleeding. Continued vomiting can produce hormone or electrolyte imbalance such as a potassium deficiency, which can lead to muscle spasms, irregular heartbeats, or even heart attacks.

Female Troubles?

It is no accident that these disorders are experienced primarily by females. It is also no accident that their onset is usually during puberty (for anorexia) and the late teenage years (for bulimia). This is because during this period in their lives, most females come to believe that their self-worth is dependent on their physical appearance. Unfortunately, as has been stated many times, this is part of "femininity," as our society defines it. To be feminine is to be desirable, and to be desirable is to be thin.

Our current concept about ideal body weight for females, epitomized by the actresses and models we all aspire to be like, is 10 to 20 percent *below* what is considered normal by medical professionals and insurance charts. Furthermore, a book about feminine ideals of beauty shows that the *Playboy* centerfold has steadily become 2 to 3 pounds thinner every year for the past twenty years.[2]

At the same time, our interest in food is constantly being stimulated. Television commercials are an unremitting procession of exquisitely photographed food temptations. Any major city or shopping mall boasts specialty restaurant sections featuring gourmet cookies, fancy fast foods, and a variety of takeouts to tempt even the most fastidious eater. A day of shopping is also a day of overeating for many Americans. There is even a revived interest in cooking utensils to meet every culinary need. Food and drink have long been recognized as both status symbols and tools of recreation.

To make matters still worse, females are traditionally the ones to be most involved with food and its preparation. At the same time that girls become acutely aware of the need to be thin in order to be attractive, they begin to prepare meals and other tempting goodies for their boyfriends, both as gestures of love and as proof of their feminine abilities in the kitchen. Unfortunately, the compelling need to be thin forbids consumption of the food they have prepared. (This paradox is graphically exposed in women's magazines whose slick covers display moist, chewy chocolate brownies—"the recipes can be found inside"— juxtaposed to feature stories on dieting, fitness, and weight control.) The society creates the classic no-win situation and thus causes what has become an epidemic of eating disorders among females. It would be funny if it weren't so tragic.

In the junior and senior high schools in my school district, it is common for the cheerleaders and pep-club girls to prepare and present the "athletes" with an elaborately decorated cake during the pep rally before the game. (Imagine the boys doing this for the female athletes.) If there is any type of party at school, it is *always* the girls who prepare and bring the food. These girls often spend a great deal of time baking party treats and other goodies which the boys consume. It is heartbreaking to watch the girls trying to resist the food they have so carefully prepared or make pathetic apologies when they eat it, or sneak the food into their mouths when the boys aren't looking—behaviors I have witnessed firsthand many times over.

A Different Kind of Substance Abuse

Eating disorders are complex. Their appearance on such a wide scale among the female population is a relatively new phenomenon, which only compounds the problem. One way to begin to understand the nature of these illnesses is to compare them to drug and alcohol abuse, to which they are akin.

Alcohol abuse and drug abuse, whether in adolescents or adults, are self-destructive methods of coping with the stressful factors of life. They can be vehicles of expressing rebellion or techniques for exercising control over others. At the bottom line, they should be seen as cries for help. While the self-destructive male is most likely to display this type of behavior through the abuse of alcohol and drugs, many females accomplish the same thing with food. In other words, in some ways, an eating disorder is like *substance abuse*. Only the substance is different.

The important thing to remember is that food becomes a way to cope with distressing feelings of pressure and inadequacy. Food is used for emotional purposes rather than as a source of fuel. We all do this to some degree, but those suffering from eating disorders behave with food much as substance abusers do with alcohol and drugs.

Unfortunately, there tends to be more sympathy for abuse of alcohol and drugs. The society is familiar with such abuse, and tends to display more compassion for the highly publicized symptoms of physical addiction. But the miserable victims of eating disorders are in no less a viselike grip than their brothers and sisters who abuse drugs and alcohol.

Because they are not "addicted" in the classic sense of the word, the superficial answer seems to be so easy. Our tendency is to tell them to simply "quit" the behavior and all will be well. Unfortunately, for the bulimic or anorexic, it is not that simple, as we shall see. Our job is to recognize that their disorders are the manifestations of psychological problems and must be treated as such.

"If I Am Not Perfect . . ."

Anorexia and bulimia have some characteristics in common. First, of course, is the fear of fat, which according to Dr. Thomas Giles, director of the Eating and Anxiety Disorders Clinic at Rose Medical Center in Denver, amounts to a phobia.[3]

"In both anorexics and bulimics the fear of gaining weight is so severe that all the symptoms of a phobia are present," says Giles. "There is an extreme amount of anxiety, which is considered irrational. By this I mean there is an actual physiological response (rapid breathing, accelerated heartbeat, clammy palms) as if she were in danger when no danger is present."

Second, both disorders usually begin with a diet and "evolve" into chronic dieting. As dieters, these perfectionists are not satisfied simply to limit their caloric intake, but typically attempt to adhere to the kind of stringent limitations that would tax a monk.

Dr. Giles again:

"The question is: How come these particular females establish such rigid rules about eating? How come they diet to such an extreme? That's where you get into the self-esteem issue. They are perfectionists because they feel they *have* to be in order to be loved, or even accepted.

"For example, if you have them fill in the blank to this sentence: 'If I am not perfect, then I am —————,' they usually fill it in with something like 'worthless,' 'inferior,' 'inadequate,' 'stupid,' or some other equally derogatory term. Trouble is, they actually mean they are worthless, inadequate, and inferior as a person.

"We are finding these particular individuals are extremely sensitive to criticism and rejection. More so than the average person. There again, it's, 'Everyone must like me or I'm nothing.' They have low self-esteem and an incredible sensitivity to *what other people think.*

"So what we are finding, and this is the very newest research," continues Giles, "is that a social anxiety or social phobia often predates the eating disorder. This is what really seems to make them so sensitive to what is 'expected' of them. It makes them take the Madison Avenue image of women to heart."

Finally, there is a great deal of pain and suffering involved. The constant tension created by having one's self-acceptance vulnerable to the minute-by-minute evaluation of one's behavior is a devastating pressure to live under. These miserable individuals literally judge every bite of food that enters their mouth. (Did I eat one bite too many? Did I eat the wrong food? How many hours must I exercise to make up for that bite? are the common and unremitting castigations to which they subject themselves.) Most human beings simply could not thrive if subjected to that kind of intense and relentless scrutiny, yet this is the cloud under which both bulimics and anorexics live their lives.

The victims, who are attempting to control their consumption of food, ironically become consumed by their passion to control. The victims become engaged in what can be a life or death struggle to meet an unrealistic ideal and control what they perceive as their "sinful" impulses to eat.

"Because they are so sensitive to criticism and so desperate to be accepted," explains Dr. Giles, "they try to be as good as possible. You know, 'This is what a good girl does. She does this, she does that.'

"The female with an eating disorder thinks, 'As long as I'm not fat, no one is going to criticize me.' She feels that if people don't like her, she is nothing. So the sensitivity to being acceptable sets up the whole thing, and food just becomes the vehicle.

For the bulimic, the hunger and sense of deprivation she has forced on her body become so overpowering they explode without warning, and she is unable to eat a normal meal. She gorges uncontrollably, feels morbidly guilty, and induces vomiting. The anorexic, on the other hand, may just be able to hold out longer than the bulimic. Eventually (as we have learned from starvation studies) she loses the desire to eat, although according to Dr. Giles a minimum of 50 percent of anorexics also binge.

"We know that dieting causes binging. But what caused the extreme and rigid dieting? The self-esteem issue, which predates the eating problem. This is where upbringing plays an important role."

What a Father Can Do: Prevention

Since treatment of these disorders is still rather new and uncertain, prevention is paramount. If your daughter is between birth and puberty, you are lucky, for there is still time. If she is already an adolescent, you must handle her emergence into womanhood with the care and sensitivity required to keep her self-esteem intact. If she is no longer an adolescent, you can still change the nature of your relationship if need be by paying attention to the way the two of you interact.

Certainly, full responsibility does not necessarily rest entirely on your shoulders. However, fathers do play an important role, and they must recognize what they can do to avoid the paternal behaviors that contribute to the onslaught of eating disorders in their female children. The advice given below falls into four basic categories:

1. Build self-esteem in your daughter through encouragement not pressure.
2. Examine your own beliefs about women.
3. Don't monitor your daughter's eating habits with a microscope or pass on your incorrect beliefs about food and eating.
4. Provide information to counter her fears.

BUILD SELF-ESTEEM IN YOUR DAUGHTER THROUGH ENCOURAGEMENT NOT PRESSURE

Establishing your daughter's sense of self-worth must go beyond the classic, "I'm-too-fat-No-you're-not" seesaw argument so common between fathers and daughters. In reality, this accomplishes very little. As has been said before, unless your words are supported by your actions, your daughter will assume, perhaps rightfully, that you don't mean what you say.

As you already know, self-esteem is a most precious commodity. But it can be very elusive. Even a girl who *appears* to have self-confidence may find herself striving toward an unattainable ideal that leaves her feeling constantly inadequate. This is particularly true if she is a high-achieving perfectionist, for as we have said before, if thin is good, thinner is better.

Furthermore, an emotionally absent or disengaged father can make matters still worse. "A father's distance contributes to low self-esteem. If he is unavailable to provide the feedback the girl needs regarding her self-worth, he leaves her more sensitive to the negative impacts of the culture like the drive for thinness, appetite control and the view of emaciation as beautiful,"[4] says Dr. Maine. One subject in her study even said, "I had always wanted to win his approval. . . . The only way to get his attention was to do something drastic."[5]

Your job, then, as a father, is to make sure, to the best of your ability, that you never undermine your daughter's self-esteem. Of course, undermining her is not something you would do intentionally, but the road to hell is paved with good intentions, and many fathers make some serious mistakes with severe consequences.

The correct approach is to work on building self-esteem from the day she is born, building her self-confidence gradually and constantly over time. (Reread Chapters 5 and 8 on self-concept and building self-esteem to refresh your memory for specific ideas.) Take every opportunity to compliment a job well done, to show joy in her accomplishments, and to enjoy her companionship. As she approaches puberty, make a special effort to flatter her appearance and reassure her that she is already an attractive person just as she is. This will go much further toward building her sense of worth than constantly pressuring her to always do better.

Remember the earlier discussions concerning encouragement versus pressure and discipline versus discouragement? Remember the common male approach, which is to continually pressure a child toward more and better accomplishments? Bear in mind that the father who insists a child must always run faster, climb higher, and throw farther inadvertently sends the subtle message that the current performance, no matter how good, is never good enough.

To the child who is ultrasensitive to criticism, this can have a devastating effect. It can make her feel perpetually inadequate. Therefore, always temper your criticism or advice with frequent and generous amounts of love and praise at the same time. Remember that it is almost impossible to lavish too much approval on your daughter. Review Chapter 8 for the difference between discipline and discouragement if you have forgotten it. And remember, you are not alone. Many parents have difficulty with this one.

If unrealistic expectations and unrelenting criticism cause your daughter to doubt herself chronically, it will be easy for her to make a small leap and attribute these feelings of inadequacy to a problem with her physical appearance. She may come to feel that once she is thin, she will finally be "OK." Thinness becomes the yardstick by which she measures her entire worth as a person. Some fathers inadvertently encourage this.

Kate G., a psychotherapist, explains it like this. "My father didn't really care what kind of grades I got. Oh, he would go and tell his bar buddies about something I did. I was a constant overachiever, but he never gave *me* any recognition. Instead he'd say, 'Are you gaining a little weight?' Or, 'Did you lose a little weight?'

It's the same thing whenever I see him now. He lives in a different state, and whenever I go to see him, the first thing he says is, 'Oh, you're still thinner. I see you kept that weight off.' It's like other families say, 'Hello, how's the weather.'

"It pisses the hell out of me. Nothing else I do seems to matter. I've told him a couple of times, 'Don't talk about that subject to me anymore.' But it's like he doesn't hear me. He goes right on."

An adolescent who feels too controlled by parental expectations and/or criticism may begin to express her anger by exerting control over the only area in which her parents lack control—her consumption of food. One of Dr. Maine's subjects said, "I think my anorexia was a challenge to my father to . . . get him to break the cycle of demands and control my mother had over me."[6] In this way, the anorexic can gain control of her life and her parents and at the same time achieve her ideal of perfection. Constant criticism or nagging pleas to alter her figure or change her eating habits will only aggravate the problem.

One woman, who is both a borderline anorexic and a bulimic, described it in the following way.

"My father was so critical that no matter what I did, I couldn't please him. He had some kind of puritan idea that if he ever showed us kids any approval, we would become 'spoiled.' Criticism was supposed to make us better people.

"Looking back on it now, I realize this resulted in some really bizarre and damaging behavior.

"Like, my father was always warning me about getting fat. So I would diet chronically. If I didn't take more than one helping at dinner, my father would make some comment suggesting I was an ungrateful kid and didn't appreciate my mother's efforts. If I broke down and *did* take more than one helping, he would tell me I was going to get fat. This didn't happen just once, but constantly.

"I remember one Thanksgiving in particular. My father kept passing me the dressing. When I finally took some, he made a remark the whole gathering could hear about how I ate too much and was getting fat.

"It made me hate him because no matter what I did, I lost. When I realized that even the most perfect behavior, like being thin and getting straight A's wasn't good enough, I went the other direction. I thought, 'Well, fuck you.' I got into teenage rebellion in a big way. I even got pregnant to escape him."

Granted, this is a rather extreme example of a no-win situation, but it illustrates the point. This father's warped view was that one must never "let up" on children. If you do, they just go to the dogs. This same woman became pregnant at sixteen to get away from her ultracritical father, and still managed to acquire a Ph.D. Granted, she did achieve, but despite her achievements she continues to feel inadequate and strives for an always unattainable model of perfection. To this day she uses her weight and food to beat herself up whenever she encounters the usual failures of life all human beings encounter.

Finally, don't forget one of the oft-repeated themes of this book—that your approval is interpreted not just as parental approval but as *male approval* as well. This is precisely why it is so important.

Your power and influence reside in the fact that during adolescence your daughter's need for male approval intensifies and you are the most important male in her life. It is from you that she will learn if she is "acceptable" to the male population. Therefore, encouraging her belief in her own unique beauty is critical *regardless of whether she measures up to your personal standard of beauty.*

EXAMINE YOUR OWN BELIEFS ABOUT WOMEN

"Fathers must take a hard look at their own beliefs about women because it will be reflected in the way they treat their daughters," says Dr. Giles. "Fathers should examine their own beliefs about what a woman is. Is a woman only worthwhile if she's a pretty young thing you can walk on your arm? If so, he's going to impart that in one way or another to his daughter.

"The whole idea that men are what they do and women are what they look like, and how pernicious this concept is, is something most fathers have never really examined."

Most men fail to see the subtle ways they contribute to the "fear of fat" in females they come into contact with. Some powerful messages are sent to a daughter via her father's treatment of her mother. One bulimic woman, whom I'll call Gloria, put it the following way.

"My father seemed to like me OK, but I think my bulimia really started with his disapproval of my mother and my identification with her.

"She was always battling her weight because my father didn't like the way she looked. At the same time she was a secret eater and wanted company in her 'sin' so she would try to coax me to overeat with her. She would say things like, 'Have some more spaghetti,' or 'How about another cookie,' that sort of thing. When I did, my father would get that disgusted look on his face and leave the room. Sometimes he would even stop speaking to us. I learned from my father that you are not an acceptable human being if you eat an extra cookie. You are a bad, disgusting person.

"To this day, I am always shocked with the open way in which some people enjoy their food. I have always felt as though I had to hide my enjoyment of food because it was wrong. Of course, this is an oversimplification of what was going on at our house, but when you're a kid, that's how you think."

Another way fathers contribute to the fear of fat in their daughters is by making disparaging remarks about other females they consider to be overweight. One father, upon hearing his son had a date with a particular girl, made the comment, "What do you want to go out with her for? She's too fat." His daughter overheard the comment and never forgot it.

Still another way is to make comments about your daughter's weight.

"Some men say terrible things to their daughters," says Giles. "Like this one father would actually say to his friends, 'Have you met my daughter, the horse?' He started calling her even crueler names like 'fat pig' when she was only four years old! Hard to believe, isn't it? But it happens."

DON'T MONITOR YOUR DAUGHTER'S EATING HABITS

According to Dr. Giles, this bit of advice is crucial.

"Some fathers start making comments about every bite that goes into their daughter's mouth. 'Should you be eating that?' 'Is that food OK for you to have?' This sets up lying, sneaking food, stealing food, and binging."

Gloria, the bulimic woman whose father made his daughter feel like an "unacceptable human being" over an extra cookie, can attest to that.

"Because my father made me feel as though the enjoyment of food was wrong, I could only enjoy it in secret. It still gives me tremendous guilt feelings to enjoy eating, even though I see other people do it. Even now, I never enjoy food in public. When I'm out, I pick at my food and pretend not to want it. Then, I go home and gorge."

Do not make a big-deal-federal-case out of the teenage propensity for high-calorie foods and poor eating habits. All teenagers eat poorly. It goes with the territory. Remember how you ate when you were a teenager?

"Some fathers are forever saying things like, 'See how I eat?' " remarks Giles. "Mostly, they are just passing on erroneous beliefs they have about food."

Recognize that to underplay food is to help diminish its power. This point bears repeating: by harping on food, you inadvertently make it more important than it is. You transform a simple source of fuel into a power tool, a punishment, and a reward. Your daughter will learn this technique and begin to use it herself as a symbolic tool for power, punishment, and reward.

When you underplay its importance, you accomplish two things. First, you diminish its power, for it is only a fuel after all, devoid of any powers of its own. (Remember the physiological phobic reactions of the bulimic or anorexic when exposed to "forbidden foods"?) Second, ignoring food is the first step in realizing the problem exists in the individual, not the food itself. No doughnut, all by itself, ever made anybody fat. Treating the individual is the answer.

Since, when we see our children overeat, the tendency is to stress discipline, control, and willpower (a concept which is extremely counterproductive), it will be very difficult not to criticize and nag. However, it is absolutely crucial to realize that in so doing, you increase the odds of your daughter turning to food as a solace, or a tool to punish herself, or a means to gain control of others.

Finally, the research shows that it is not unusual for a girl suffering from an eating disorder to have at least one parent who has a food or body-image problem. She may have learned fear of the dreaded fat from her mother, who has unconsciously passed on her own fears. Or perhaps her father has contributed to her anxiety by gently teasing her about her new curves or a few extra pounds in an effort to get her to slim down. It is not that these parents seek to make their daughters neurotic, but they recognize the pain involved in being an overweight female so they endeavor to make life as painless as possible by coaxing a daughter to become weight-conscious. Ironically, they may make the problem worse.

Finally, if you see a real problem developing, take action as quickly as possible, since the habitual nature of these disorders is insidious and they tend to worsen over time. This action should take the form of acquiring professional help with a clinic or individual therapist trained in the techniques of treating eating disorders, since a traditional therapist may try to stress discipline and control.

"It is important for parents to carefully choose a therapist if their daughter has an eating disorder," cautions Giles. "Clinics and treatment centers have sprung up all over the place, but not everybody knows the proper treatment or research. It is still a very new field. It seems like anybody who has read about it hangs out their shingle.

"I recommend that parents seek out real specialists who know the literature and have experience. Ask them the hard questions."

PROVIDE INFORMATION TO COUNTER HER FEARS

"Fathers can be an excellent source of information to counter all the current junk floating around by making statements like, 'Why is it so important what other people think?' " says Giles.

This, of course, refers back to the earlier statement that females who develop eating disorders try very hard to be "good girls." Fathers who are concerned that their daughters conform to some socially acceptable standard of feminine behavior and appearance; or those who insist on paternal authority, contribute to and exacerbate the problem. This may be particularly difficult for the type of father who believes that being feminine means pleasing men.

A father must teach his daughter that she doesn't have to please everyone all the time, and he can reinforce his teachings tenfold *by not always insisting that she please him.* Avoiding remarks like, "Be a good girl and go and do such and such for me," would be a good start. Not insisting that his wife or girlfriend cater to him, a behavior his daughter will witness, would be another step in the right direction.

Above all, continue to express as often as possible your love and approval of your daughter as a person. If your own hang-ups about weight and physical appearance get in the way, then at least do no harm. Keeping quiet is infinitely better than criticizing her. Remember, if she is overweight, she is probably already having trouble with her self-concept, and she doesn't need any additional help in this department.

The key, of course, is unconditional love. A frequently repeated theme throughout this book, which has emerged from the interviews I have conducted with women, is the perception that their fathers' love is conditional. This belief is frightening to a daughter, since it carries the constant threat of the loss of his love and the potential for abandonment. Release her from this terrifying threat by loving her as she is, whatever her weight and physical appearance. Once you realize that the greatest gift of life you can give your daughter is an unfailing feeling of self-worth, it will be easy to love her unconditionally.

EPILOGUE

The nature of the power structure in our society demands that the focus of this book be on the "masculine" behaviors a female must cultivate in order to achieve and succeed in a power structure founded primarily on war and sports models. The emphasis on risk taking and assertive behavior is mandatory to enable girls and women to achieve in this power structure. Bear down, toughen up.

As one father said to me at the end of a workshop, "You know, everything you said is right. I tell my daughter all the time not to be such a pansy. When she gets hurt, I don't give her sympathy. I teach her not to cry, to be tough, like her brother."

This breaks my heart. It is not the message of this book. This man may have his heart in the right place, but he is not a nurturing father. He is a drill sergeant, and while he may have some worthwhile lessons to teach his daughter, I would venture to guess she never really feels his love, his warmth, or his humanity.

My point is this: let no one use this book to support an argument for the masculinization of females, without the corresponding process of the feminization of males. Let no one use this book to justify the lament of Prof. Henry Higgins, "Why can't a woman be more like a man?" The great danger is that some readers will see flexible behavior as important, as long as it is limited to the masculinization of females. They will fail to see they are perpetuating the devaluation of the feminine in our society and stop at only half the solution. Our out-of-balance world will tilt a little closer toward extinction.

My goal is not the overthrow of men and male power, nor is it the transformation of females into pseudo-males. My hope is for the achievement of balance, the creation of a truly flexible society, where a trait is just a trait, without the label of masculine or feminine, and where all are encouraged to express their natures, talents, and visions free of the shackles of gender restraints.

If you, too, embrace this concept and can envision the great freedom contained within its practice, then you must encourage the feminization of your son as well. To develop different behaviors and potentials in your daughter but fail to do so in your son treats only half the problem and increases by 50 percent the length of time required to attain these lofty goals. Please join me in the creation of a truly egalitarian society. It's not too late.

CHECKLIST II

1. Allow yourself to grieve over the loss of your little girl when she starts to show signs of becoming a woman.

2. Do not misinterpret your daughter's flirtatious behavior. She is merely practicing her "femininity."

3. Give plenty of male approval for her appearance, regardless of whether or not she meets your standards for female beauty.

4. Try to curb any jealous feelings that arise when her boyfriends start to come over to the house. They are natural feelings, but if you let them get out of hand, they can cause you to become aloof, withdrawn, or short-tempered.

5. *Do not* withdraw your love and affection when your daughter reaches puberty. Learn new ways of expressing your affection.

6. If you feel there is any potential for sexual abuse or if you feel out of control in any way around your daughter, *Get help immediately!!!*

7. Do not make her feel somehow guilty or dirty about becoming a woman. It is a beautiful and natural process, one to be appreciated and enjoyed.

8. Realize that sexual experimentation (to one degree or another) is a natural part of adolescence. If you are a single father, find an understanding female willing to discuss birth control with your daughter.

9. If she becomes pregnant, do not rage at her. Do not take it personally. Realize she is already in a lot of emotional pain. Be loving and kind, and help her solve her problem.

10. Never tease your daughter about her body no matter how innocently you may mean it.

11. If your daughter has a weight problem, remember, the worst thing you can do is harp at her about her weight. She already knows, without you telling her, that she has a weight problem. She needs your love to bolster her self-esteem more than she needs your criticism.

12. Know the facts about eating disorders. Do not assume that if your daughter is at a normal weight, she does not have an eating disorder. Learn the symptoms and what to look for.

13. Do not be a perfectionist or insist your daughter always be a "good girl." Some of the most serious bulimics and anorexics are "good girls." That may be part of their problem.

14. Help your daughter learn that it is not important what everybody else thinks, or that everybody like her. Many anorexics and bulimics are trying hard to either be perfect or be "liked."

15. Build self-esteem through encouragement not pressure.

16. Examine your own beliefs about women.

17. Don't monitor your daughter's eating habits or pass on your incorrect beliefs about food.

18. Love your daughter unconditionally. Love her just because she is who she is. Don't send the message you would love her more if she would just act or look a certain way.

19. *Do not* criticize and nag your daughter about her eating

habits or what you may perceive as her "lack of will-power." Reread the chapter on eating disorders if your daughter's weight concerns you. Particularly in the area of weight control, it is possible to make some *serious* mistakes, so reread Chapter 11 before doing anything else.

20. If you suspect or already know that your daughter is gifted, reread Chapter 4. Remember that being gifted and female in our culture is a double burden; first, because there is a general anti-intellectualism in the American culture, and second, because the demands of femininity come into direct conflict with the demands of giftedness. Be prepared to do some double duty as a father to help your daughter learn to carry her burden.

21. Support the feminist movement in general in order to create a world where the talents and contributions of your daughter will be accepted and valued.

22. Present both sides of the marriage and family issue. Do not concentrate on only the joys of marriage and family, but also on the sacrifices that must be made, particularly in terms of time. Make your daughter aware of how this sacrifice can sidetrack her from her goals and aspirations.

23. Support your wife's goals and aspirations in tangible, observable ways, giving your own time to help her achieve her goals. This is real evidence of male support.

24. Be involved in all aspects of housekeeping and child care.

25. Seek and act on your wife's opinions and advice to show your daughter that female ideas are valued.

26. Don't expect your wife to be an aggressive, vital career woman during the day and transform herself into a passive, acquiescent wife at night. It creates a chaotic message.

27. Stand up for females and their rights in front of other men. Attempt to change some male attitudes.

APPENDIX A

❧

Biographies of
Successful Women

Scholars and Scientists

MARGARET MEAD

This formidable figure in anthropology—author of *Coming of Age in Samoa*—so dominated her field with her quest for adventure and understanding that she brought the study of primitive societies out of the realm of purely academic interest and into the lives of average people.

FLORENCE SABIN

The working of the human lymphatic system was discovered by Ms. Sabin after thirty-eight years of study. The governor of Colorado, in 1944, appointed her to an "honorary" position on a committee for public health. However, once in this post, she implemented tough new laws in the area of public health.

KAREN HORNEY

The awesome figure of Freud—characterized by his theory of biological determinants of personality and perception of women as "castrated men"—dominated the field of psychoanalysis until Dr. Horney challenged and broke with the traditional orientation. She postulated that personality is shaped by one's culture, not biology, and in the 1920s she established a new school of psycho-analysis in New York. Her contributions expanded the field and have led to exciting research in psychiatry and psychology.

RUTH BENEDICT

Patterns of Culture is Ms. Benedict's classic work, studying how personality is formed in primitive societies. Following Dr. Mead, she became the foremost anthropologist in the 1940s and used what might have been serious limitations—partial deafness and her own periodic depressions—to focus attention on her own interest in the development of human personality.

MARIA GOEPPERT MAYER

In 1948, Dr. Mayer discovered the structure of the atom's nucleus, which was termed the "shell theory." For her intense research, this physicist was awarded the Nobel prize.

HELEN TAUSSIG

A heart defect manifesting itself as an oxygen deficiency once took the lives of newborns diagnosed as "blue babies." These babies were given the chance to live and thrive when Dr. Taussig identified the cause of the disorder and suggested the operation which was to become the life-saving treatment for decades to come.

ALICE HAMILTON

As a resident of Hull House, Dr. Hamilton saw workers who were suffering permanent damage to their brains and lungs due to industrial poisons. Even by 1910, no American physician had investigated poisonous substances found in the workplace, no one, that is, until this pathologist decided to enter industrial settings, detecting the origins of poisons in the air and dust. Her investigations, carried out despite protests of angry employers, led to passage of Illinois' first worker's compensation laws and eventually to laws stipulating nationwide standards for working conditions.

EDITH HAMILTON

Reading ancient Greek writers by the age of seven, Ms. Hamilton (the elder sister of Alice Hamilton, above) continued to be fascinated with Greek culture throughout her adult years. She had a full life as an academician and headmistress of Bryn Mawr preparatory school in Baltimore, and she completed her scholarly and popular manuscript, *The Greek Way*, at the age of fifty-five. When she was 90, in 1957, the mayor of Athens awarded her official citizenship to the city she had loved since youth.

ELIZABETH BLACKWELL

The first female to practice medicine in America, Dr. Blackwell was refused admittance to twenty-nine medical schools before Geneva College accepted her, the all-male student body voting it might be "amusing" to have a "hen-medic" among them. Though she graduated at the head of her class, city hospitals still did not believe a female could heal the sick. Consequently, she opened a dispensary in a New York slum which ultimately became her own hospital—the New York Infirmary for Women and Children.

Social Reformers

FRANCES PERKINS

Boston aristocrat Frances Perkins became the first woman to be appointed to a cabinet post when, in 1933, she was named secretary of labor. Ten years' experience as a labor lobbyist and a New York State official prior to her appointment enabled her to help draft New Deal laws directed at improvement of workers' lives.

HARRIET BEECHER STOWE

The author of *Uncle Tom's Cabin* (which sold 10,000 books in a week and 300,000 total the first year of its publication) brought the injustice of slavery into sharp focus. In 1862 she met with President Abraham Lincoln, encouraging him to sign the Emancipation Proclamation. At this meeting he is alleged to have said, "So this is the little lady who made this big war."

EMMA GOLDMAN

Emma came to the United States from Russia in 1885, at which time she began her ceaseless campaigns advocating free love, anarchism, violence against specific capitalists, birth control, Bolshevism, and feminism. This Russian-born Jew did not seek to advance suffragism, however, apparently believing the right to vote would not aid women.

ANGELA DAVIS

A striking political and social figure of the 1970s, Ms. Davis was removed from her UCLA faculty position in the philosophy department due to her avowed communism. She was accused and acquitted of murdering the judge who presided over the Soledad Brothers trial. As a woman not yet thirty years of age, she was a symbol of radicalism in America.

HARRIET TUBMAN

The north star was Ms. Tubman's sole guide when she escaped from the Maryland farm where she was born a slave. A $12,000 bounty did not stop her from returning to the south nineteen times in order to lead 300 slaves to freedom. Her role as scout and spy behind enemy lines aided the north during the Civil War, making her a leader not only to blacks but to freedom-seeking people of all colors.

"MOTHER" JONES

A prominent figure in the struggle for the rights of laboring people, "Mother" Jones went from the coal mines of Pennsylvania to the copper mines of Colorado, driving off those who threatened miners' jobs. She even went directly to President Theodore Roosevelt with a group of children who worked in a factory—a journey of 145 miles—to persuade him of the horror of child labor.

DOROTHEA DIX

An early proponent of humane treatment of those suffering from mental illness, Ms. Dix visited people shackled and chained in filthy asylums. As a lobbyist for these helpless individuals, she presented reports of abuses to various state legislatures and was foremost in the attempt to cease maltreatment of those who were most in need of compassionate care.

GLORIA STEINEM

As a journalist and the editor of *Ms.* magazine, Gloria Steinem became the spokeswoman for women's liberation. Her intelligence, personal style of humor, and determination gave many women a rallying point and a means by which they could define some of their own goals.

BETTY FRIEDAN

Founder of the National Organization for Women (NOW), Ms. Friedan gave voice to the contemporary struggle for women's liberation. *The Feminine Mystique*, published in 1963, clarified for women "the problem that has no name," that is, the discontent some women felt in assuming traditional roles. She thus became the catalyst of major social changes to take place in America in the mid-twentieth century.

CLARA BARTON

Almost single-handedly the founder of the American Red Cross, Clara Barton left a legacy of initiating appropriate responses to the urgent needs of others. During the Civil War she was named the "Angel of the Battlefield" because she led Army mule teams, often in the face of enemy fire, in order to bring food and medical supplies to the troops in the field.

JANE ADDAMS

Co-winner of the Nobel peace prize in 1931, Ms. Addams was described by President Theodore Roosevelt as "the most useful citizen in America." Her career was one devoted to serving the underprivileged, most notably by establishing Hull House, which began with one tenement in Chicago and grew to a thirteen-building complex aiding 2,000 people per day with needed social services. The profession of social work was born of her efforts.

ELEANOR ROOSEVELT

Her husband was one of America's most powerful Presidents, yet Ms. Roosevelt never lived in the shadow of his greatness. She went to the ghettos and coal mines, spoke in support of minority rights during an era when our country's conscience was not ready to hear. Though she witnessed the extremes of poverty and injustice, Ms. Roosevelt believed "people matter" and spoke to what is humane in all of us.

MARGARET SANGER

Making information on birth control available to women—allowing them control over a crucial area of their lives—was Ms. Sanger's mission. Her 1913 article, "What Every Girl Should Know," ignited charges that she was a "lascivious monster." Her determination resulted in religious, political, and professional battles, along with eight arrests and one term spent in jail. America's first contraceptive clinic was founded by her in 1923, and by 1937 her efforts were recognized by a court decision effectively legalizing contraception.

Women in a Man's World

LILLIAN GILBRETH

A woman who managed to "have it all," Lillian Gilbreth combined the exigencies of raising eleven children with an industrial-engineering partnership with her husband, Frank Gilbreth. Their time-motion studies streamlined American industry as well as our household chores.

CLARE BOOTHE LUCE

Achieving success in three different careers—magazine editor, playwright, and congresswoman—Ms. Luce stated, "Success by a woman makes it easier for other able women." Her appointment by President Dwight Eisenhower as ambassador to Italy marked the first time a woman served in that capacity to a major U.S. embassy.

BARBARA JORDAN

Ms. Jordan reminded the nation in 1974 that the phrase "We the people" would not have applied to her when the Constitution was written because she is a black woman. However, this woman of considerable personal and political presence became the first black member of the Texas state senate since Reconstruction and was elected to the House of Representatives in 1972.

ABIGAIL ADAMS

Abigail Adams and her husband, John Adams, the second U. S. President, shared a nontraditional life as equal partners during a period when women played a subordinate role to men. During

John's absence, she was in control of their farm and increased their holdings. In correspondence with John, she urged resistance to tyranny on two fronts: America's independence from Britain and restraint of men's power because "all Men would be tyrants if they could."

HELENA RUBINSTEIN

Although the competitive cosmetics industry, in which Rubinstein amassed a $100 million personal fortune, idealized traditional feminine beauty, she stated, "I am a worker; I have no time for it." This consummate salesperson began by selling for $1 per jar a homemade cream created by her mother in Poland and ended by presiding over an international industry.

TILLIE LEWIS

The pear-shaped tomato which is required for spaghetti sauce once grew only in Italy. However, Tillie Lewis believed it could be grown in America, and in 1934, she gained financing, imported the seeds, and convinced wary Stockton, California, farmers to plant them, thereby creating a business with annual sales of $145 million.

BELVA LOCKWOOD

Ms. Lockwood's decision to pursue a career in law was constantly confronted with obstacles. It took two years before a law school admitted her, then, when her degree was "unaccountably withheld," she needed to petition the school's honorary president—Ulysses S. Grant—in order to receive it. In 1879 she became the first woman to argue a case before the U.S. Supreme Court, but before she could do so, she had to persuade Congress to pass a special bill allowing a woman to bring a case before any federal court.

KATHERINE GRAHAM

Upon the death of her husband, Philip, Ms. Graham assumed leadership of the Washington Post Company—which includes *Newsweek* and five television stations in addition to the *Washington Post* newspaper. Despite a twenty-week union walkout by pressmen, she continued to print the paper and report profits. In 1972, although facing attacks from the White House, she allowed Carl Bernstein and Bob Woodward to pursue their investigation of the Watergate burglary, which culminated in the resignation of President Richard Nixon.

BELLA ABZUG

Unlike traditional first-term congressional representatives, Bella Abzug began early to advance causes in which she believed, including civil rights, civil liberties, and peace in Vietnam. The congressional career of "Battling Bella" is imprinted with her distinct style of forcefulness and concern for individuals.

MARY WELLS LAWRENCE

In 1966, Ms. Lawrence helped found Wells, Rich, Greene, Inc., and ten years later, she earned $350,000 a year—making her the highest paid female executive in America in 1976. As chairwoman of her advertising agency, she developed notable campaigns for Braniff Airlines and Benson and Hedges.

JULIA MORGAN

William Randolph Hearst's San Simeon castle was the creation of Julia Morgan. In the early 1900s, Julia headed her own successful architectural firm in San Francisco, itself quite an unusual accomplishment for a female in a field almost totally dominated by males.

CALAMITY JANE

Traveling with construction gangs and occasionally being jailed for drunkenness and prostitution, Martha Jane Canary participated in the wildness of her era. Wearing men's clothes, cussing, chewing tobacco and, when drunk, howling like a coyote and shooting her rifles were common pastimes. One of the men she settled down with and called her husband for a time was Wild Bill Hickok.

BERYL MARKHAM

This author, aviator, horse breeder and trainer defies categorization—perhaps the word "adventurer" says it best. Beryl flew passengers, mail, and supplies to remote areas of the Sudan, Tanganyika, Kenya, and Rhodesia from 1931–1936. She scouted elephant herds by air for rich hunters on safari—an activity so hazardous that the best pilots of her day tried to discourage her.

Calling it "a release from routine," she did not stop. In 1936, she was the first person to successfully fly solo from east to west across the Atlantic Ocean. She survived the crash landing that she had to make in Nova Scotia 21 hours and 25 minutes from the time she took off. Her book *West With the Night*, which chronicles her adventures, is highly recommended.

BELLE STARR

A gang of horse thieves, cattle rustlers, and bootleggers was led by this "Bandit Queen," generally attired in fringed buckskins and a gun belt loaded with six-shooters. She was able to combine family with her professional life, giving birth in 1866, at eighteen, to a daughter sired by Cole Younger—Jesse James's cohort. Before she was shot to death by a bushwhacker, Belle had as lovers some of the west's most famous outlaws.

Artists

SARAH CALDWELL

A musical prodigy from Arkansas, at the age of twenty-nine Ms. Caldwell gathered $5,000 to found the Opera Company of Boston, her goal being to keep opera from being "a crashing bore." Personal supervision of all aspects of the performance and arduous rehearsal have resulted in Ms. Caldwell being not only the first woman to conduct at the Met (in 1976) but also—according to some musical authorities—the *finest* operatic director in America.

IMOGENE CUNNINGHAM

Beginning her career in high school before the turn of the century, Ms. Cunningham ordered her first camera—a "view box"—for $15 from a correspondence school. Her creative genius for composition, lighting, and capturing what is uniquely human in her subjects has made Ms. Cunningham one of this century's foremost photographers.

TWYLA THARP

Choreographer and dancer Twyla Tharp stands as an innovative leader in her art form. The theme of urban life is strong in her work, yet the diversity of her scope can encompass movements from Bach to Fats Waller.

MARTHA GRAHAM

Ms. Graham broke with tradition in 1920, creating her own group which embodied her revolutionary choreography, costuming, and sets. She focuses intently upon the expression of basic human emotion through dance. Her contemporaries in the audience were not initially supportive or appreciative of her style, yet her name has become synonymous with modern dance. She herself performed well into her seventies.

GEORGIA O'KEEFFE

Portraying the desert landscape of New Mexico as she saw it, O'Keeffe caught the attention of art critics seventy years ago when she first exhibited her charcoals. Diverse in her medium, one of her major retrospectives exhibited oils at the Whitney Museum in the 1970s. She commented that she painted "beautiful shapes that I see in my mind."

DOROTHEA LANGE

The faces of migrant American farmers displaced by the poverty of the Depression in the Dust Bowl were captured by Ms. Lange's camera. Her photographs became a part of American history as she worked in the Farm Security Administration photo project.

HELEN FRANKENTHALER

When her abstract paintings can be obtained, Frankenthaler commands prices of $30,000. Sometimes she pours the paint from the can onto canvas. Her work has been exhibited in major galleries, including the Museum of Modern Art in New York and the Smithsonian.

ISADORA DUNCAN

Isadora's internally motivated desire to move and flow led her to start her own dance school at the age of six in her San Francisco home. She was unconventional in all aspects of her life. The novelty of her dance style—barefoot and in loose gowns—captivated audiences. Author Edith Wharton said of her performance, "Suddenly I beheld the dance I had always dreamed of . . . satisfying every sense as a flower does."

GRANDMA MOSES

Respected and appreciated for her American primitive paintings, Grandma Moses spent the first seventy-eight years of her life working a farm with her husband and raising five surviving children of the ten she bore. Having time to devote to the expression of her innate talent, she used paint found in the barn to re-create the joyful images she cherished from her youth.

LOUISE NEVELSON

Boxes within boxes was how sculptor Louise Nevelson came to express her understanding of the world to herself. She studied under Diego Rivera, but it was many years before her genius was accorded recognition. Her years of struggle culminated in commanding six-figure sums for her work.

MARY LOU WILLIAMS

Ms. Williams, as a musical arranger, worked with the greats—Armstrong, Goodman, and Ellington. But her powerful influence in the world of jazz has come as a composer; her work—from symphony and ballet to original religious hymns—has been performed by the New York Philharmonic and the Alvin Ailey dance company. Her compositions have won her recognition as one of the nation's top figures in jazz.

Writers

PEARL BUCK

This daughter of American missionaries in China became in 1938 the first woman writer to receive the Nobel prize. Ms. Buck has spoken to people around the world, her works having been translated into sixty languages.

EMILY DICKINSON

Emily Dickinson is perhaps the most well known and widely read female poet in the English language; however, only seven of her poems were published during her lifetime. She obeyed her father's wish that she stay at home, yet upon her death, hundreds of her poems were found in her room. The poems were published eventually, thus reaching people all around the world.

LILLIAN HELLMAN

Powerful both as a novelist and dramatist, Ms. Hellman uses her characters to unmask the truth inherent in both interpersonal relationships and implicit moral principles. In her own life, she was summoned before the House Un-American Activities Committee, where, jeopardizing her own career as a screenwriter, she stated, "to hurt innocent people whom I knew many years ago in order to save myself is, to me, inhuman and indecent and dishonorable. I cannot and will not cut my conscience to fit this year's fashion."

WILLA CATHER

Willa Cather worked in the male-dominated city room of a newspaper and a magazine office. Having grown up in an era epitomized by individualism on the farmlands of Nebraska, she learned that in order to survive in any inhospitable environment, one has to have faith in oneself. Written in her clear descriptive style, Ms. Cather's novels keep the strength of the nineteenth-century homesteaders alive for us today.

EDNA ST. VINCENT MILLAY

Because of the fiery spirit of this 1920s poet, she was described by a contemporary as "spokesman for the human spirit." "My candle burns at both ends," she said—her goal being to "knock 'em cold."

GERTRUDE STEIN

Poet, playwright, novelist—Gertrude Stein gained worldwide recognition not only for her personal genius, but also for the role she played in shaping an era of creative talent. During the early years of their careers, contemporary artists such as Picasso and Hemingway sought intellectual refuge in her Paris salon.

Risk Takers

AMELIA EARHART

A risk taker whose career began joyriding with barnstormer Frank Hawks in 1920, Amelia Earhart went on to achieve many "firsts" in aviation: from first woman to be issued a license to first woman to cross the Atlantic. Her disappearance in 1937 over the South Pacific may have been in conjunction with a spying mission for her country.

JEANNETTE PICCARD

Together with her husband, Jean—an aerospace scientist— Jeannette piloted a balloon to an altitude of 57,559 feet, thereby becoming the first woman to reach the stratosphere. In 1974, having become a deacon in the Episcopal church, she and fourteen other women were ordained as priests. They found their ordination was ruled invalid, as women still were not allowed to rise to the level of priesthood in the Episcopal church.

Religious Leaders

AIMEE SEMPLE MCPHERSON

In 53 years, Aimee established 400 churches, 200 missionaries, a Bible college, and a radio station—all from money gathered in preaching to crowds of up to 5,000 in her $1.5 million Angelus Temple. This charismatic and colorful recipient of "divine inspiration," also known as the "Barnum of religion," evolved a lifestyle which embraced the "miracle" of faith healing along with dipping into the collection plate to pay for trips to Parisian nightclubs.

MARY BAKER EDDY

The belief that mental processes can cure physical ailments was unquestionably held and preached by Ms. Eddy, who founded the Christian Science religion. Her precept that "matter and death are mortal illusions" was shared by 22,000 people in the 420 churches she established. The religion she founded in the late nineteenth century is today a powerful force in the lives of many.

Athletes

BILLIE JEAN KING

Ms. King's career in tennis has been characterized by firsts: first female athlete to earn $100,000 a year, first female athlete to admit to an abortion, first female athlete to publicly acknowledge a lesbian relationship. Her fame is in large measure due to personal integrity—she has been a fighter for professionalism in her sport, equal rights for female athletes, and women's right to live up to their potential and be proud of their accomplishments. She is the holder of the most Wimbledon titles.

BABE DIDRIKSON ZAHARIAS

A champion in a wide range of sports—holding track records in five events, capturing two gold medals and worldwide attention in the 1932 Olympics—Babe chose golf as her main sport. She went on to win seventeen consecutive tournaments in the 1940s. It was her effort and determination which brought the women's pro tour into existence.

WILMA RUDOLPH

Scarlet fever and pneumonia during her early years left Ms. Rudolph unable to walk normally until she was eleven years of age. Yet, as a sprinter in the 1960 Olympic games, this incredible athlete won three gold medals—in the 100- and 200-meter dashes and as the anchor of a 400-meter relay team—thereby breaking one world record and tying another.

APPENDIX B

❦

Questions to Pose Concerning the Gifted Program at Your School

1. *What is the school district's philosophy concerning IQ scores for identification of gifted students?*
2. *What are your own personal beliefs about IQ scores?*
3. *If you use IQ scores, what is the cutoff point?*

The cutoff point is usually between 125 and 130. My school arbitrarily picked 128, but we were not steadfast in this if there were other indications of giftedness.

It is important to realize that IQ scores tell educators and parents basically only one thing: how well a student will perform in a traditional school setting. J. P. Guilford, in his "structure of the intellect" (SOI), designates 120 different cognitive functions of which the brain is capable.* To get some perspective: IQ tests measure only 8 of them. Furthermore, the variables that can influence a child's score on any given day give a false picture of a child's abilities; instead, they give a picture of how the child felt *that day*.

If possible, a student should be given an individual rather than a group test. (This is difficult because an individual test is much more expensive for the school district to provide. On the other hand, it is more accurate.)

*J. P. Guilford, *The Nature of Human Intelligence*, McGraw-Hill, New York, 1967.

4. How do you identify the gifted student? How many different criteria do you use?

Since IQ tests are so limited and grades are irrelevant, a multi-level assessment should be done. Test scores (on creativity and developmental maturity as well as intelligence), grades, teacher testimonials, a product review of something the child has created, a personal interview, and an autobiography should all be part of the identification criteria.

The following anecdote, shared with me by Jana Waters, co-founder of the Gifted Child Development Center in Denver, illustrates the need for personal interviews with gifted children as well as autobiographies and product reviews.

"We had this one little boy whose mother came to us for testing," said Jana, "because the school said he was emotionally immature and therefore not 'gifted material.'"

"When the mother asked why they came to this conclusion, they informed her that he had been observed frequently playing alone in the sandbox.

"We pursued it and asked him why he played alone so often. He told us he had been classifying crystals."

Stories like these about gifted children abound. For this reason, encourage your school district to use a personal interview or an autobiography or a product review (or all three!) as part of their identification process so that they don't overlook some relevant aspects of the child's intellectual life.

5. What do you use to measure developmental maturity and creativity?

There are a variety of tests available to help gauge a child's creativity and developmental maturity. Again, as with any test, each has its drawbacks and should not be taken as the final word. However, the moral of the story is that a battery of tests should be given, and a variety of criteria consulted, so that no one test or aspect is the final determiner.

6. How would you (or the school district) define a gifted individual?

Defining a gifted individual is a difficult task and one with which teachers become justifiably impatient. Is it a matter of demonstrated achievement or potential ability? Is it a matter of performance or thinking? How much of it is culturally determined and defined? Renzulli's intersecting circles (see Chapter 4) are a good pictorial representation because they can apply to any culture. Generally speaking, the following is the accepted definition:* A gifted child is one who has been identified by qualified professionals as showing outstanding ability or potential for high performance in one or more of the following areas:

- General intellectual ability
- Specific academic aptitude
- Creative or productive thinking
- Leadership ability
- Visual and performing arts
- Psychomotor ability

7. *What specifically is being done to meet the needs of gifted girls, either in your own classroom or district-wide?*
8. *Are all classes open to both boys and girls? Are both sexes encouraged to enroll in any class?*

The special strategies for helping a gifted girl cope with the pressures she feels within school have been outlined and discussed in Chapter 4, "A New Look at Underachieving Girls."

*Subcommittee on Labor and Public Welfare, U.S. Senate, *Education of the Gifted and Talented,* March 1972, p. 10.

NOTES AND SOURCES

Chapter 1

1. The interested reader is referred to the bibliography for further material on this subject.

Also, the book jacket of a recent book entitled *Unnecessary Choices: The Hidden Life of the Executive Woman*, by Edith Gilson, suggests that the idea that a father strongly influences a woman's success is a fallacy and that the mother-daughter relationship is the best predictor of a daughter's future success. While I agree with Ms. Gilson that a mother's influence is extremely important (and will be covered at length in this book), I cannot agree with her conclusions on the role of the father. First, virtually every other study of successful women comes to the opposite conclusion—that fathers play a dominant role in the lives of successful women. Second, my own interviews of successful women as well as my observations of adolescent girls for the last eleven years lead me to a different conclusion. Third, Ms. Gilson herself states, "I would have liked a larger group of women who were favored by their mothers. Statistically, the 5 percent of those surveyed is too small a sample from which to draw detailed conclusions." Finally, upon close reading, I find that what Ms. Gilson *actually* states in her text is that the mother-daughter relationship is not a predictor of a daughter's ultimate success, but rather an indicator of whether or not a successful adult daughter will be *content* with her income and her career.

Chapter 3

1. I have been pleasantly surprised to discover a more varied audience in my seminars than I would have predicted. Besides fathers of daughters, I have had mothers of daughters, adult daughters seeking to understand their relationship with their fathers, and, most encouraging of all, men in relationships with high-achieving women seeking ways to be supportive of them!

2. A few points about these lists are in order before continuing with our discussion of success.

First, as you may have already noted, there are some adjectives which appear in both categories, positive and negative. This occurs because the definition of the word can vary according to the circumstance. Nuances of words like "sensitive," "emotional," and "aggressive" are particularly dependent on situation; however, it should come as no great surprise that the so-called masculine traits denote action and dominance, while the so-called feminine traits denote passivity and submissiveness.

Second, the feminine list features a number of adjectives descriptive of childlike behavior, while the adjectives in the masculine list describe a more worldly perspective. For example, men are more likely to be described as "intelligent," while women are described as "curious."

Third, many women who have participated in the seminar have taken exception to some of the traits listed as positive. They object to items like "passive," "soft," "dainty," "fragile," "sweet," "submissive," and "in need of protection" being thought of as positive feminine traits.

3. M. C. Shaw and J. T. McCuen, "The Onset of Academic Underachievement in Bright Children," *Journal of Educational Psychology*, 51:103–108 (1960).

4. As reported in the *Philadelphia Enquirer*, March 6, 1986, Associated Press article by Maud Beelman.

5. Eleanor E. Maccoby and Carol N. Jacklin, *The Psychology of Sex Differences*, Stanford University Press, Stanford, Calif., 1974, pp. 114–117, 134–142.

6. Lynn H. Fox and Laura D. Turner, "Gifted and Creative Female: In the Middle School Years," *American Middle School Education*, 4: 17–18 (1981).

7. W. Ickes and M. Layden, "Attributional Styles," in J. H. Harvey, W. Ickes and R. F. Kidd (eds.), *New Directions in Attributional Research*, Vol. 2, Erlbaum Associates, Hillsdale, N.J., 1978, pp. 121–147.

8. G. Gallup, *Gallup Youth Survey*, Gallup Organization, Princeton, N.J., 1983.

9. All these studies can be found in a special issue of *Sex Roles*, 13 (1985), devoted to the first empirical evidence regarding the determinants and consequences of sex-related differences in computer use by adults and children. Interested readers are referred to this journal for further study.

10. *USA Today*, Oct. 16, 1984.

11. Marlaine E. Lockheed, "Women, Girls and Computers: A First Look at the Evidence," *Sex Roles*, 13:118. (1985).

12. E. Fennema, "Girls, Women and Mathematics," in E. Fennema and M. J. Ayer (eds.), *Women and Education: Equity or Equality*, McCutchen, Berkeley, Calif., 1984, pp. 137–164.

13. Fox and Turner, p. 19.

14. P. L. Casserly, "Factors Affecting Female Participation in Advanced Placement Programs in Mathematics, Chemistry and Physics," in L. H. Fox, L. Brody, and D. Tobin (eds.), *Women and the Mathematical Mystique*, Johns-Hopkins University Press, Baltimore, 1980.

15. Alice Baumgartner Papageorgiou, *My Daddy Might Have Loved Me: Students' Perceptions of Differences Between Being Male and Being Female*, Institute for Equality in Education, University of Colorado at Denver, 1982.

16. It is both interesting and arresting that this slang term used primarily by males is so violent, almost as if they were hit men about to bag their prey.

17. "Games Stay Out in Front," *Time*, May 23, 1983, p. 61.

18. Robert D. Hess and Irene T. Miura, "Gender Differences in Enrollment in Computer Camps and Classes," *Sex Roles*, 13:200–201 (1985).

19. Mary Catherine Ware and Mary Frances Stuck, "Sex-Role Messages vis-à-vis Microcomputer Use: A Look at the Pictures," *Sex Roles*, 13:205–213 (1985).

20. Hess and Miura, pp. 193–203.

21. Marlaine E. Lockheed, A. Nielsen, and M. K. Stone, "Sex Differences in Microcomputer Literacy," paper presented at the National Educational Computer Conference, Baltimore, 1983.

22. Marlaine E. Lockheed, "Women, Girls and Computers: A First Look at the Evidence," *Sex Roles*, 13:117 (1985).

23. Elizabeth Tidball, "Baccalaureate Origins of Entrants into American Medical Schools," *Journal of Higher Education*, 56:385–402 (1985).

24. This issue of "pleasing Daddy" is one that will surface many times throughout this text. As you will see, it is not a good motivation to give a daughter, because she may be trying to succeed for the wrong reasons. Later, you will see how trying to be a "good girl" to please Daddy can even have devastating effects.

Chapter 4

1. Telephone interview with Dr. Silverman, Sept. 1986.

2. Joseph Renzulli, "What Makes Giftedness: Reexamining a Definition," *Phil Delta Kappan*, 60:180–184 (1978).

3. Study by Betty Walker, University of Southern California, reported in *Glamour*, Sept. 1986, p. 403.

4. Kasimierz Dabrowski, *Positive Disintegration*, Gryf, London, 1964.

5. Carol Gilligan, *In a Different Voice*, Harvard University Press, Cambridge, 1982, p. 10.

Chapter 5

1. Dana W. Birnbaum and William L. Croll, "The Etiology of Children's Stereotypes About Sex Differences in Emotionality," *Sex Roles*, 10:679–691 (1984).

2. For a more in-depth discussion of the formation of self-concept, interested readers are referred to Morris Rosenberg, *Conceiving the Self*, Basic Books, New York, 1979, from which this material was taken.

3. Alice Baumgartner Papageorgiou, *My Daddy Might Have Loved Me.: Students' Perceptions of Differences Between Being Male and Being Female*, Institute for Equality in Education, University of Colorado, Denver, 1982.

4. Papageorgiou, p. 12.

5. Ross D. Parke and D. B. Sawin, "The Family in Early Infancy: Social Interactional and Attitudinal Analyses," in F. A. Pederson (ed.), *The Father-Infant Relationship: Observational Studies in the Family Setting*, Praeger, New York, 1980.

6. E. Redina and J. D. Dickerscheid, "Father Involvement with First-Born Infants," *Family Coordinator*, 25:373–379 (1976); A. M. Frodi, M. E. Lamb, M. Frodi, C. P. Hwang, B. Forsstrom, and T. Corry, "Stability and Change in Parental Attitudes Following an Infant's Birth into Traditional and Nontraditional Families," unpublished manuscript, University of Michigan, 1980, as referenced in *Fathers* by Ross Parke, Harvard University Press, Cambridge, 1981.

7. Norma Radin, "Childrearing Fathers in Intact Families: An Exploration of Some Antecedents and Consequences," paper presented to study group on the role of the father in child development, social policy and the law, University of Haifa, Israel, July 15–17, 1980, as referenced in *Fathers* by Ross Parke, Harvard University Press, Cambridge, 1981.

8. Jean H. Block, "Another Look at Sex Differentiation in the Socialization Behaviors of Mothers and Fathers," in J.A. Sherman and F.L. Denmark (eds.), *Psychology of Women: Future Directions of Research*, Psychological Dimensions, New York, 1979.

9. Interested readers are referred to Martin Seligman's fascinating work on this subject. Besides the Seligman reference, which can be found in the bibliography, an entire issue of the *Journal of Abnormal Psychology*, 87 (1) (February 1978), dealt with this issue.

10. Jefferey Rubin, F. J. Provenzano, and Zella Luria, "The Eye of the Beholder: Parents' Views on Sex of Newborns," *American Journal of Orthopsychiatry*, 44:512–519 (1974).

11. Studies vary from one-half hour per day to several hours. This may be due in part to the new commitment to parenting evidenced by today's fathers. Still, it is important to bear in mind that most children spend a good deal more time with mommy than with daddy.

12. Lois Hoffman, "Changes in Family Roles, Socialization and Sex Differences, *American Psychologist*, 32:649 (1977).

13. Papageorgiou, p. 5.

14. Papageorgiou, p. 3.

15. Kristen Yount, "A Theory of Productive Activity: The Relationships Among Self-Concept, Gender, Sex-Role Stereotypes, and Work Emergent Traits," *Psychology of Women Quarterly*, 10:63-88 (1986).

16. Telephone conversation with Dr. Kristen Yount, professor of sociology, University of Kentucky, May 1986.

Chapter 6

1. Marjorie Honzik, "Environmental Correlates of Mental Growth: Prediction from the Family Setting at Twelve Months," *Child Development*, 38:337–364 (1967).

2. Allow me to interject here that if your values or religious persuasion dictate that the traditional role of wife and mother is "natural" and "right," I am not here to dissuade you. What I *am* here for is to remind you of the double message to your daughter, if and only if, you are simultaneously encouraging her to achieve something *in the world outside the home*. If you are only interested in making sure she can take of herself until a man comes along to lead her, a man to stand in for you, one to ensure she takes her "rightful" place, then perhaps our goals as author and reader are more widely discrepant than we thought!

3. According to a study presented by Helen Cleminshaw, associate professor of child and family development at the University of Ohio, Akron, in a panel at the American Psychological Association Annual Convention, 1986.

4. Elyce Wakerman, *Father Loss: Daughters Discuss the Man That Got Away*, Doubleday, New York, 1984, p. 263.

5. Wakerman, p. 265.

6. If your problem is a custody battle, you will need legal advice, which I am not qualified to give and which will vary from state to state anyway. The purpose of this section is to help you if you already have some time allotted, either through the courts or by arrangement with your ex-wife, to be with your daughter.

Chapter 7

1. Robert Frost, "On Looking Up by Chance at the Constellations," in Edward Connery Lathem and Lawrence Thompson (eds.), *Robert Frost: Poetry and Prose*, Holt, Rinehart and Winston, New York, 1972, p. 109.

2. Michael Castleman, *Crime Free*, Simon & Schuster, New York, 1986.

Chapter 8

1. As reported in the *Rocky Mountain News*, May 13, 1986, excerpted from research by John Anderson, director of the counseling center at the U. S. Air Force Academy in Colorado Springs, Colorado.

2. A Michigan State University study on eating disorders and athletes, as reported in *Runner's World*, May 1986, p. 22.

Chapter 9

1. This is extraordinary in itself when you consider it took place during the Victorian period in England, when females were thought to be intellectually inferior and primarily decorative. They were the property of their fathers and husbands and their sole purpose in life was to bear and rear children.

2. My former principal used to do this in front of the entire faculty and then get indignant if we complained about not being treated like professionals. We were supposed to join good-naturedly in the fun, but none of us thought it was very funny. He thought we were just being overly sensitive and said so publicly.

Chapter 10

1. This comment should not be read as an excuse by men who *are* sick and may be candidates for sexual abuse of their daughters. This anecdote was not meant for you. If you are a man who feels out of control around your daughter, or any underage female, turn to the section of this chapter entitled, "Special Note to the Sexually Abusive or Potentially Abusive Father" and read it immediately.

2. Actually, he *can* correct his mistake, as we saw in the section "Delivering Difficult Communications," in Chapter 8.

Chapter 11

1. Margo Maine, "Engaging the Disengaged Father in the Treatment of Eating Disordered Adolescents," paper presented at the annual conference sponsored by the Center for the Study of Anorexia and Bulimia, New York, November 1985.

2. David Garner, Karl Garfinkel, Donald Schwartz, and Michael Thompson, "Cultural Expectations of Thinness in Women," *Psychological Reports*, 47 (1980).

3. Personal interview with Dr. Thomas Giles, director, Eating and Anxiety Disorders Clinic, Rose Medical Center, Denver, Colorado, April 1986.

4. In the research report on anorexics, Dr. Margo Maine says, "The father's absence alone does not cause anorexia nervosa, but compounds diffculties in the mother/child relationship, in family dynamics, in developmental mastery, in self-acceptance, in psycho-sexual development, and in management of the cultural demands placed on young women." Maine, p. 11.

5. Maine, p. 6.

6. Maine, p. 6.

BIBLIOGRAPHY AND SUGGESTED READINGS

Books

Appleton, William S.: *Fathers and Daughters: A Father's Powerful Influence on a Woman's Life*, Doubleday, Garden City, N.Y., 1981.

Bell, Ruth, and Leni Zeiger Wildflower: *Talking With Your Teenager: A Book for Parents*, Random House, New York, 1983.

Briggs, Dorothy Corkille: *Your Child's Self-Esteem*, Doubleday, New York, 1970.

Cassell, Carol: *Swept Away: Why Women Confuse Love and Sex . . . And How They Can Have Both*, Bantam, New York, 1984.

Castleman, Michael: *Crime Free*, Simon & Schuster, New York, 1986.

Cath, Stanley H., Alan R. Gurwitt, and John Munder Ross (eds.): *Father and Child: Developmental and Clinical Perspectives*, Little, Brown, Boston, 1982.

Chernin, Kim: *The Hungry Self: Women, Eating and Identity*, Times Books, New York, 1985.

Colangelo, Nick, and R. T. Zaffran: *New Voices in Counseling the Gifted*, Kendall/Hunt, Dubuque, Iowa, 1979.

Dabrowski, Kasimiez: *Positive Disintegration*, Gryf, London, 1964.

Dodson, Fitzhugh: *How To Father*, New American Library, New York, 1974.

Dowling, Colette: *The Cinderella Complex: Women's Hidden Fear of Independence*, Pocket Books, New York, 1981.

Edel, Leon: *Bloomsbury: A House of Lions*, Avon, New York, 1979.

Faber, Adele, and Elaine Mazlish: *How To Talk So Kids Will Listen & Listen So Kids Will Talk*, Rawson Associates, New York, 1980.

Fields, Suzanne: *Like Father, Like Daughter*, Little Brown, Boston, 1983.

Fishel, Elizabeth: *The Men in Our Lives: Fathers, Lovers, Husbands, Mentors*, Morrow, New York, 1984.

Frieze, Irene H., et al.: *Women and Sex Roles: A Social, Psychological Perspective*, Norton, New York, 1978.

Gallagher, James J.: *Teaching the Gifted Child*, 2d ed., Allyn and Bacon, Boston, 1975.

Gilligan, Carol: *In a Different Voice: Psychological Theory and Women's Development*, Harvard University Press, Cambridge, 1982.

Gilson, Edith: *Unnecessary Choices: The Hidden Life of the Executive Woman*, Morrow, New York, 1987.

Ginot, Haim C.: *Between Parent and Child*, Macmillan, New York, 1965.

Goertzel, Victor, and Mildren G. Goertzel: *Cradles of Eminence*, Little, Brown, Boston, 1962.

Gowan, John C., et al.: *Educating the Ablest: A Book of Readings*, Peacock Publishers, Itasca, Illinois, 1979.

Hammer, Signe: *Passionate Attachments: Fathers and Daughters in America Today*, Rawson Associates, New York, 1982.

Kaplan, A. G., and J. P. Bean (eds.): *Beyond Sex-Role Stereotypes: Readings Toward a Psychology of Androgyny*, Little Brown, Boston, 1976.

Konopka, Gisela: *Young Girls: A Portrait of Adolescence*, Prentice-Hall, Englewood Cliffs, N.J., 1976.

Leonard, Linda: *The Wounded Woman: Healing the Father-Daughter Relationship*, Shambhala, Boston, 1982.

Lockheed, M. E., A. Nielson and M. K. Stone: "Sex Differences in Microcomputer Literacy," paper presented at the National Educational Computer Conference, Baltimore, 1983.

Maccoby, Eleanor E., and Carol N. Jacklin: *The Psychology of Sex Differences*, vol. 1, Stanford University Press, Stanford, Calif., 1974.

Owen, Ursula (ed.): *Fathers: Reflections by Daughters*, Pantheon, New York, 1985.

Parke, Ross D.: *Fathers*, Harvard University Press, Cambridge, 1981.

Rosenberg, Morris: *Conceiving the Self*, Basic Books, New York, 1979.

Seligman, Martin: *Helplessness: On Depression, Development and Death*, W. H. Freeman, San Francisco, 1975.

Silverman, Linda K.: *Gifted Education: A Developmental Approach*, in preparation, Charles E. Merrill, Columbus, Ohio.

Stacey, Judith, et al.: *And Jill Came Tumbling After: Sexism in American Education*, Dell, New York, 1974.

Storaska, Frederic: *How To Say No to a Rapist and Survive*, Warner, New York, 1975.

Wakerman, Elyce: *Father Loss: Daughters Discuss the Man That Got Away*, Doubleday, New York, 1984.

Williams, Juanita H.: *The Psychology of Women: Behavior in a Biosocial Context*, Norton, New York, 1977.

Woolf, Virginia: *A Room of One's Own*, Harcourt, Brace and World, New York, 1929.

Woolfolk, William, with Donna Woolfolk Cross: *Daddy's Little Girl: The Unspoken Bargain Between Fathers and Their Daughters*, Prentice-Hall, Englewood Cliffs, N.J., 1982.

Articles

Abromowitz, Robert H., Anne C. Petersen, and John E. Schulenberg: "Changes in Self-Image During Early Adolescence," *New Directions for Mental Health Services*, 22:19–28. (1984).

Almquist, E. M., and S. S. Angrist: "Role Model Influences on College Women's Career Aspirations," *Merrill-Palmer Quarterly*, 17:263–279 (1971).

Anyon, Jean: "Intersections of Gender and Class: Accommodation and Resistance by Working-class and Affluent Females to Contradictory Sex Role Ideologies," *Journal of Education*, 166:25–48 (1984).

Benbow, C. P. and J. C. Stanley: "Sex Differences in Mathematical Reasoning Ability: More Facts," *Science*, 222:1029–1031 (1983).

Birnbaum, Dana W., and William L. Croll: "The Etiology of Children's Stereotypes About Sex Differences in Emotionality," *Sex Roles*, 10:679–691 (1984).

Block, Jean H.: "Another Look at Sex Differentiation in the Socialization Behaviors of Mothers and Fathers," in J. A. Sherman and F. L. Denmark (eds.), *Psychology of Women: Future Directions of Research*, Psychological Dimensions, New York, 1979, p. 25.

Cash, Thomas F., and Claire A. Trimer: "Sexism and Beautyism in Women's Evaluations of Peer Performance," *Sex Roles*, 10:87–98 (1985).

Casserly, P. L.: "Helping Able Young Women Take Math and Science Seriously in School," in Nick Colangelo and R. T. Zaffran. (eds.) *New Voices In Counseling the Gifted*, Kendall/Hunt, Dubuque, Iowa, 1979, pp. 346–369.

Cherry, L.: "The Preschool Teacher-Child Dyad: Sex Differences in Verbal Interaction," *Child Development*, 46:532–535 (1975).

de Chesnay, Mary: "Father-Daughter Incest: Issues in Treatment and Research," *Journal of Psychosocial Nursing and Mental Health Services*, 22:9–16 (1984).

Dunn, J. F., and B. Antonis: "Caretaking and the First Year of Life: The Role of Fathers' and Mothers' Social Isolation," *Child: Care, Health and Development*, 3:23–26 (1977).

Dweck, Carol: "Motivational Processes Affecting Learning," *American Psychologist*, 41:1040–1048 (1986).

——and C. S. Bush: "Sex Differences in Learned Helplessness: I. Differential Debilitation with Peer and Adult Evaluators," *Developmental Psychology*, 12:147–156 (1976).

——W. Davidson, S. Nelson, and B. Enna: "Sex Differences in Learned Helplessness: II. The Contingencies of Evaluative Feedback in the Classroom, and III. An Experimental Analysis," *Developmental Psychology*, 14:268–276 (1978).

——and E. S. Elliot: "Achievement Motivation," in E. M. Heatherington (ed.), *The Handbook of Child Psychology: Volume 4: Socialization, Personality and Social Development*, 4th ed., Wiley, New York, 1983, pp. 643–691.

Edwards, Steven W., Richard D. Gordin, and Keith P. Henschen: "Sex Role Orientations of Female NCAA Championship Gymnasts," *Perceptual and Motor Skills*, 58:625–626 (1984).

Fennema, E.: "Girls, Women and Mathematics," in E. Fennema and M. J. Ayer (eds.), *Women and Education: Equity or Equality*, McCutchen, Berkeley, Calif., 1984, pp. 137–164.

Fetler, Mark: "Sex Differences on the California Statewide Assessment of Computer Literacy," *Sex Roles*, 13:181–191 (1985).

Fox, Lynn H., and Laura D. Richmond: "Gifted Females: Are We Meeting Their Counseling Needs?" *Personnel and Guidance Journal*, 58:256–259 (1979).

——and L. D. Turner: "Gifted and Creative Female: In the Middle School Years." *American Middle School Education*, 4:17–23 (1981).

Frey, K. S.: "Differential Teaching Methods Used With Girls and Boys of Moderate and High Achievement Levels," paper presented to the Society for Research in Child Development, San Francisco, March 1979.

Frodi, A. M., C. P. Hwang, B. Forsstrom, and T. Corry: "Stability and Change in Parental Attitudes Following an Infant's Birth in Traditional and Nontraditional Families," unpublished manuscript, University of Michigan, 1980, as referenced in *Fathers* by Ross Parke, Harvard University Press, Cambridge, 1981.

Garner, David, Karl Garfinkel, Donald Schwartz, and Michael Thompson: "Cultural Expectations of Thinness in Women," *Psychological Reports*, 47 (1980).

Giles, Thomas R., Renee R. Young, and David E. Young: "Behavioral Treatment of Severe Bulimia," *Behavior Therapy*, 16:393–405 (1985).

Gladding, Samuel T., and Charles H. Huber: "The Position of the Single-Parent Father," *Journal of Employment Counseling*, 21:13–18 (1984).

Hennig, Margaret: "Family Dynamics and the Successful Woman Executive," in R. Knudsin (ed.), *Women and Success*, Morrow, New York, 1973.

Hess, Robert D., and Irene T. Miura: "Gender Differences in Enrollment in Computer Camps and Classes," *Sex Roles*, 13 (1985), 193–203.

Hock, Robert A., and John F. Curry: "Sex Role Identification of Normal Adolescent Males and Females as Related to School Achievement," *Journal of Youth and Adolescence*, 12:461–470 (1983).

Hoffman, Lois: "Changes in Family Roles, Socialization and Sex Differences," *American Psychologist*, 32:649 (1977).

Honzik, Marjorie P.: "Environmental Correlates of Mental Growth:

Prediction from the Family Setting at Twelve Months," *Child Development*, 38:337–364 (1967).

Kotelchuck, M.: "The Infant's Relationship to the Father: Experimental Evidence," in M. E. Lamb (ed.), *The Role of the Father in Child Development*, Wiley, New York, 1976.

Kourilsky, Marilyn, and Michael Campbell: "Sex Differences in a Simulated Classroom Economy: Children's Beliefs About Entrepreneurship," *Sex Roles*, 10:53–66 (1984).

Kranz, Bella: "From Lewis Terman to Matina Horner: What Happens To Gifted Girls," *Talents and Gifts*, 17:31–36 (1975).

Lemkau, Jeanne Parr: "Women in Male-Dominated Professions: Distinguishing Personality and Background Characteristics," *Psychology of Women Quarterly*, 8:144–165 (1983).

Like Father, Like Daughter. Narr. Barbara Walters. Television interview, "20/20," Feb. 20, 1986, with Dr. Margaret Hennig.

Linn, Marcia C.: "Fostering Equitable Consequences from Computer Learning Environments," *Sex Roles*, 13:229–240 (1985).

Lockheed, Marlaine E.: "Women, Girls and Computers: A First Look at the Evidence," *Sex Roles*, 13:115–122 (1985).

Maine, Margo: "Engaging the Disengaged Father in the Treatment of Eating Disordered Adolescents," paper presented at the annual conference sponsored by the Center for the Study of Anorexia and Bulimia, New York, November, 1985.

Marini, Margaret Mooney, and Mary C. Brinton: "Sex Typing in Occupational Socialization," in Barbara F. Reskin (ed.), *Sex Segregation in the Workplace: Trends, Explanations, Remedies*, National Academy Press, Washington, 1984, pp. 192–232.

Martin, Elaine: "Power and Authority in the Classroom: Sexist Stereotypes in Teaching Evaluations," *Signs*, 9:482–492 (1984).

Martin, Ruth E., and Harriett K. Light: "Sex Role Orientation of University Students," *Psychological Reports*, 54:316 (1984).

McBride, Angela, and Kathryn N. Black: "Differences that Suggest Female Investment In, and Male Distance From, Children," *Sex Roles*, 10:231–246 (1984).

Papageorgiou, Alice Baumgartner: *My Daddy Might Have Loved Me: Students' Perceptions of Differences Between Being Male and Being Female*, Institute for Equality in Education, University of Colorado, Denver, 1982.

Parke, Ross D., and D. B. Sawin: "The Family in Early Infancy: Social Interactional and Attitudinal Analysis," in F. A. Pederson (ed.), *The Father-Infant Relationship: Observational Studies in the Family Setting.* Praeger, New York, 1980.

Plumb, Pat, and Gloria Cowan: "A Developmental Study of Destereotyping and Androgynous Activity Preference of Tomboys, Nontomboys and Males," *Sex Roles,* 10:703–712 (1984).

Radin, Norma: "Childrearing Fathers in Intact Families: An Exploration of Some Antecedents and Consequences," paper presented at the annual meeting of the American Psychological Association, Toronto, Sept. 1978, as referenced in *Fathers* by Ross Parke, Harvard University Press, Cambridge, 1981.

Redina, E., and J. D. Dickerscheid: "Father Involvement with First-Born Infants," *Family Coordinator,* 25:373–379 (1976).

Renzulli, Joseph: "What Makes Giftedness: Reexamining a Definition," *Phi Delta Kappan,* 60: 180–184 (1978).

Rubin, Jeffrey, Z., Frank J. Provenzano, and Zella Luria: "The Eye of the Beholder: Parents' Views on Sex of Newborns," *American Journal of Orthopsychiatry,* 44:512–519 (1974).

Shaw, M. C., and J. T. McCuen: "The Onset of Academic Underachievement in Bright Children," *Journal of Educational Psychology,* 51:103–108 (1960).

Tidball, M. Elizabeth: "Baccalaureate Origins of Entrants into American Medical Schools," *Journal of Higher Education,* 56:385–402 (1985).

Wahlberg, H. J.: "Physics, Femininity and Creativity," *Developmental Psychology,* 1:47–54 (1969).

Ware, Mary Catherine, and Mary Frances Stuck: "Sex-Role Messages vis-à-vis Microcomputer Use: A Look at the Pictures," *Sex Roles,* 13:205-212 (1985).

Weintraub, Marsha, et al.: "The Development of Sex Role Stereotypes in the Third Year: Relationships to Gender Labeling, Gender Identity, Sex-typed Preference, and Family Characteristics," *Child Development,* 55:1493–1503 (1984).

Wilder, Gita, Diane Mackie, and Joel Cooper: "Gender and Computers: Two Surveys of Computer Related Attitudes," *Sex Roles,* 13:215–228 (1985).

Williams, Sue Winkle, and John C. McCullers: "Personal Factors Related to Typicalness of Career and Success in Active Professional Women," *Psychology of Women Quarterly*, 7:343–356 (1983).

Yount, Kristen R.: "A Theory of Productive Activity: The Relationships Among Self-Concept, Gender, Sex Role Stereotypes, and Work-Emergent Traits," *Psychology of Women Quarterly*, 10:63–88 (1986).

INDEX

ABOUT THE AUTHOR

NICKY MARONE holds a Master's degree in Education of Gifted Children. She was a teacher of junior high school students in Denver for eleven years and also the coordinator and founder of a pilot program for gifted children. She has been leading workshops on "How to Father a Successful Daughter" at hospitals and corporations and in cities across the country since 1984. She lives in Denver, Colorado.